The Best of
Clean Eating 3

Improving your life one meal at a time.

The Best of Clean Eating 3

Improving your life one meal at a time.

FROM THE EDITORS OF **Clean Eating** MAGAZINE

ROBERT KENNEDY PUBLISHING

Published by Robert Kennedy Publishing
400 Matheson Blvd. West
Mississauga, ON
L5R 3M1 Canada
Visit us at www.rkpubs.com
and www.cleaneating.com

Library and Archives Canada Cataloguing in Publication

The best of Clean eating 3 : improving your life one meal
at a time / from the editors of Clean eating magazine.

Includes index.
ISBN 978-1-55210-118-6

1. Cooking (Natural foods). 2. Cooking. 3. Reducing
diets--Recipes. 4. Cookbooks.

TX741.B485 2012   641.5'63   C2012-906174-3

10 9 8 7 6 5 4 3 2 1

Distributed in Canada by
NBN (National Book Network)
67 Mowat Avenue, Suite 241
Toronto, ON
M6K 3E3

Distributed in USA by
NBN (National Book Network)
15200 NBN Way
Blue Ridge Summit, PA
17214

Printed in Canada

Robert Kennedy Publishing
BOOK DEPARTMENT

MANAGING DIRECTOR
Wendy Morley

SENIOR EDITOR
Amy Land

EDITOR, ONLINE AND PRINT
Meredith Barrett

ASSOCIATE EDITOR
Rachel Corradetti

ONLINE EDITOR
Kiersten Corradetti

EDITORIAL ASSISTANTS
Brittany Seki, Chelsea Kennedy

ART DIRECTOR
Gabriella Caruso Marques

ASSISTANT ART DIRECTOR
Jessica Pensabene Hearn

EDITORIAL DESIGNER
Brian Ross

PROP/WARDROBE STYLIST
Kelsey-Lynn Corradetti

SENIOR WEB DESIGNER
Chris Barnes

Table of Contents

It is as simple as coming to the realization that you don't have to give up the foods you love in order to eat clean.

Introduction

You *Can* Have it All!

Welcome to the third installment of *The Best of Clean Eating*. Time flies, doesn't it? Before I sat down to write this, I brewed a comforting cup of herbal tea and took a little trip back to 2008. As I reread my Editor's Letter from the very first issue of *Clean Eating*, I was flooded with memories. I realized that although a lot has changed since then (popular ingredients, trends and even hairstyles) a lot has remained the same – first and foremost, our mission of "Improving your life one meal at a time."

Those were exciting times – they still are. And one of the most thrilling aspects of my job is receiving your feedback. Not just discovering which recipes became scrape-the-plate favorites in your household (the type of feedback that makes the job of choosing the recipes for this book such a breeze), but also the stories of how your lives have been improved by clean eating.

For some, it may mean breaking away from the debilitating symptoms of a food allergy. For others, it could mean transforming from a skinny-fat, junk-food junkie who once lacked energy to someone who found well-being through nutritious whole foods that adequately fueled her demanding days. Or maybe it is as simple as coming to the realization that you don't have to give up the foods you love in order to eat clean.

Speaking of foods you love, this book is absolutely full of them. Inside you'll find eleven chapters containing exactly what you've told us you want most: quick and easy family dinners, budget-friendly suppers, meatless meals, classic comfort foods and decadent desserts.

Recreating classic recipes that seem too indulgent to be healthy is a big part of our mission statement. A few of the dishes that brought in such rave reviews that we knew we had to include them in this book include the Southwestern Cheddar Steak Fries (p. 55), the Lobster Mac & Cheese (p. 199), the Chicken Fingers with Ranch-Style Dipping Sauce (p. 152) – yes, you read that right! – and the Chocolate Chunk Banana Bread (p. 250).

As an added benefit, the recipes in this book feature something other recipes don't. You'll notice *Clean Eating*'s Nutritional Bonuses peppered throughout the book. These chunks of easy-to-digest information have been designed to help you discover the health benefits of each recipe, including which vitamins, minerals, antioxidants and phytonutrients you're getting and how they will benefit your body.

Inside this book you'll also enjoy mouthwatering food photography that practically leaps off the page. And you'll uncover the secret ingredient to a lifetime of happiness and love: the food. It really is the star ingredient in life – and one that never goes out of style!

To fabulous food and vigorous health!

Alicia Rewega
Editor in Chief

Breakfast, Brunch & Beverages

Strawberry-Banana Slush, p. 22

There's nothing like a fresh morning start with a nutritious meal! Wake up your loved ones with the tantalizing aroma of Mango-Coconut Pancakes touched with Citrus Honey Syrup. Or if you're on the go, grab a homemade Raspberry-Almond Muffin and avoid those fatty pastries at the coffee shop. *Clean Eating* offers you weekend-ready brunches complete with tasty, vitamin-rich drinks, like our relaxing Savory Breakfast Cocktail. Morning meals will never be the same!

Baked Eggs Benedict

Serves 4. **Hands-on time:** *15 minutes.* **Total time:** *22 minutes.*

Traditional Eggs Benedict with Hollandaise may not be the poster child for healthy fare, but our clean take on the breakfast classic has you covered.

INGREDIENTS:

- Olive oil cooking spray
- ½ oz extra-lean, uncured, cooked ham, finely diced
- 4 large eggs
- 1 Tbsp organic unsalted butter
- 1 Tbsp brown-rice flour
- ¾ cup 1% milk
- ½ oz low-fat Monterey Jack cheese, grated
- ¼ tsp each sea salt and fresh ground black pepper
- 2 cups baby spinach leaves
- 2 whole-grain English muffins, split and toasted
- 1 Tbsp chopped fresh tarragon

INSTRUCTIONS:

ONE: Preheat oven to 375°F. Bring a kettle or saucepan of water to a boil.

TWO: Mist 4 4-oz ramekins with cooking spray. Place ramekins into a 9 x 9-inch baking pan and fill with enough boiling water to reach halfway up sides of ramekins. (Alternatively, fill pan with very hot tap water.) Divide ham among ramekins and crack an egg into each. Transfer pan to oven and bake until eggs are just set, 7 to 10 minutes; do not over-bake. Remove from oven and let ramekins rest in pan to cool slightly.

THREE: Meanwhile, in a medium saucepan, melt butter on medium. Add flour and cook for 30 to 45 seconds, whisking constantly. Gradually add milk, whisking constantly until thickened, about 2 minutes. Remove from heat and add cheese, stirring until completely melted. Stir in salt and pepper; set aside.

FOUR: In a large sauté pan on medium-high heat, add 2 tsp water and spinach and sauté, stirring occasionally, until wilted, 45 to 60 seconds. Drain.

FIVE: Top each muffin half with spinach, dividing evenly. Run a knife around the inside edge of each ramekin to loosen eggs. Using a spoon, remove egg-ham mixture from ramekins and place over top of spinach, dividing evenly. Stir tarragon into cheese mixture and pour over top of egg-ham mixture, dividing evenly. Serve warm.

Nutrients per serving (1 egg, ⅛ oz ham, ½ muffin, ¼ cup cheese sauce): *Calories: 215, Total Fat: 10 g, Sat. Fat: 4 g, Monounsaturated Fat: 2 g, Polyunsaturated Fat: 1 g, Carbs: 20 g, Fiber: 3 g, Sugars: 5 g, Protein: 13 g, Sodium: 443 mg, Cholesterol: 226 mg*

Nutritional Bonus:
Baby spinach is an excellent source of antioxidants and vitamin C, while low-fat Monterey Jack contributes a mere 4 oz of fat per serving and fresh tarragon adds a kick of low-sodium, low-cal flavor.

14

Mango-
Coconut
Pancakes

Mango-Coconut Pancakes
WITH CITRUS HONEY SYRUP

*Serves 4. **Hands-on time:** 30 minutes. **Total time:** 30 minutes.*

Savory clove and nutmeg add a touch of warmth to these tropical-inspired pancakes. Serve them with a delicate drizzle of our Citrus Honey Syrup.

INGREDIENTS:

- ¾ cup whole-wheat pastry flour
- ¾ cup shredded low-fat unsweetened coconut
- 1 Tbsp organic evaporated cane juice
- 1½ tsp baking powder
- ¼ tsp sea salt
- ¼ tsp ground clove
- ¼ tsp ground nutmeg
- ¾ cup liquid egg whites or 6 large egg whites
- ½ cup 2% milk
- Zest ½ orange
- Zest ½ lime, plus additional for garnish
- 1 small mango, peeled, pitted and cut into ⅓-inch dice, plus additional chunks for garnish
- Olive oil cooking spray

CITRUS HONEY SYRUP

- 1¼ cups peeled, pitted and cubed fresh mango (about 1 mango)
- 2 Tbsp raw honey
- 3 Tbsp fresh orange juice
- 1 Tbsp fresh lime juice

INSTRUCTIONS:

ONE: In a large bowl, whisk flour, coconut, cane juice, baking powder, salt, clove and nutmeg. In a medium bowl, whisk egg whites, milk, orange zest and lime zest. Add milk mixture to flour mixture and stir until just moistened. Fold in mango.

TWO: Heat a large nonstick skillet or griddle on medium and mist with cooking spray. Working in batches, add 3 Tbsp batter to skillet per pancake, spreading each with the back of a spoon to form 3- to 4-inch circles. Cook until bubbles form on the surface and bottoms are golden brown, 1 to 2 minutes. Flip and cook until golden brown and centers are cooked through, 1 to 2 minutes; if pancakes brown too quickly, reduce heat to medium-low. (TIP: While remaining pancakes are cooking, wrap cooked pancakes in foil and transfer to a 300°F oven to keep warm.)

THREE: Prepare Citrus Honey Syrup: In a medium saucepan, combine mango, honey, orange juice and lime juice. Heat on medium and bring to a simmer. Reduce heat to low and simmer, stirring frequently, until slightly thickened, 4 to 6 minutes.

FOUR: To serve, top pancakes with additional mango and lime zest, and drizzle with Citrus Honey Syrup.

Nutrients per serving (3 pancakes with 1¼ Tbsp syrup): *Calories: 328, Total Fat: 8.5 g, Sat. Fat: 6 g, Monounsaturated Fat: 0 g, Polyunsaturated Fat: 0 g, Carbs: 57 g, Fiber: 8 g, Sugars: 30 g, Protein: 10.5 g, Sodium: 212 mg, Cholesterol: 2 mg*

Savory Waffles

*Makes 12 waffles. **Hands-on time:** 20 minutes. **Total time:** 35 minutes.*

Who says crêpes are the only breakfast food that can wear both sweet and savory hats? Not us! Soft and cheesy on the inside, crispy on the outside, and topped with tangy apples and sweet syrup, these waffles wear several hats – all of them delicious! In fact, this exciting combination of flavors and textures will have you saying, "Hats off" to *Clean Eating* for sharing this recipe.

INGREDIENTS:

- 2 apples, peeled, cored and cubed
- 2 eggs
- 1¾ cups 1% milk
- ¼ cup safflower oil
- 1 cup light spelt flour
- 1 cup quinoa flour
- ¼ tsp sea salt
- 4 tsp baking powder
- 2 oz low-fat sharp cheddar cheese, shredded
- 2 Tbsp chopped chives
- 3 Tbsp pure maple syrup, optional

INSTRUCTIONS:

ONE: In a medium saucepan, combine apples and ½ cup water. Place on medium heat and bring to a simmer; reduce heat to low and continue simmering until apples soften, 8 to 10 minutes, stirring occasionally. Remove from heat; set aside.

TWO: Preheat a waffle iron. In a large bowl, whisk eggs, milk and oil until combined, about 45 seconds. In a separate large bowl, combine both flours, salt and baking powder. Add to egg mixture and mix until just blended. Using a spatula or wooden spoon, fold in cheese and chives. Pour ⅓ cup batter onto each section of waffle iron and close lid; cook until golden brown and crispy, 3 to 5 minutes, checking for doneness when steam escaping from waffle iron slows. Repeat with remaining batter. Top waffles with apple mixture, dividing evenly, and maple syrup, if desired.

Nutrients per serving (1 waffle and 2 Tbsp apple mixture): *Calories: 167, Total Fat: 7 g, Sat. Fat: 1 g, Monounsaturated Fat: 4 g, Polyunsaturated Fat: 1 g, Carbs: 21 g, Fiber: 3 g, Sugars: 5 g, Protein: 6 g, Sodium: 104 mg, Cholesterol: 38 mg*

Shrimp & Vegetable Sauté
WITH CHEESY-BAKED GRITS

Serves 6. Hands-on time: 40 minutes. Total time: 1 hour.

This dish is packed with filling lean protein, yet it remains very low in calories – leaving you plenty of room to enjoy a muffin on the side!

INGREDIENTS:

- Olive oil cooking spray
- 1 cup quick-cooking grits
- 4 oz low-fat garlic and herb spreadable cheese
- 3 large fresh egg whites
- 1 lb medium shrimp, peeled and deveined, tail on or off
- 1 tsp mild chile powder
- ⅓ tsp sea salt, divided
- Fresh ground black pepper, to taste
- 2 Tbsp olive oil, divided
- 2 small zucchini, quartered lengthwise and cut into ½-inch pieces
- ½ red onion, chopped
- 3 cloves garlic, finely chopped
- 1½ cups no-salt-added diced tomatoes with juice
- 1 Tbsp chopped fresh basil

INSTRUCTIONS:

ONE: Preheat oven to 325°F and coat a 2-qt baking dish with cooking spray. Prepare grits according to package directions. When done, remove from heat and stir in cheese. Partially cover and let cool slightly.

TWO: Add egg whites to a clean, stainless steel bowl and beat with an electric mixer on medium-high speed until stiff peaks form. Gently fold one-third of egg whites into grits. Fold remaining egg whites into grits in 2 batches. Transfer mixture to prepared baking dish and bake for 40 minutes or until puffed and lightly browned. Let cool for 10 minutes before serving.

THREE: Meanwhile, season shrimp with chile powder, ¼ tsp salt and black pepper. Place a large, heavy skillet on medium-high and add 2 tsp oil. When skillet is hot, add half of shrimp. (TIP: Cooking in batches means that the shrimp will have enough space in the hot pan to brown and develop flavor, rather than steam.) Cook without moving shrimp until browned on bottom, about 2 minutes. Turn and cook until opposite sides are browned, 1 to 2 more minutes. Transfer shrimp to a plate and repeat with additional 2 tsp oil and remaining shrimp.

FOUR: Pour remaining 2 tsp oil into same, empty skillet on medium-high. Add zucchini and onion, season with remaining salt and black pepper, and cook until softened and lightly browned, 6 to 8 minutes. Add garlic and cook for 1 minute, stirring constantly. Add tomatoes with their juice and cook until mixture thickens slightly. Add shrimp with any juices that have accumulated on the plate and stir until just heated through. Remove from heat and stir in basil. Spoon grits onto each of 6 plates, dividing evenly, then top with about ¾ cup shrimp mixture. Serve immediately.

Nutrients per serving (1 cup grits and ¾ cup shrimp mixture): Calories: 284, Total Fat: 8 g, Sat. Fat: 2 g, Monounsaturated Fat: 4 g, Polyunsaturated Fat: 1 g, Omega-3s: 430 mg, Omega-6s: 640 mg, Carbs: 26 g, Fiber: 2 g, Sugars: 3 g, Protein: 22 g, Sodium: 511 mg, Cholesterol: 124 mg

Mexican Breakfast Bake

Serves 4. Hands-on time: 20 minutes. Total time: 35 minutes.

Craving a casserole, but only have a few folks to feed? This zesty dish will fit the bill (and fill your stomach) without mountains of leftovers because it is baked and served in individual ramekins.

INGREDIENTS:

- 1 tsp olive oil
- 1 medium onion, chopped
- 2 cloves garlic, chopped
- 1 large Anaheim or New Mexican green chile pepper or 2 small hot chile peppers, cut into ¼-inch dice
- 1 medium sweet potato, peeled and cut into ¼-inch dice
- 2 medium tomatoes, cut into ¼-inch dice
- 2 cups BPA-free canned black beans, drained and rinsed well (or cooked black beans)
- 1 tsp ground cumin
- 1 tsp chile powder
- 1 tsp smoked paprika
- Olive oil cooking spray
- 4 large eggs
- 4 Tbsp finely chopped cilantro leaves
- 1 oz queso fresco cheese, separated into 4 pieces
- 2 oz avocado, thinly sliced

INSTRUCTIONS:

ONE: Preheat oven to 450°F. In large saucepot on medium-high, heat oil. Add onion, garlic, pepper and sweet potato. Sauté for 5 minutes. Add tomatoes, beans, cumin, chile powder and paprika. Cover and cook for 20 minutes, until sweet potatoes soften.

TWO: Mist 4 16-oz ramekins with cooking spray. Place 1 cup vegetable mixture into each ramekin and spread to outside edges, making a well in the center. Carefully crack 1 egg in center well of each ramekin.

THREE: Bake for 5 minutes, until eggs are set; remove from oven. Set oven to broil on high. Add ramekins back to oven and broil for 5 minutes, until eggs are soft set (for firmer eggs, broil for 5 more minutes). Remove from oven and sprinkle each dish with 1 Tbsp cilantro, ¼ oz cheese and 2 or 3 slices avocado. Serve immediately.

TIP: If you don't want to bake all 4 ramekins, save leftovers for the next day! Simply prepare this recipe through Step One and refrigerate. When ready to eat, mist ramekins with cooking spray, pour in vegetable mixture and microwave for 1 to 2 minutes. Continue with Step Two.

Nutrients per ramekin: Calories: 285, Total Fat: 9 g, Sat. Fat: 2 g, Monounsaturated Fat: 4 g, Polyunsaturated Fat: 1 g, Carbs: 35 g, Fiber: 10 g, Sugars: 7 g, Protein: 16 g, Sodium: 134 mg, Cholesterol: 214 mg

Mexican
Breakfast
Bake

Savory
Breakfast
Cocktail

Ruby Crush

Tropical
Tonic

Need a surefire way to sneak a few healthy servings of produce into your daily routine? Skip the juice bar lineup and make your own fresh-squeezed glass of fruits and vegetables instead!

Tropical Tonic

Serves 2. **Hands-on time:** *5 minutes.* **Total Time:** *5 minutes.*

A sweet breakfast treat, this sunny drink is full of vitamin-rich ingredients. And since these fruits are available fresh or frozen year-round, you're going to want to keep this recipe handy during winter's cold and flu months as well.

INGREDIENTS:

- 3 oz pineapple, peeled, cored and cut into chunks
- 1 mango, peeled, pitted and cut into chunks
- 2 kiwi, peeled and cut into chunks
- Ice, as desired

INSTRUCTIONS:

Juice pineapple, mango and kiwi. Stir well and serve over ice, if desired.

Nutrients per 5-oz serving: *Calories: 135, Total Fat: 1.5 g, Sat. Fat: 0 g, Carbs: 34 g, Fiber: 5 g, Sugars: 26 g, Protein: 1.5 g, Sodium: 4 mg, Cholesterol: 0 mg*

Savory Breakfast Cocktail

Serves 1. **Hands-on time:** *5 minutes.* **Total time:** *5 minutes.*

Bloody Mary fans will love this hearty drink, especially if you spike it with a dash of Worcestershire sauce.

INGREDIENTS:

- 2 stalks celery
- 1^{1}₂ oz fresh spinach
- 1 tomato (about 5 oz), cored
- ^{1}₂ lemon, peeled (seeded, if desired), plus lemon wedges for garnish
- Ice, as desired

INSTRUCTIONS:

Juice produce in the following order: celery, spinach, tomato and lemon. Stir well. If desired, serve over ice and garnish glass with lemon wedge.

Nutrients per 6.5-oz serving: *Calories: 64, Total Fat: 0 g, Sat. Fat: 0 g, Carbs: 16 g, Fiber: 6 g, Sugars: 6 g, Protein: 2 g, Sodium: 202 mg, Cholesterol: 0 mg*

Ruby Crush

Serves 2. **Hands-on time:** *5 minutes.* **Total time:** *5 minutes.*

Phytonutrient-rich beets give this juice its dark red color and earthy flavor. Ginger adds a surprisingly spicy bite and packs a nutritional punch – it's known to aid digestion.

INGREDIENTS:

- ½-inch piece ginger, peeled
- 2 oranges, peeled
- 4 oz beets (about 3 small)
- Ice, as desired

INSTRUCTIONS:

Juice produce in the following order: ginger, oranges and beets. Stir well and serve over ice, if desired.

Nutrients per 8-oz serving: *Calories: 95, Total Fat: 0.5 g, Sat. Fat: 0 g, Carbs: 22 g, Fiber: 2 g, Sugars: 17 g, Protein: 2 g, Sodium: 46 mg, Cholesterol: 0 mg*

TIP: Juicing citrus fruit in a centrifugal or masticating juicer can give it a little bitterness from the pith and seeds. If you prefer a sweeter taste, juice oranges separately with a reamer.

Chocolate Espresso Crêpes
WITH CARAMELIZED BANANAS

*Serves 6. **Makes** 12 crêpes. **Hands-on time:** 20 minutes. **Total time:** 20 minutes.*

Everyone knows that chocolate and coffee make a perfect pair, but throw in some warm, caramelized bananas and you've got yourself an unforgettable trio of tastes!

INGREDIENTS:

- ¼ cup unsweetened cocoa powder
- ¾ cup light spelt flour
- 1 tsp instant espresso powder
- 1½ Tbsp organic evaporated cane juice
- ¼ tsp sea salt
- 1 cup 1% milk
- 2 large eggs
- 1 tsp safflower oil
- Olive oil cooking spray
- 1 tsp organic unsalted butter
- 4 bananas, thinly sliced
- 3 Tbsp pure maple syrup, optional

INSTRUCTIONS:

ONE: In a large bowl, combine cocoa powder, flour, espresso powder, cane juice and salt.

TWO: In a small bowl, combine milk, eggs and oil. Add to cocoa mixture and whisk until well combined.

THREE: Coat an 8-inch nonstick pan with cooking spray and place on medium heat. Drop 3 Tbsp batter into pan and swirl to coat bottom; cook until edges start to dry, 45 to 60 seconds. Using a thin, flexible spatula, flip and cook for 30 to 45 seconds. Transfer to a large plate and repeat with remaining batter, making 12 crêpes.

FOUR: In same pan, melt butter on medium heat. Working in batches, add bananas in a single layer and cook, flipping once, for 45 to 60 seconds, until browned on both sides. Spoon bananas into center of crêpes, dividing evenly, and top with syrup, if desired. Fold and serve.

Nutrients per serving (2 crêpes and ⅓ cup bananas): Calories: 185, Total Fat: 5 g, Sat. Fat: 2 g, Carbs: 33 g, Fiber: 4 g, Sugars: 14 g, Protein: 7 g, Sodium: 128 mg, Cholesterol: 75 mg

Hearty Sausage & Cheese Frittata

*Serves 6. **Hands-on time:** 7 minutes. **Total time:** 15 minutes.*

Does clean, comforting and ready in 15 minutes sound too good to be true? One bite of this frittata and we know you'll become a believer.

INGREDIENTS:

- Olive oil cooking spray
- 10 oz deli-fresh low-fat chicken or turkey sausage (about 3 sausages), casings removed
- 1½ cups chopped broccoli florets
- ½ red or green bell pepper, diced
- 2 green onions, thinly sliced
- 6 egg whites
- 2 eggs
- ½ cup low-fat ricotta cheese
- ½ cup grated low-fat cheddar cheese

INSTRUCTIONS:

ONE: Heat a 9- or 10-inch ovenproof, stick-resistant (or seasoned) skillet on medium-high; mist with cooking spray. Add sausage, broccoli, pepper and onions and cook, breaking up sausage with a wooden spoon, until sausage is crumbled and no longer pink, about 3 minutes.

TWO: Meanwhile, in a medium bowl, whisk egg whites, eggs and ricotta until foamy and just a few lumps remain. Pour over top of sausage mixture; cover, reduce heat to medium and cook until bottom and sides are firm and top is almost set, about 7 minutes.

THREE: Preheat broiler to high. Uncover skillet and sprinkle cheddar over top of egg mixture. Broil until center is set and cheddar is melted and bubbly, 2 to 3 minutes.

NOTE: If skillet handle is not ovenproof, simply wrap it in foil. Alternatively, cover skillet and cook on stove top on medium heat until set in center and cheddar is melted, about 4 minutes.) Slide or invert onto a cutting board and cut into 6 wedges.

Nutrients per serving (⅙ of frittata or about 1½ cups): Calories: 166, Total Fat: 7 g, Sat. Fat: 3 g, Monounsaturated Fat: 1 g, Polyunsaturated Fat: 0.5 g, Carbs: 5 g, Fiber: 1 g, Sugars: 3 g, Protein: 19 g, Sodium: 460 mg, Cholesterol: 118 mg

Blueberry Cheesecake-Stuffed French Toast Casserole

Serves 10. **Hands-on time:** *40 minutes.* **Total time:** *1 hour, 10 minutes.*

Cheesecake AND French toast?! Nothing sounds more perfect than your 2 favorite comfort foods combined in one glorious breakfast! Plus, you can start your day with the antioxidant power of blueberries along with cinnamon to pump up your immune system.

INGREDIENTS:

- Olive oil cooking spray
- 13 to 14 slices whole-wheat sandwich bread, crusts removed
- 1 cup low-fat ricotta cheese
- ½ cup ⅓-less-fat plain cream cheese
- 4 large eggs, divided
- 5 Tbsp organic evaporated cane juice, divided
- 1¾ cups fresh blueberries
- 1 cup 2% milk
- 2 egg whites
- 2 tsp pure vanilla extract
- 1 tsp ground cinnamon
- ¼ tsp sea salt
- ¼ cup sliced unsalted almonds

BLUEBERRY SAUCE

- 2¼ cups fresh blueberries
- ¼ cup organic evaporated cane juice

INSTRUCTIONS:

ONE: Preheat oven to 350°F. Coat a 9 x 13-inch baking dish with cooking spray. Place half of bread on bottom of dish, trimming as necessary to fit in a snug single layer.

TWO: In a food processor or blender, combine ricotta, cream cheese, 1 whole egg and 2 Tbsp cane juice. Process until smooth. Pour mixture over bread layer and spread to coat evenly. Top with blueberries. Cover with remaining bread, trimming to fit in a single layer.

THREE: In a large bowl, whisk remaining 3 whole eggs, 1 Tbsp cane juice, milk, egg whites, vanilla, cinnamon and salt. Pour evenly over bread. Place almonds in a zip-top bag and lightly crush with a rolling pin. Add remaining 2 Tbsp cane juice and shake to combine. Sprinkle over bread. Cover with foil and bake in center of oven for 25 minutes. Uncover and bake for an additional 10 minutes, until center is slightly puffed and set (filling will remain creamy). Then broil for 2 to 3 minutes, until top is lightly browned. Remove from oven and let cool for 10 minutes.

FOUR: Prepare blueberry sauce: In a medium saucepan, combine blueberries, ½ cup water and cane juice. Bring to a boil, then reduce heat to low and simmer, uncovered and stirring often, until berries begin to burst and liquid thickens slightly, about 10 minutes. Divide French toast into 10 portions and top each with 3 Tbsp blueberry sauce.

Nutrients per serving: *Calories: 285, Total Fat: 9 g, Sat. Fat: 4 g, Carbs: 39 g, Fiber: 4 g, Sugars: 22 g, Protein: 13 g, Sodium: 378 mg, Cholesterol: 101 mg*

Enjoy happy hour early! There's no need to wait till 5 pm to indulge in one of these clean cocktails. Each of the following five beverages will quench your thirst with fruit, vegetables and herbs ... not alcohol.

Muddle Up

Serves 2. **Hands-on time:** 5 minutes. **Total time:** 7 minutes.

Crush mint, lime and basil together and you've got a refreshing blast of flavor! While basil may seem unconventional in a beverage, it's actually botanically related to mint, adding a light floral essence.

INGREDIENTS:

- ½ cup torn fresh basil leaves
- ½ cup torn fresh mint leaves
- 1 large lime, cut into small wedges
- 1 tsp organic evaporated cane juice
- 2 cups sparkling water
- Ice, as desired
- Fresh mint sprigs for garnish, optional

INSTRUCTIONS:

ONE: Place basil, mint, lime and cane juice in the bottom of a large martini shaker. Using a wooden spoon, crush mixture until lime releases most of its juice and herbs are slightly bruised, about 2 minutes.

TWO: Top with sparkling water and stir to combine. Fill 2 glasses with ice and divide mixture evenly among glasses. If desired, garnish with mint sprigs.

TIP: The act of crushing the herbs and lime together is referred to by bartenders as "muddling." The idea is to get the aromatic ingredients to release their essential oils, providing maximum flavor!

Nutrients per 8-oz serving: Calories: 30, Total Fat: 0 g, Sat. Fat: 0 g, Carbs: 8 g, Fiber: 3 g, Sugars: 2 g, Protein: 1 g, Sodium: 8 mg, Cholesterol: 0 mg

NUTRITIONAL BONUS: Basil has been shown to possess both anti-bacterial and anti-inflammatory properties thanks to the volatile oils within its leaves. Components such as estragole, linalool, eugenol and limonene, to name a few, in the basil may help restrict the growth of bacteria.

Strawberry Banana Slush

Serves 2. **Hands-on time:** 5 minutes. **Total time:** 7 minutes.

If you're craving a cool summer daiquiri, you're in luck! With half the calories and less than a third of the sugar of your standard Cuban cocktail, our slushy sipper will cool you down in no time. We'll drink to that!

INGREDIENTS:

- 1 cup sliced strawberries, plus 2 whole strawberries for garnish
- 1 medium banana, frozen and peeled
- Juice 1 large lime
- 2 tsp organic evaporated cane juice
- ½ cup fresh orange juice
- 1 cup crushed ice

INSTRUCTIONS:

In a blender, combine all ingredients and purée until smooth. (Mixture will be very thick and slushy.) Divide between 2 8-oz glasses and garnish with additional strawberries, if desired.

Nutrients per 8-oz serving: Calories: 128, Total Fat: 1 g, Sat. Fat: 0 g, Carbs: 32 g, Fiber: 3 g, Sugars: 21 g, Protein: 2 g, Sodium: 5 mg, Cholesterol: 0 mg

NUTRITIONAL BONUS: Thanks to the strawberries and banana, not only is a single cup of this daiquiri-inspired beverage chock-full of vitamin C and fiber, but it also provides a good source of potassium (15% DV). The mineral plays an integral role in heart function, plus it's vital in skeletal and smooth muscle contraction and, as a result, healthy digestion.

Tea-Killa Sunrise

Serves 4. **Hands-on time:** 5 minutes. **Total time:** 25 minutes (includes tea cooling time).

Caffeine-free and boasting a mild fruity flavor, our jazzed-up brew makes a perfect addition to your next backyard barbecue.

INGREDIENTS:

- Ice, as needed
- 1 large navel orange
- 3 cups prepared rooibos tea (regularly brewed), cooled to room temperature
- Juice ½ lemon
- 2 Tbsp raw honey
- Fresh mint sprigs for garnish, optional

INSTRUCTIONS:

ONE: Fill a large pitcher halfway with ice. Slice orange in half. Juice first half into a small bowl and set aside. Cut remaining half into slices and add to pitcher.

TWO: Pour orange juice, tea, lemon juice and honey into pitcher and stir until chilled, about 1 minute. To serve, pour mixture into tall glasses filled with ice and garnish with mint sprigs, if desired.

Nutrients per 8-oz serving: Calories: 57, Total Fat: 0 g, Sat. Fat: 0 g, Carbs: 17 g, Fiber: 0 g, Sugars: 11 g, Protein: 0.5 g, Sodium: 0.5 mg, Cholesterol: 0 mg

Not-a-Colada

*Serves: 2. **Hands-on time:** 5 minutes. **Total time:** 5 minutes.*

Do you like piña coladas? At over 560 calories, 62 grams of sugar and six grams of fat per typical eight-ounce serving, you may want to say "no" and try our cleaned-up version instead! We kept that signature velvety texture thanks to a small helping of light coconut milk, and fresh, succulent pineapple ensures your taste buds get whisked away to the islands.

INGREDIENTS:

- Juice 1 lime
- ½ tsp unsweetened shredded coconut, toasted
- 1 cup coconut water
- ⅓ cup light coconut milk
- 1 cup fresh pineapple chunks
- ½ tsp pure coconut extract
- 1 tsp pure maple syrup
- 1 cup crushed ice

INSTRUCTIONS:

ONE: Place lime juice and shredded coconut into 2 separate shallow dishes. Dip rims of 2 8-oz hurricane glasses in lime juice, then shredded coconut. (Coconut should stick to rim of glass.)

TWO: In a blender, mix any leftover lime juice from dish with coconut water, coconut milk, pineapple, coconut extract, maple syrup and ice until well combined, about 45 seconds. Pour into prepared glasses, dividing evenly.

Nutrients per 8-oz serving: Calories: 106, Total Fat: 3 g, Sat. Fat: 3 g, Carbs: 20 g, Fiber: 3 g, Sugars: 14 g, Protein: 1 g, Sodium: 135 mg, Cholesterol: 0 mg

NUTRITIONAL BONUS: You may have noticed the many coconut water-based products on the market, often targeted towards athletes. What's the deal? Coconut water is rehydrating and naturally isotonic, which means it contains a balance of electrolytes – sodium, potassium and other minerals – that matches the concentration found within your blood and that is lost through sweat and exercise.

All Hail Caesar

*Serves 2. **Hands-on time:** 5 minutes. **Total time:** 7 minutes.*

This mocktail is an eye-opener thanks to its spicy finish (hello, hot sauce!). Wow friends and family by serving it at your next weekend brunch.

INGREDIENTS:

- Juice 1 lime
- 1 tsp celery seed
- Juice ½ lemon
- 1 tsp fresh grated horseradish
- 2-inch chunk English cucumber, peeled and chopped
- 1½ cups low-sodium tomato juice
- Pinch fresh ground black pepper
- 2 dashes hot pepper sauce (such as Tabasco), optional
- Ice, as desired
- English cucumber slices or celery stalks for garnish, optional

INSTRUCTIONS:

ONE: Place lime juice and celery seed into 2 separate shallow dishes. Dip rims of 2 old-fashioned tumblers into lime juice, then celery seed. (Celery seed should stick to rims of glasses.) Set aside.

TWO: In a blender, mix any leftover lime juice and celery seed from dishes with lemon juice, horseradish, cucumber, tomato juice, black pepper and hot pepper sauce, if desired. Blend until smooth, about 3 minutes. Fill prepared glasses with ice and divide mixture evenly among them. Garnish each with 1 slice English cucumber, if desired.

Nutrients per 8-oz serving: Calories: 55, Total Fat: 0 g, Sat. Fat: 0 g, Carbs: 12 g, Fiber: 2 g, Sugars: 7 g, Protein: 2 g, Sodium: 137 mg, Cholesterol: 0 mg

24

Raspberry-Almond Muffins

Raspberry-Almond Muffins

Makes 12 muffins. *Hands-on time:* 15 minutes. *Total time:* 45 minutes.

Light, fluffy and bursting with juicy red raspberries, these three-step muffins get a savory touch with a dash of nutmeg and cardamom. For a milder flavor, substitute one or both of these spices with twice the amount of cinnamon.

INGREDIENTS:

- 2 cups whole-wheat pastry flour
- ⅔ cup organic evaporated cane juice
- 3 Tbsp ground flaxseeds
- 2 tsp baking powder
- ½ tsp baking soda
- ½ tsp sea salt
- ¼ tsp ground nutmeg
- ¼ tsp ground cardamom
- ¾ cup low-fat vanilla yogurt
- ½ cup 2% milk
- 3 Tbsp walnut or safflower oil
- 1 large egg
- ½ tsp pure almond extract
- 6 oz fresh or frozen raspberries, thawed (TIP: If using frozen, thaw on paper towels to absorb maximum moisture.)
- 3 Tbsp sliced raw unsalted almonds

INSTRUCTIONS:

ONE: Preheat oven to 350°F. Line a 12-cup muffin tin with paper muffin liners.

TWO: In a large bowl, whisk flour, cane juice, flaxseeds, baking powder, baking soda, salt, nutmeg and cardamom. In a medium bowl, whisk yogurt, milk, oil, egg and almond extract.

THREE: Add yogurt mixture to flour mixture and stir until just moistened. With a rubber spatula, gently fold in raspberries; do not over-mix. Spoon into muffin liners, dividing evenly. Sprinkle almonds over top, pressing gently to adhere. Bake until edges are golden and a toothpick comes out clean when inserted in center, 20 to 22 minutes. Let cool in tin for 5 minutes. Remove muffins from tin and transfer to a cooling rack.

TIP: Freeze muffins in a sealed zip-top bag for up to 2 months. To serve, defrost at room temperature.

Nutrients per muffin: Calories: 192, Total Fat: 6 g, Sat. Fat: 1 g, Monounsaturated Fat: 3 g, Polyunsaturated Fat: 2 g, Carbs: 31 g, Fiber: 4 g, Sugars: 13 g, Protein: 4 g, Sodium: 153 mg, Cholesterol: 19 mg

Stuffed French Toast

Serves 4. *Hands-on time:* 15 minutes. *Total time:* 20 minutes.

Not your typical French toast, this is truly some next-level stuff. Be warned, though…. Not only does it taste mind-blowingly delicious, but tucking into one of these babies may evoke a bit of an existential dilemma, namely: Do you use a fork and knife or dive in with both hands?

INGREDIENTS:

- 2 large eggs
- ¼ cup 1% milk
- 1 tsp pure vanilla extract
- 2 Tbsp hazelnut butter
- 8 thin slices country wheat or whole-wheat bread
- 1 banana, sliced
- ½ cup sliced strawberries
- 4 Tbsp pure maple syrup, optional

INSTRUCTIONS:

ONE: In a shallow dish, beat eggs, milk and vanilla; set aside.

TWO: Spread ¼ Tbsp hazelnut butter onto 1 side of each bread slice; place slices on a work surface or cutting board, buttered side up. Layer 4 slices with bananas and strawberries, dividing evenly. Top with remaining 4 bread slices, buttered side down, to form sandwiches. Press each down gently to squeeze filling together slightly.

THREE: Heat a large nonstick pan on medium-high. Carefully dip each sandwich into egg mixture, turning to coat. Working in batches, transfer sandwiches to pan and cook until golden, flipping once, 1 to 2 minutes per side. Serve warm with maple syrup, if desired.

Nutrients per sandwich: Calories: 263, Total Fat: 9 g, Sat. Fat: 1 g, Carbs: 32.5 g, Fiber: 6 g, Sugars: 8 g, Protein: 12 g, Sodium: 234 mg, Cholesterol: 107 mg

Nutritional Bonus:

If you're wondering how French toast can be considered slimming, check out the fiber content of this recipe. At almost a quarter of your required daily amount, the fiber in this dish will not only help keep you feeling full and satisfied, it will also help keep your weight in check.

Live Longer and *Stronger*

10 habits that may extend your life.

1 Treat Yourself with Dark Chocolate

It's been said before, but it's been proven again: Eating chocolate can be good for you, and according to current studies, in varied ways. Some of the latest research, reported in the *Journal of the American College of Cardiology*, shows that women who eat two bars of dark chocolate per week have a 20% lower risk of stroke, probably due to the flavonoids in cocoa. An earlier study found that eating only one square, or 6.3 grams, of dark chocolate per day may also help reduce blood pressure. Irrespective of the amounts that women ate, the message is clear: Cocoa continues to showcase benefits, assuming you eat reasonable quantities.

2 Smile

People who feel happy tend to live longer lives, found a British study published in late 2011 in the *Proceedings of the National Academy of Sciences*. Earlier studies have shown that simply smiling will actually make you feel happier, too.

3 Consume Fewer Calories

Scientists at Sweden's University of Gothenburg found that restricting calories helps the enzyme peroxiredeoxin to function, countering damage to genetic material. They speculate that a caloric reduction of one-third might slow the aging process.

4 Reduce Alcohol Intake

Cocktails are no cause for celebration: Heavy drinking is also linked to lung cancer and stomach cancer, a pair of separate new studies reveal. The first, presented at the annual meeting of the American College of Chest Physicians, found that people who had three or more drinks per day had a 30% higher risk of lung cancer than teetotalers. The second, published in the *American Journal of Clinical Nutrition*, suggested that beer in particular might up your risk of stomach cancer. To reduce your risk, opt for a seltzer or plain water with lemon.

5 Drink More Water

You learned back in grade school that your body is about 60% water – now, a new study shows just how important it is to replenish those fluid stores. Researchers at the French national research institute INSERM found that adults who drink two or fewer glasses of water each day are more likely to have abnormally high blood sugar, a precursor to diabetes. Aim to consume at least nine cups of beverages (including tea and coffee) per day; that's equivalent to the 2.2 liters that the Institute of Medicine has determined as adequate for most women.

6 Get Some Vitamin Z

We don't need another trigger to keep us up at night, but here's one: A new study published in the journal *Circulation* has found that insomnia could increase our risk of a heart attack. Other recent studies reveal that poor sleep quality is tied to high blood pressure. Since sleep habits and preferences vary, it's important to do whatever it takes – from drinking a glass of warm milk to turning off the computer at least an hour before bedtime – to get adequate Zs.

7 Consume Less Salt

Despite doctors' advice, Americans are still eating far too many sodium-packed foods, according to a recent announcement by the Centers for Disease Control and Prevention. You should have no more than 2,300 milligrams of sodium each day, and no more than 1,500 mg if you are 51 or older, are African American, have high blood pressure, or have diabetes or chronic kidney disease.

8 Make Sure You Get Enough Fiber

This one is simple: Eating a high-fiber diet could help you live longer. A recent study in the *Archives of Internal Medicine* followed nearly 400,000 men and women between the ages of 50 and 71 for a period of nine years. It found that those who ate the most fiber from whole grains were 22% less likely to die from natural causes than those who ate the least. Women should aim for at least 25 grams of fiber per day through whole foods, while men should aim for 38 grams per day.

9 Lean On Friends and Family

That is, if they have healthy habits. Edelman's 2011 Health Barometer survey reveals that people who hang out with healthy people tend to be healthier. If your pals are chip-scarfing couch potatoes, you may be able to turn them toward a more healthy lifestyle by serving nutritious meals and organizing walks. Of course, make sure that you yourself have a strong cohort of healthy, inspiring friends.

10 Get Your Vitamin D

Study after study is pushing the sunshine vitamin to the top of the health charts. One of the latest, from Germany, shows that people who consume enough D could lower their risk of type 2 diabetes. Another found an association with low levels of vitamin D and advanced cancer. A new blood test can determine how much more vitamin D you can get from your diet. At your next physical, ask your doc about the latest test.

Don't Worry Be Happy Today

The top foods and supplements proven to help boost your mood.

You've noticed her in the grocery store or in line at the post office: the woman who's always in a good mood, quick with a smile and unflustered by the typical daily annoyances. Chances are, she hasn't won the lottery. She just knows – as an increasing number of studies show – that what you consume has a profound impact on not only your body, but also your brain. Here are the best foods and supplements for eternal happiness, and some other positive side effects, too.

A single three-ounce serving of **wild salmon** has more omega-3 fatty acids than just about any other type of seafood. Further, omega-3 fatty acids can help stabilize your mood and even make you more agreeable, found researchers from the University of Pittsburgh School of Medicine. You can also feel good knowing that omega-3s may reduce your heart disease risk by as much as 90%, according to a Danish study of women aged 15 to 49, published in December 2011 in *Hypertension: Journal of the American Heart Association*. Lead researcher Marin Strøm, PhD, says women should eat fish as a main course at least twice a week.

Scientists have shown that **B vitamins**, especially vitamin B12, improve mental health. In one Finnish study, researchers found that depressive outpatients with the highest levels of B12 battled their symptoms better than those who had lower levels of the vitamin. Additional studies also now link B vitamins with improved memory – which is good, because how can you stay cheery if you forget where you left your iPhone? Because B12 is found naturally only in animal products, and because foods fortified with the vitamin may be chock-full of chemicals, a supplement could be the answer. Look for one that will give you at least the recommended dietary allowance of 2.4 micrograms of B12 per day.

One cup of **yogurt** contains nearly a quarter of your daily need for tryptophan, an amino acid that converts to the neurotransmitter serotonin, a critical regulator of mood, sleep and agreeability. Since your body can't produce tryptophan, you have to get it from your diet. Yogurt is also rich in B12, and a study by the Northwestern University Feinberg School of Medicine, published in the *Proceedings of the National Academy of Sciences*, found that the probiotics in yogurt may have the ability to fight inflammatory bowel disease. Another reason to smile!

While recent studies have shown that the yellow-flowered plant has little benefit in treating major depression, experts still say that scientific evidence suggests that **St. John's Wort** can be useful for milder depression. Just be sure to talk with your doctor about the supplement, since it can have interactions with other drugs and supplement regimens.

According to the National Institutes of Health, the chemical **SAMe** – found naturally in the body but also produced as a supplement – can be beneficial in reducing symptoms of depression. Some women also take SAMe to mitigate PMS. Look for a supplement containing 400 to 1,600 milligrams per day, and be sure to talk with your doctor before taking it, as it can interact with other drugs and supplements such as St. John's Wort.

There's no doubt about it – **kale** is king when it comes to leafy greens. The plant beats broccoli, Swiss chard and spinach when it comes to potassium, calcium and vitamins A and K. Kale is also rich in folic acid and magnesium, which could help improve your mood, according to the American Academy of Family Physicians. A new study published in the October 2011 issue of *Journal of the Academy of Nutrition* *and Dietetics*, meanwhile, shows that kale and other vegetables in the brassica family may also reduce our risk of developing colon cancer.

You're not just imagining the happy feeling you get from munching on a bowl of **popcorn** while watching a movie. Like yogurt, whole-grain carbohydrates contain serotonin-boosting tryptophan. Plus, crunching on popcorn can help alleviate the stress of a bad day at the office, and a 2009 study by researchers at the University of Scranton in Pennsylvania found that popcorn is a good source of fiber and antioxidants. Just be sure to skip the butter and salt – sprinkle it with chile powder, smoked paprika, or even a little anti-inflammatory cinnamon instead.

Used since ancient Greek and Roman times, **valerian** has long been thought to battle sleep disorders and anxiety. The plant, some scientists believe, may help increase amounts of the chemical gamma-aminobutyric acid in the brain – producing a similar but weaker effect to such drugs as Valium. If you find that sleep deprivation is putting you in a bad mood, steep a cup of boiling water and two to three grams of dried root for five to 10 minutes and drink the tea an hour or two before bedtime.

Sandwiches

AWARD WINNING
**Kimchi Quesadillas
with Salsa Roja, p. 36**

We've ditched the ham and cheese same-olds to offer you *Clean Eating*'s best creations between two pieces of bread! Need to whip up a quick after-work dinner? Treat the kids to Turkey Sloppy Joes – full of flavor and ready in 15 minutes. Savor the waistline-friendly, European tastes of Grilled Italian and French Dip Sandwiches, or try the more worldly Falafel Pitas and Kimchi Quesadillas. These budget-friendly meals are simple to make and take with you wherever you go!

Veggie Melt

Serves 4. ***Hands-on time:*** *25 minutes.* ***Total time:*** *1 hour, 15 minutes.*

Packed with fresh shaved fennel, smoky tomatoes, arugula and balsamic syrup, this is not your typical grilled cheese! Sprinkling a little smoked sweet paprika on the tomatoes adds a hint of smokiness without having to grill them or fire up your food smoker.

INGREDIENTS:

- 6 plum tomatoes, halved lengthwise
- 1 tsp olive oil
- ½ tsp smoked sweet paprika
- Sea salt and fresh ground black pepper, to taste
- ¾ cup balsamic vinegar
- 2 Tbsp raw honey or Sucanat
- ½ small bulb fennel, trimmed
- 8 1-oz slices whole-grain bread
- 2 Tbsp olive oil buttery spread
- 8 1-oz slices low-fat Swiss cheese
- 2 cups baby arugula

INSTRUCTIONS:

ONE: Preheat oven to 425°F. Arrange tomatoes, cut side up, on a parchment-lined baking sheet. Drizzle with oil and sprinkle with paprika, salt and pepper. Roast in center of oven for 50 to 60 minutes, until shriveled, lightly caramelized and lightly browned on top.

TWO: Meanwhile, prepare balsamic syrup: In a small saucepan on high heat, bring vinegar and honey to a boil. Reduce heat to medium and simmer for 8 to 10 minutes, until mixture is reduced to about ⅓ cup. Remove from heat and set aside.

THREE: Using a vegetable peeler or Japanese mandoline, shave fennel into ⅛-inch-thick slices. Set aside.

FOUR: Arrange bread on a flat surface. Brush buttery spread evenly on 1 side of each slice. Flip 4 slices over, buttered side down, and layer with 1 slice cheese. Add tomatoes, fennel and arugula, dividing evenly. Drizzle each with 2 tsp balsamic syrup, top with another slice cheese and sandwich with remaining bread slices, butter side up.

FIVE: Heat a large nonstick sauté pan on medium. Place 2 sandwiches in pan and cook, turning once, until cheese melts, filling is warm and bread is golden brown, 4 to 5 minutes. Cover and keep warm. Repeat with remaining sandwiches. Slice each sandwich in half and serve immediately.

TIP: Reducing vinegar emits a very acidic steam – resist the temptation to put your face over the pot to smell it while cooking!

Nutrients per sandwich: *Calories: 396, Total Fat: 10 g, Sat. Fat: 3.5 g, Monounsaturated Fat: 2 g, Polyunsaturated Fat: 2 g, Carbs: 47 g, Fiber: 6 g, Sugars: 20 g, Protein: 27 g, Sodium: 494 mg, Cholesterol: 22 mg*

Turkey
Sloppy
Joes

Turkey Sloppy Joes
WITH NUTTY CARROT SLAW

*Serves 6. **Hands-on time:** 15 minutes. **Total time:** 15 minutes.*

A clean dinner for six in 15 minutes? File this one under "crowd pleaser" for sure! In fact, this dish is so easy to whip up that the person who prepares it is bound to be quite pleased as well.

INGREDIENTS:

- 1 lb lean ground turkey or chicken breast
- 1 yellow onion, chopped
- 1 red bell pepper, chopped
- 1½ cups no-salt-added tomato-vegetable juice
- 1 6-oz jar no-salt-added tomato paste
- ½ cup fresh or frozen corn kernels (thawed, if frozen)
- 2 tsp apple cider vinegar
- 2 tsp chile powder
- 1 tsp dry mustard
- 6 whole-grain burger buns, split

SLAW

- ⅓ cup low-fat plain yogurt
- 3 Tbsp light olive oil mayonnaise
- 2 tsp apple cider vinegar
- 2 tsp raw honey
- Sea salt and fresh ground black pepper, to taste
- 4 cups peeled and shredded carrots (about 3 large carrots)
- 1 green onion, thinly sliced
- ¼ cup unsweetened golden raisins
- ⅓ cup chopped raw unsalted peanuts

INSTRUCTIONS:

ONE: Heat a large nonstick skillet on medium-high. Add turkey, yellow onion and bell pepper and cook, breaking up turkey with a wooden spoon, until no longer pink, about 4 minutes. Stir in tomato-vegetable juice, tomato paste, corn, vinegar, chile powder and mustard; bring mixture to a boil. Reduce heat to medium-low and simmer until thickened, about 5 minutes.

TWO: Prepare slaw: In a large bowl, add yogurt, mayonnaise, vinegar, honey, salt and black pepper and stir until combined. Mix in carrots, green onion, raisins and peanuts.

THREE: Spoon turkey mixture between buns, dividing evenly, and serve with slaw alongside.

Nutrients per serving (1 bun, 1 cup turkey-tomato mixture, ¾ cup slaw): Calories: 384, Total Fat: 10 g, Sat. Fat: 1 g, Monounsaturated Fat: 3 g, Polyunsaturated Fat: 4 g, Carbs: 50 g, Fiber: 8.5 g, Sugars: 20 g, Protein: 27 g, Sodium: 448 mg, Cholesterol: 40 mg

Thanksgiving Griller
*Serves 1. **Hands-on time:** 5 minutes. **Total time:** 8 minutes.*

Put those holiday dinner leftovers to good use with this ready-in-a-snap sandwich. Bonus: You can cut the ridiculously short prep time down further if you've already got some cranberry sauce on hand.

INGREDIENTS:
- 2 thin slices pumpernickel bread, divided
- 2 oz roasted, boneless, skinless turkey breast, sliced
- ½ oz low-fat brie cheese, sliced
- ¼ cup baby spinach leaves
- ½ small green apple, cored and thinly sliced

CRANBERRY SAUCE
- 1 cup fresh or frozen cranberries
- 3 Tbsp organic evaporated cane juice

INSTRUCTIONS:

ONE: Prepare cranberry sauce: In a small saucepan, combine cranberries, ½ cup water and cane juice. Place on medium-high heat and bring to a boil. Reduce heat to medium-low and simmer until thickened, 6 to 8 minutes. (Makes ½ cup sauce. Save leftover sauce for another sandwich or as a dressing for chicken or turkey.)

TWO: Spread 1 Tbsp cranberry sauce on 1 slice of bread. Add turkey, cheese, spinach and apple; top with remaining slice of bread. Place sandwich in a hot panini press and grill until bread toasts and cheese melts, 2 to 3 minutes. (Alternatively, toast sandwich in a nonstick skillet on medium-high heat, flipping once.)

Nutrients per sandwich: Calories: 273, Total Fat: 4 g, Sat. Fat: 0 g, Carbs: 35 g, Fiber: 5 g, Sugars: 13 g, Protein: 24 g, Sodium: 425 mg, Cholesterol: 55 mg

Kimchi Quesadillas
WITH SALSA ROJA

*Serves 8. **Hands-on time:** 25 minutes. **Total time:** 45 minutes.*

Serve the extra Salsa Roja on the side with baked tortilla chips.

INGREDIENTS:

- 4 medium green tomatillos
- 6 medium plum tomatoes
- 10 dried chiles de arbol
- 1 medium yellow onion, chopped
- 3 cloves garlic, divided
- 2 Tbsp low-sodium tamari
- 3 tsp chopped fresh ginger, divided
- 1½ cups kimchi cabbage, strained and 2 Tbsp liquid reserved, divided
- 4 tsp sesame seeds
- 2 tsp sesame oil
- Sea salt, to taste
- Olive oil cooking spray
- 3 cups shredded Napa cabbage
- 4 10-inch whole-wheat tortillas
- ½ cup fresh cilantro leaves
- ¾ cup shredded low-fat cheddar cheese
- ¾ cup shredded low-fat mozzarella cheese

INSTRUCTIONS:

ONE: Prepare Salsa Roja: Place oven rack in top third of oven and preheat broiler to high. Arrange tomatillos and tomatoes on a foil-lined baking sheet and broil until lightly blackened, turning once, about 18 minutes. Transfer tomatillos, tomatoes and juices to a medium saucepan. Add chiles, onion, 2 cloves garlic, tamari, 2 tsp ginger, reserved kimchi liquid and ½ cup water. Bring to a boil on high heat. Reduce heat to medium-low and simmer for 20 minutes, stirring occasionally.

TWO: Meanwhile, in a large nonstick sauté pan on medium heat, toast sesame seeds until light brown and fragrant, shaking pan continuously, about 4 minutes. Remove seeds from pan and set aside.

THREE: With a fine strainer over a medium bowl, drain tomato-chile mixture, reserving ½ cup liquid. In a blender, purée tomato-chile solids and reserved liquid until almost smooth. Transfer to medium bowl and stir in oil, 3 tsp sesame seeds and salt. Cover and refrigerate until needed.

FOUR: Heat pan on medium-high. Mist with cooking spray, add remaining 1 clove garlic, remaining 1 tsp ginger, Napa cabbage and 2 Tbsp water. Cook for 3 to 4 minutes, until cabbage is wilted. Add kimchi and cook, stirring frequently, until golden and wilted, about 8 more minutes. Transfer to a small bowl and wash pan.

FIVE: Lay tortillas on a flat surface. Top half of each with cilantro, cheddar, mozzarella and kimchi mixture, dividing evenly. Fold each tortilla to create a half-circle and press gently to flatten. Mist both sides with cooking spray. Return pan to medium heat. Working in batches, place quesadillas in pan and cook, turning once, until they are golden and cheese is melted, about 4 minutes total. Transfer to a cutting board and let sit for about 2 minutes. Cut each quesadilla into 4 wedges and drizzle each with 2 tsp Salsa Roja. Sprinkle with remaining 1 tsp sesame seeds.

Nutrients per serving (2 wedges and 4 tsp Salsa Roja): Calories: 237, Total Fat: 6 g, Sat. Fat: 1 g, Carbs: 25 g, Fiber: 3 g, Sugars: 4 g, Protein: 11 g, Sodium: 754 mg, Cholesterol: 6 mg

For a photo of this recipe, see page 30.

Chèvre, Spinach & Mushroom Calzones

*Serves 2. **Hands-on time:** 30 minutes. **Total time:** 50 minutes.*

When you think of fiber-packed foods, calzones probably aren't the first things that pop to mind. With nine grams of fiber per serving, though, these calzones will have you well on your way to getting the 29 grams per day that the National Cancer Institute recommends.

INGREDIENTS:

- Olive oil cooking spray
- 1 tsp olive oil
- 1 cup chopped yellow onion
- 1 cup sliced button mushrooms
- 2 cups baby spinach, coarsely chopped
- 2 oz goat cheese (chèvre)
- 2 Tbsp fresh basil, chopped
- Whole-wheat flour, as needed for rolling
- 8 oz frozen whole-wheat pizza, roll or bread dough, thawed

INSTRUCTIONS:

ONE: Place a rack at lowest level in oven and preheat to 400°F. Mist a small baking sheet with cooking spray; set aside.

TWO: In a medium sauté pan, heat oil on medium-high. Add onion and mushrooms and cook, stirring constantly, until mushrooms soften, onion is golden and oil has cooked off. Add spinach and cook, stirring constantly, until wilted. Remove from heat and stir in goat cheese and basil until well blended. Set aside and let cool to room temperature, about 10 minutes.

THREE: On a clean, floured surface, divide dough and form into 2 balls; flatten each into an oval, about 5 inches long. Using a rolling pin, roll each piece of dough out into a larger oval, 6 inches long by 4 inches wide. Spoon spinach mixture onto lower half of each dough oval, dividing evenly and leaving a ¾-inch border. Dampen edges, then fold top half of each oval over spinach mixture to create a half-moon. Seal by pressing dough edges together with a fork and poke top of each to form a vent. Transfer to baking sheet and bake on bottom rack in oven for 20 minutes or until dough is golden brown and bottoms are crisp. Let cool on baking sheet for 5 minutes before serving.

Nutrients per calzone: Calories: 410, Total Fat: 12 g, Sat. Fat: 4.5 g, Monounsaturated Fat: 3 g, Polyunsaturated Fat: 0.5 g, Carbs: 59 g, Fiber: 9 g, Sugars: 4 g, Protein: 16 g, Sodium: 148 mg, Cholesterol: 13 mg

Two-Time Award Winner!
Thanks to this spicy fusion dish, Chef Jo was voted in as Toronto's Hottest Chef in 2012! Her Kimchi Quesadilla recipe was also reprinted in the *Toronto Star* newspaper, where it was then granted a Golden Whisk award as one of the 10 best recipes of 2011!

Chèvre, Spinach & Mushroom Calzones

38

Grilled
Cuban

Grilled Cuban

Serves 1. ***Hands-on time:*** *5 minutes.* ***Total time:*** *8 minutes.*

Melted Swiss, tangy pickles, rich mushrooms and savory ham ... How could you not love this waistline-friendly version of the classic Cuban sandwich?

INGREDIENTS:

- ½ tsp organic unsalted butter
- 2 white mushrooms, sliced
- 2 slices country wheat or whole-wheat bread
- 2 thin slices low-fat Swiss cheese (½ oz), divided
- 1½ oz extra-lean, uncured, roasted ham, sliced
- 2 slices bread-and-butter pickles, optional

INSTRUCTIONS:

In a small sauté pan, melt butter on medium heat. Add mushrooms and sauté, stirring occasionally, until golden, about 5 minutes. Between bread slices, layer 1 slice cheese, ham, pickles (if desired), mushrooms and remaining slice cheese. Place sandwich in a hot panini press and grill until bread toasts and cheese melts, 3 to 4 minutes. (Alternatively, toast sandwich in a nonstick skillet on medium-high heat, flipping once.)

Nutrients per sandwich: Calories: 231, Total Fat: 6 g, Sat. Fat: 3 g, Carbs: 24 g, Fiber: 4 g, Sugars: 4 g, Protein: 20 g, Sodium: 617 mg, Cholesterol: 36 mg

Nutritional Bonus:
Small but mighty, this sandwich provides 81% of your daily requirement for manganese, a trace mineral that aids in both calcium absorption and carbohydrate metabolism. Our Cuban is also light on sodium and saturated fat, making it a satisfyingly smart mealtime decision.

Grilled Italian

Serves 1. ***Hands-on time:*** *5 minutes.* ***Total time:*** *8 minutes.*

This recipe calls for prepared pesto, but if you'd rather whip up your own pesto at home, simply add the following to the bowl of a small food processor: 1 clove garlic, 2 tsp olive oil and 10 large basil leaves. Process until finely chopped, 1 to 2 minutes.

INGREDIENTS:

- 2 slices whole-grain Italian bread
- 2 tsp prepared pesto
- 1½ oz part-skim mozzarella cheese, sliced
- 1 plum tomato, sliced
- 2 large basil leaves

INSTRUCTIONS:

Place bread on a work surface and spread 1 tsp pesto on each slice. On 1 slice, layer cheese, tomato and basil. Top with remaining slice of bread, pesto side down. Place sandwich in a hot panini press and grill until bread toasts and cheese softens, about 4 minutes. (Alternatively, toast sandwich in a nonstick skillet on medium-high heat, flipping once.)

Nutrients per sandwich: Calories: 306, Total Fat: 14 g, Sat. Fat: 5 g, Monounsaturated Fat: 6 g, Polyunsaturated Fat: 2 g, Carbs: 27 g, Fiber: 5 g, Sugars: 5 g, Protein: 18 g, Sodium: 485 mg, Cholesterol: 27 mg

NUTRITIONAL BONUS: Who needs mayo when you have the bold flavors and nutrient-dense ingredients of pesto to bring this sandwich to life? The basil has potent antioxidant, antiviral and antimicrobial properties; the olive oil contains heart-healthy unsaturated fats; and the garlic contains powerful immune-boosting compounds.

Pulled Pork Sandwiches
WITH CRUNCHY SLAW

Serves 4. *Hands-on time:* 20 minutes. *Total time:* 2 hours, 20 minutes.

This recipe uses pork tenderloin instead of the more traditional pork shoulder (aka Boston butt), which keeps things lean – and it means you don't have to cook a several-pound hunk of meat.

INGREDIENTS:

- 1 tsp ground cumin
- 1 tsp ground coriander
- 1 tsp chile powder
- ¼ tsp each sea salt and fresh ground black pepper
- 1 1-lb pork tenderloin, trimmed of visible fat
- 2 tsp olive oil
- 1 yellow onion, diced
- 1 clove garlic, minced
- 26 oz boxed diced tomatoes with juices
- 1 Tbsp pure maple syrup
- 1 Tbsp Sucanat
- 3 Tbsp apple cider vinegar, divided
- ½ cup low-fat plain yogurt
- 4 cups shredded Napa cabbage
- 1 cup shredded red cabbage
- 2 Tbsp chopped green onion
- 4 whole-grain buns, split

INSTRUCTIONS:

ONE: Preheat oven to 300°F.

TWO: In a small bowl, combine cumin, coriander, chile powder, salt and pepper. Rub mixture over entire surface of pork.

THREE: In a large heavy-bottomed pot or Dutch oven, heat oil on medium. Add yellow onion and garlic and sauté, stirring occasionally, until softened, 2 to 3 minutes. Spoon onion-garlic mixture to sides of pot; place pork in center and cook, turning, until browned on all sides, 1 to 2 minutes per side. Add tomatoes, maple syrup, Sucanat and 2 Tbsp vinegar. Cover and transfer to oven; bake until very tender, about 2 hours.

FOUR: Meanwhile, prepare slaw: In a separate small bowl, combine yogurt and remaining 1 Tbsp vinegar. In a large bowl, combine both cabbages and green onion. Spoon yogurt mixture over top and toss to combine. If desired, refrigerate until serving.

FIVE: Remove Dutch oven and transfer pork to a large bowl. Using 2 forks, shred pork and cover to keep warm. Using an immersion hand blender, purée onion-tomato mixture in pot until smooth, 45 to 60 seconds. Return pork to pot and mix until well combined. Spoon pork mixture between buns, dividing evenly. Serve with slaw on the side and/or pile a bit of slaw on top of pulled pork for added crunch.

Nutrients per serving (1 sandwich and 1 cup slaw): *Calories: 384, Total Fat: 8 g, Sat. Fat: 2 g, Monounsaturated Fat: 3 g, Polyunsaturated Fat: 2 g, Carbs: 45 g, Fiber: 7 g, Sugars: 20 g, Protein: 32 g, Sodium: 500 mg, Cholesterol: 76 mg*

Cobb Salad-Style Sandwiches
WITH BLUE CHEESE MAYONNAISE

Serves 4. *Hands-on time:* 5 minutes. *Total time:* 12 minutes.

With two types of meat, slices of velvety avocado and a creamy blue cheese mayonnaise, you might find yourself thinking, "Can this sandwich really be *Clean Eating* approved?" Well, here's the good news: It is and it's spectacular.

INGREDIENTS:

- Olive oil cooking spray
- 2 4-oz boneless, skinless chicken breasts, cut in half horizontally
- 2 oz deli-sliced, low-sodium, nitrate-free lean ham
- 8 slices whole-grain bread
- 4 leaves lettuce
- 1 vine-ripened tomato, thinly sliced
- ½ ripe avocado, pitted, peeled and thinly sliced

MAYONNAISE

- 3 Tbsp light olive oil mayonnaise
- 2 Tbsp crumbled blue cheese
- ½ tsp white or red wine vinegar or apple cider vinegar
- Fresh ground black pepper, to taste

INSTRUCTIONS:

ONE: Prepare mayonnaise: In a small bowl, combine mayonnaise, cheese, vinegar and pepper; set aside at room temperature.

TWO: Heat a large nonstick skillet on medium-high; mist with cooking spray. Add chicken and cook, turning once, until no longer pink inside, about 8 minutes. Transfer chicken to a plate and set aside. Add ham to skillet and cook, turning once, until golden and heated through, about 1 minute.

THREE: To assemble sandwiches, spread 1 tsp mayonnaise onto each slice of bread. Top each of 4 bread slices, mayonnaise side up, with lettuce, tomato, ham, chicken and avocado, dividing evenly. Top with remaining 4 bread slices, mayonnaise side down. (Alternatively, skip spreading mayonnaise on each slice of bread and pile it on top of avocado instead.)

Nutrients per serving (1 sandwich and 2 tsp mayo): *Calories: 287, Total Fat: 10 g, Sat. Fat: 2 g, Monounsaturated Fat: 4 g, Polyunsaturated Fat: 2 g, Carbs: 32 g, Fiber: 12 g, Sugars: 3 g, Protein: 22 g, Sodium: 443 mg, Cholesterol: 47 mg*

Cobb
Salad-Style
Sandwiches

Nutritional Bonus:
Chickpeas are an excellent
source of protein, vitamin
B6 and folate – also known
as vitamin B9 or folic acid.
Just one serving of our falafel
sandwich provides almost
half of your daily need for
folate, a key player in building
blocks of DNA and RNA,
which are essential for rapidly
growing tissues (like those of a
developing fetus) and rapidly
regenerating cells (like red
blood cells and immune cells).

**Falafel Pita
Sandwiches**

Falafel Pita Sandwiches
WITH TAHINI SAUCE

Serves: 6. ***Hands-on time:*** *20 minutes.* ***Total time:*** *20 minutes.*

Save any leftover tahini sauce in the refrigerator for up to one week. It's great drizzled over chicken, brown rice or steamed vegetables.

INGREDIENTS:

- ¼ cup tahini
- 2 Tbsp fresh lemon juice
- 2 cloves garlic, minced
- ¼ tsp paprika
- 6 6-inch whole-wheat pitas
- 12 falafel patties (see recipe, right)
- 1 head green leaf or red leaf lettuce, coarsely shredded
- 1 tomato, cut into thin wedges
- ½ cucumber, peeled and sliced
- 1 low-sodium dill pickle, sliced
- ¼ small red onion, thinly sliced
- Harissa or other hot sauce, optional

INSTRUCTIONS:

ONE: In a small bowl, whisk together tahini, ¼ cup water, lemon juice, garlic and paprika. Set aside.

TWO: Cut about 1 inch off the top of each pita, forming a pocket. Add 2 falafel to each pita with equal amounts of lettuce, tomato, cucumber, pickle and onion. Drizzle each with tahini sauce and, if desired, hot sauce.

NOTES:

Tahini (sesame paste) can be found in the ethnic or health food section of most major supermarkets.

Harissa is a Tunisian hot sauce that's usually made with chiles, garlic, cumin, coriander, caraway and olive oil. It can be found at some specialty stores and at Middle Eastern markets.

Nutrients per serving (1 filled pita and 5 tsp sauce): *Calories: 243, Total Fat: 7 g, Sat. Fat: 1 g, Monounsaturated Fat: 2 g, Polyunsaturated Fat: 2.5 g, Carbs: 36 g, Fiber: 7 g, Sugars: 4.5 g, Protein: 10 g, Sodium: 336 mg, Cholesterol: 0 mg*

Falafel

Makes 12 patties. ***Hands-on time:*** *15 minutes.* ***Total time:*** *25 minutes (plus soaking time).*

If you can't find dried chickpeas, or you don't have the time to soak them overnight, substitute one 15-ounce BPA-free can of no-salt-added chickpeas, drained, plus a quarter of a cup whole-wheat pastry flour. The texture will be a little less authentic, but the flavor will be just as good.

INGREDIENTS:

- ⅔ cup dried chickpeas (about 2¼ oz)
- ¼ onion, cut into 3 or 4 chunks
- 2 Tbsp fresh flat-leaf parsley
- 2 cloves garlic
- 1 tsp sodium-free baking powder
- ½ tsp ground cumin
- ½ tsp ground coriander
- ½ tsp fine sea salt
- Olive oil cooking spray

INSTRUCTIONS:

ONE: Place chickpeas in a refrigerator container and cover with cold water by at least 2 inches. Refrigerate overnight.

TWO: Drain chickpeas and transfer to a food processor. Add onion, parsley, garlic, baking powder, cumin, coriander and salt and pulse to a grainy paste, scraping down bowl as necessary. With lightly moistened hands, shape paste into 12 golf ball-size rounds, arranging on a plate.

THREE: Coat a very large nonstick skillet with cooking spray and heat on medium-low. Working in batches if necessary to avoid crowding the skillet, add balls and use a spatula to flatten to about ½ inch thick. Cook until browned on bottom, 4 to 5 minutes. Flip and brown other side, 4 to 5 minutes.

Nutrients per 2-patty serving: *Calories: 43, Total Fat: 1 g, Sat. Fat: 0 g, Carbs: 7 g, Fiber: 2 g, Sugars: 1 g, Protein: 2 g, Sodium: 83 mg, Cholesterol: 0 mg*

Baby Blues Griller

Serves 1. ***Hands-on time:*** *5 minutes.* ***Total time:*** *7 minutes.*

Baby arugula and blue cheese combine to give this sandwich its intriguing title. Throw in some Dijon, rustic bread, an Anjou pear and a bit of heat and you'll be widening *your* baby blues in amazement at how good it all tastes.

INGREDIENTS:

- 2 tsp honey Dijon mustard
- 2 slices country wheat or whole-wheat bread, divided
- ½ oz low-fat blue cheese, sliced
- ½ Anjou pear, cored and sliced
- ½ cup baby arugula leaves

INSTRUCTIONS:

Spread Dijon on 1 slice of bread. Add cheese, pear and arugula. Top with remaining slice of bread. Place sandwich in a hot panini press and grill until cheese melts and begins to bubble and bread is crisp, about 3 minutes. (Alternatively, toast sandwich in a nonstick skillet on medium-high heat, flipping once.)

Nutrients per sandwich: Calories: 244, Total Fat: 5 g, Sat. Fat: 2 g, Carbs: 36 g, Fiber: 6 g, Sugars: 13 g, Protein: 10.5 g, Sodium: 302 mg, Cholesterol: 8 mg

The King Griller

Serves 1. ***Hands-on time:*** *4 minutes.* ***Total time:*** *8 minutes.*

The sandwich that legends are made of! In fact, we can't help falling in love with this cleaned up version of the Elvis Presley favorite.

INGREDIENTS:

- 2 slices whole-wheat sandwich bread
- 1 Tbsp natural unsalted peanut butter
- ½ banana, peeled and sliced
- ½ oz low-fat medium cheddar cheese, sliced

INSTRUCTIONS:

Heat a medium nonstick pan on medium-low. Place bread on a work surface and spread each slice with peanut butter, dividing evenly. On 1 slice, layer banana and cheese. Top with remaining slice of bread, peanut-butter side down. Place sandwich in pan and cook, turning once, until bread lightly toasts and cheese melts, about 2 minutes per side.

Nutrients per sandwich: Calories: 363, Total Fat: 11 g, Sat. Fat: 2 g, Carbs: 54 g, Fiber: 8 g, Sugars: 18 g, Protein: 16 g, Sodium: 352 mg, Cholesterol: 3 mg

Nutritional Bonus:

Although this sandwich may seem simple, it's packed with protein, fiber and almost your entire daily requirement of the trace mineral manganese. Manganese aids in cholesterol metabolism, and it helps to neutralize free radicals and regulate blood sugar levels. It also helps maintain healthy bones, joints and skin.

The King Griller

Nutritional Bonus:
Piperine, a natural compound found in all peppercorns, is most abundant in black pepper and is credited with many health-promoting benefits. Regular, liberal use of black pepper may help reduce blood pressure, enhance brain function and improve the health of your digestive tract.

Western Sandwiches

Western Sandwiches

*Serves 2. **Hands-on time:** 15 minutes. **Total time:** 15 minutes.*

With just four or five ingredients and a few pantry staples, you can have a healthy breakfast, lunch or dinner almost as fast as you can say yippie-ki-yay!

INGREDIENTS:

- 4 large egg whites
- 1 Tbsp chopped fresh Italian flat-leaf parsley, optional
- ½ green bell pepper, chopped
- ½ cup diced cooked turkey or chicken breast, boneless and skinless
- 4 thin slices whole-wheat bread, toasted

PANTRY STAPLES:

- 1 Tbsp chopped yellow onion
- Olive oil cooking spray
- Fresh ground black pepper, to taste

INSTRUCTIONS:

ONE: In a medium bowl, gently whisk egg whites until blended, about 10 seconds. Add onion, parsley (if desired), bell pepper and turkey and stir with a wooden spoon. Mist a medium skillet with cooking spray. Place on medium heat, pour in egg white mixture and season with black pepper. Cook until bottom sets, 2 to 3 minutes, tilting pan to allow egg to cook around the edges.

TWO: In skillet, carefully divide cooked egg mixture into 4 wedges. Flip each to complete cooking on opposite side, 1 to 2 minutes, until eggs are completely set. Season with black pepper.

THREE: To assemble sandwiches, place 2 egg wedges between 2 slices of bread. Repeat with remaining egg wedges and bread. Serve immediately.

Nutrients per sandwich: Calories: 241, Total Fat: 4 g, Sat. Fat: 0.5 g, Carbs: 24 g, Fiber: 5 g, Sugars: 3 g, Protein: 24 g, Sodium: 328 mg, Cholesterol: 30 mg

French Dip Sandwiches

*Serves 4. **Hands-on time:** 20 minutes. **Total time:** 20 minutes.*

Substituting the beef for turkey plays a big role in keeping this diner classic clean. Actually, the savory yet skinny dipping sauce deserves some of the credit, too. And with just a few ingredients and 20 minutes you'll be able to dive right in to this delectable 187-calorie lunch!

INGREDIENTS:

- ¼ cup chopped onion
- 1 shallot, chopped
- 2 cups low-sodium chicken broth
- 8 oz deli-sliced, all-natural, low-sodium turkey breast
- 4 whole-wheat torpedo sandwich rolls, split and toasted

PANTRY STAPLES:

- 1 Tbsp extra-virgin olive oil
- 1 Tbsp whole-wheat flour
- Sea salt and fresh ground black pepper, to taste

INSTRUCTIONS:

ONE: In a large, shallow skillet, heat oil on medium. Add onion and shallot and sauté, stirring occasionally, for 2 minutes. Sprinkle flour over top and cook, stirring, for 1 minute.

TWO: Gradually whisk in broth in a steady stream. Bring sauce to a gentle boil; reduce to a simmer for 1 to 2 minutes, until sauce thickens slightly. Season with salt and pepper. Cover and keep warm until ready to serve.

THREE: In a medium bowl, toss turkey with salt and pepper. Using tongs, dip turkey into warm onion sauce and place between each roll, dividing evenly. Serve with remaining onion sauce on the side.

Nutrients per sandwich (plus ½ cup sauce): Calories: 187, Total Fat: 7 g, Sat. Fat: 1 g, Monounsaturated Fat: 3 g, Polyunsaturated Fat: 2 g, Carbs: 19 g, Fiber: 2.5 g, Sugars: 3 g, Protein: 15 g, Sodium: 552 mg, Cholesterol: 30 mg

NUTRITIONAL BONUS: Turkey offers a rich supply of the trace mineral selenium, which helps regulate thyroid hormone metabolism and immune function, and acts like an antioxidant in defending against free radicals. Plus, the poultry option's high levels of B vitamins also play a role in energy production.

Crispy Fish Tacos

WITH ROASTED CORN, GRAPEFRUIT & CUCUMBER SALSA

Serves 4. Hands-on time: *40 minutes.* **Total time:** *40 minutes.*

No need for a deep fryer! Bonus: This recipe is gluten free.

INGREDIENTS:

- 2 ears corn, husked
- 1 medium ruby red grapefruit
- ¼ medium English cucumber, diced
- ½ medium white onion, diced
- 2 plum tomatoes, seeded and diced
- 1 serrano pepper, seeded and minced
- Zest and juice of 2 limes, divided
- 2 Tbsp olive oil
- ¼ cup chopped fresh cilantro
- ½ tsp ground cumin, divided
- ½ tsp sea salt, divided
- 8 small corn tortillas
- ¼ cup brown rice flour
- 4 egg whites
- 1 cup brown rice crisp cereal
- 8 oz boneless, skinless Pacific halibut, cut into 1-oz strips
- Olive oil cooking spray
- ⅓ cup nonfat plain Greek yogurt
- ⅓ cup crumbled low-fat feta or queso cotija cheese

INSTRUCTIONS:

ONE: Prepare salsa: Arrange oven racks in center and top half of oven, and preheat oven to broil. Trim about 1 inch from tip of corn to form a flat end. Place corn on a baking sheet and transfer to top oven rack. Broil, turning once, until kernels are blistered, about 18 minutes. Remove from oven and let cool to room temperature. Over a cutting board, stand corn upright on cut end and slice kernels from cob in a downward motion. Transfer kernels to medium bowl. Cut peel and white skin from grapefruit. Working over bowl of corn, use a paring knife to segment grapefruit, adding segments to bowl. Add cucumber, onion, tomatoes, serrano pepper, zest and juice of 1 lime, oil, cilantro, ¼ tsp cumin and ¼ tsp salt to bowl. Mix well, cover with plastic wrap and refrigerate until needed.

TWO: Preheat oven to 425°F. Stack tortillas on top of each other and wrap in aluminum foil. Place packet on a parchment-lined baking sheet.

THREE: In a shallow bowl, add flour. In a separate shallow bowl, whisk egg whites, remaining ¼ tsp cumin and ¼ tsp salt. In the bowl of a food processor, pulse rice crisp cereal into a fine powder; transfer to a third shallow bowl. Pat halibut dry with paper towel. Working 1 at a time, coat each strip in rice flour, then egg mixture and, finally, rice cereal. Arrange strips in a single layer on empty side of baking sheet. Mist strips with cooking spray and bake in center of oven for 6 minutes or until golden.

FOUR: Meanwhile, in a small bowl, combine yogurt, feta and remaining lime zest and juice. Set aside.

FIVE: To assemble, carefully open tortillas and lay out in a single layer. Spoon salsa onto center of each, dividing evenly. Top each with 1 strip halibut and yogurt-feta mixture, dividing evenly. Fold closed and enjoy.

Nutrients per 2 tacos: Calories: 474, Total Fat: 14 g, Sat. Fat: 3 g, Monounsaturated Fat: 7 g, Polyunsaturated Fat: 2 g, Carbs: 65 g, Fiber: 7 g, Sugars: 12 g, Protein: 27 g, Sodium: 533 mg, Cholesterol: 29 mg

Lobsta Roll

Serves 4. Hands-on time: *15 minutes.* **Total time:** *30 minutes.*

When making this New England classic, fresh lobster meat is always best. If cooking and cracking a few lobsters seems daunting, ask your fishmonger to boil and crack the lobster for you.

INGREDIENTS:

- 2 Tbsp low-fat olive oil mayonnaise
- 2 Tbsp nonfat plain Greek yogurt
- 1 scallion or green onion, thinly sliced
- 1 Tbsp fresh lemon juice
- 2 Tbsp chopped fresh dill
- 12 oz cooked and chilled lobster meat, cut into ½-inch chunks
- Sea salt and fresh ground black pepper, to taste
- 4 whole-wheat top-cut hot dog buns

INSTRUCTIONS:

ONE: In a large bowl, combine mayonnaise, yogurt, scallion, lemon juice and dill. With a rubber spatula, fold in lobster and season with salt and pepper. Cover and refrigerate until needed. (Mixture may be prepared in advance and refrigerated overnight.)

TWO: Preheat oven to 400°F. Place buns on a baking sheet and toast for 4 to 6 minutes or until light golden brown. Scoop lobster mixture into buns, dividing evenly. Serve immediately.

Nutrients per serving (1 roll and ½ cup lobster mixture): Calories: 226, Total Fat: 4.5 g, Sat. Fat: 1 g, Carbs: 25 g, Fiber: 3 g, Sugars: 3 g, Protein: 22 g, Sodium: 417 mg, Cholesterol: 61 mg

Nutritional Bonus:
Ounce for ounce, lobster is lower in fat and calories than boneless, skinless chicken breast (90 calories versus 160 calories in a 3½-oz serving). Better yet, lobster is also rich in omega-3 fatty acids, which help to lower cholesterol and may reduce your risk of heart disease.

Lobsta
Roll

Bell Peppers

Roasted peppers are among the list of a chef's secret ingredients that really up the "Ooh!" and "Ahh!" factor of many savory dishes. They're surprisingly easy (and fun!) to make at home.

What You'll Need:

Gas flame or broiler

Metal tongs

Baking sheet (if roasting peppers in oven)

Large bowl

Plastic wrap

Paper towels

Knife

Cutting board

When you see how easy it is to make your own, you'll never spend another dime on a jar of marinated roasted red peppers. And if you've got a gas stove, the process is that much more enjoyable. While you can roast peppers successfully in an oven, the best way to achieve that smoky, flame-broiled flavor is to do it over an open flame. Once roasted, sweet red peppers take on a tender texture and readily pick up the flavors of a simple marinade. You can also roast orange or yellow peppers, but not green – their skin is too thin and they would develop a mushy texture.

Roasted peppers are a staple in Mediterranean pantries, where they're a frequent addition to many dishes. Well known for their heart-healthy fare, Mediterranean countries rank sweet peppers right up there with olives, olive oil, lemons and red wine. And there's a lesson to learn from keeping these staple foods handy – they add an array of flavors to meals without contributing a ton of added sugars or salt. For example, instead of adding sugar-laden ketchup to a grilled burger, try serving it with a more healthful topping of marinated roasted peppers. Or instead of drowning a salad in a high-sodium dressing, try tossing greens with marinated roasted peppers to up the flavor, color and antioxidants. See "5 Ways to Enjoy Your Peppers" (at right) for even more ideas on how to serve your bells.

Are you all fired up for roasted peppers? Then it's time to grab a pair of tongs and get the flame (safely) a-blazing. This is one time when burning the food is actually a good thing!

Your Step-by-Step Guide to Roasting Peppers

GAS STOVE-TOP OPTION (ONE): Turn gas stove-top flame to high. With metal tongs, turn and rotate peppers over flame until skin is blackened on all sides (about 2 minutes per pepper).

OVEN OPTION (ONE): Arrange 1 oven rack in highest position and preheat broiler to high. Halve or quarter peppers and remove stems and seeds. Place peppers, skin side up, on a large baking sheet and broil until skins are blackened and bubbling, about 15 minutes.

TWO: Immediately transfer peppers to a large bowl and cover tightly with plastic wrap. Set aside for 10 minutes for steam to loosen skin.

THREE: If the peppers were blackened over the flame, rub skins with paper towel to remove as much blackened skin as possible. If roasted in the oven, the skin will come off easily, so use your fingers to peel.

FOUR: If following stove-top method, cut peppers in half lengthwise, remove stems and seeds and slice into ½-inch strips. If following oven method, simply slice peppers into ½-inch strips. Enjoy as is or marinate and use as desired.

5 Ways to Enjoy Your Peppers

There are so many ways to enjoy delicious roasted peppers. Here are a few suggestions:

TOPPING Lay them over top of pizza, burgers, tacos and hot dogs for a punch of flavor.

TOSSED Chop some prepped peppers and toss them into a pasta dish, salad or with other roasted vegetables to add bites of sweetness.

BLENDED Add depth of flavor when blending into puréed soups and hummus or other dips.

STUFFING Your fired-up bells make a fine filling for stuffed chicken, vegetables, burgers and meatloaf.

À LA CARTE Present them on an antipasto platter along with olives, whole-grain crackers and low-fat cheeses and meats.

Salads & Sides

Left: Potato Rounds with Fresh Lemon, p. 54

Center: Southwestern Cheddar Steak Fries, p. 55

Below: Oven-Fried Squash Spears with Spicy Garlic Sour Cream, p. 55

Our sides and salads make a perfect complement to any of your *Clean Eating* favorites. We've picked the liveliest greens and zestiest potato recipes to infuse your meals with nutrition. Our Chile-Lime Roasted Sweet Potatoes are a satisfying alternative to a side of fatty fries! Experience one of our scrumptious salads, as an appetizer or meal on its own. Have you ever served a Sushi Salad to your guests? Now is the time to impress!

Potato Rounds
WITH FRESH LEMON

*Serves 4. **Hands-on time:** 8 minutes. **Total time:** 28 minutes.*

Pop one of our "coins" into your mouth for a burst of fresh lemon flavor – the generous addition of grated lemon rind, tossed in at the last second, gets credit for that citrus zing. While fingerling potatoes are often thought of as a specialty potato served with more sophisticated fare, the elongated, knobby taters are actually extremely versatile and can add interest to casual dishes.

INGREDIENTS:

- 1 lb fingerling potatoes, scrubbed and sliced into ⅛-inch-thick rounds
- 1 Tbsp extra-virgin olive oil, divided
- 2 tsp dried oregano
- ¼ tsp coarsely ground black pepper
- ¼ tsp sea salt
- 1 Tbsp grated lemon zest

INSTRUCTIONS:

ONE: Preheat oven to 450°F. Line a large baking sheet with foil. Place potatoes on baking sheet, drizzle evenly with 2 tsp oil and sprinkle with oregano and pepper. Toss to coat, then arrange potatoes in a single layer. Bake in center of oven for 20 to 22 minutes or until golden, stirring occasionally.

TWO: Remove from oven. Sprinkle with remaining 1 tsp oil, salt and lemon zest and toss gently yet thoroughly. Serve immediately or at room temperature.

Nutrients per ⅔-cup serving: *Calories: 130, Total Fat: 3.5 g, Sat. Fat: 0.5 g, Carbs: 21 g, Fiber: 2 g, Sugars: 0.25 g, Protein: 3 g, Sodium: 127 mg, Cholesterol: 0 mg*

For a photo of this recipe, see page 52.

Nutritional Bonus:
These fingerling potato rounds are the perfect timesaver because there's no peeling required. Plus, their delicate skin packs a punch of fiber, vitamin C and potassium!

Southwestern Cheddar Steak Fries

Serves 4. **Hands-on time:** 8 minutes. **Total time:** 27 minutes.

Red and Yukon gold potatoes generally weigh two to six ounces each. When shopping, select taters that weigh about six ounces in order to achieve these long spear-like wedges (ideal for holding a substantial helping of our bright toppings!).

INGREDIENTS:

- 1 lb red or Yukon gold potatoes, scrubbed and cut lengthwise into ¾-inch wedges
- 1 Tbsp extra-virgin olive oil
- 2 tsp smoked paprika
- ½ tsp ground cumin
- ½ tsp garlic powder
- ¼ tsp sea salt
- 1 oz finely shredded reduced-fat sharp cheddar cheese
- ⅓ cup finely chopped red bell pepper
- 2 Tbsp finely chopped cilantro

INSTRUCTIONS:

ONE: Preheat oven to 425°F. Line a large baking sheet with foil. Place potatoes on baking sheet, drizzle evenly with oil and toss to coat lightly. In a small bowl, combine paprika, cumin and garlic powder. Sprinkle paprika mixture evenly over both sides of potatoes, then arrange potatoes in a single layer. Bake in center of oven for 10 minutes, then flip and stir, and bake for 7 minutes or until lightly golden and tender when pierced with a fork.

TWO: Remove from oven. Sprinkle with salt, cheese and pepper. Bake for 2 minutes more or until cheese has melted slightly. Sprinkle with cilantro and serve immediately for peak flavor.

Nutrients per ⅔-cup serving: *Calories: 154, Total Fat: 5 g, Sat. Fat: 1.5 g, Carbs: 22 g, Fiber: 2 g, Sugars: 0.5 g, Protein: 5 g, Sodium: 187 mg, Cholesterol: 5 mg*

NUTRITIONAL BONUS: **Oranges may get all the glory, but our southwestern fries also offer an excellent supply of vitamin C – nearly 70% of your daily need. If you're someone who happens to slack on your intake of the immunity-boosting vitamin when cold and flu season is long gone, here's something to ponder: You need vitamin C for the growth and repair of all bodily tissues. Plus, your body doesn't make or store the nutrient.**

For a photo of this recipe, see page 52.

Oven-Fried Squash Spears
WITH SPICY GARLIC SOUR CREAM

Serves 4. **Hands-on time:** 12 minutes. **Total time:** 27 minutes.

Branch out a bit and take your fries beyond the potato. Being creative with vegetables such as crookneck squash and zucchini offers personality, variety and flavor dimension to even the simplest menus.

INGREDIENTS:

- 2 egg whites
- ⅓ cup skim milk
- 2 1-oz slices reduced-calorie whole-grain bread
- 1 tsp paprika
- 1 tsp dried thyme
- 1 tsp onion powder
- ½ tsp garlic powder
- ⅛ tsp ground cayenne pepper
- 2 medium zucchini, cut in eighths lengthwise
- 1 medium yellow squash (such as crookneck), cut in eighths lengthwise
- Olive oil cooking spray
- ¼ tsp sea salt
- 1 lemon, quartered

SAUCE
- ½ cup reduced-fat sour cream
- 1 clove garlic, minced
- 2 tsp mild Louisiana hot sauce

INSTRUCTIONS:

ONE: Preheat oven to 450°F. In a medium bowl, whisk together egg whites and milk until well blended. Place bread in a blender or food processor and process into coarse bread crumbs. In a shallow pan, combine bread crumbs, paprika, thyme, onion powder, garlic powder and cayenne.

TWO: Place zucchini and squash wedges in egg mixture. Toss gently, yet thoroughly, to coat well. Working with a few spears at a time, coat zucchini and squash wedges with bread crumb mixture, pressing lightly with fingertips to allow breadcrumbs to adhere.

THREE: Coat a large nonstick baking sheet with cooking spray, arrange zucchini and squash in a single layer on sheet and bake for 12 minutes. Flip over and bake for 3 minutes more, until lightly golden and tender when pierced with a fork.

FOUR: Meanwhile, prepare sauce: In a small bowl, whisk together sour cream, garlic and hot sauce.

FIVE: To serve, sprinkle squash evenly with salt and squeeze lemon over top. Serve immediately with sauce.

Nutrients per serving (6 spears and 2 Tbsp sauce): *Calories: 80, Total Fat: 3 g, Sat. Fat: 3 g, Carbs: 18 g, Fiber: 4 g, Sugars: 7 g, Protein: 8 g, Sodium: 272 mg, Cholesterol: 18 mg*

For a photo of this recipe, see page 53.

Snow Peas
WITH SWEET & SOUR DRESSING

Serves 6. *Hands-on time:* 8 minutes. *Total time:* 10 minutes.

This simple seasonal dish is sure to become a staple in your summertime menus.

INGREDIENTS:

- 1 Tbsp pure maple syrup
- 1 Tbsp rice wine vinegar
- 2 tsp sesame oil
- 3 cups snow peas, trimmed
- 1 tsp toasted sesame seeds

INSTRUCTIONS:

ONE: Prepare dressing: In a small bowl, combine maple syrup, vinegar and oil. Set aside.

TWO: Fill a large saucepan with water and bring to a boil. Drop peas into boiling water and cook until tender, about 1 to 2 minutes. Drain and transfer peas to a medium bowl. Drizzle with dressing, tossing to coat, and sprinkle with seeds. Serve at room temperature.

Nutrients per 3-oz serving: Calories: 73, Total Fat: 2 g, Sat. Fat: 0 g, Carbs: 10 g, Fiber: 3.5 g, Sugars: 6 g, Protein: 4 g, Sodium: 15 mg, Cholesterol: 0 mg

NUTRITIONAL BONUS: While most people classify snow peas as vegetables, they're actually a legume within an edible pod. And, like all legumes, they are an excellent source of protein. But the goodness doesn't end there: They're also low-cal and packed with vitamins A and C, which are vital for eye and skin health.

Salt & Pepper Shrimp over Jalapeño Slaw
WITH COCONUT-LIME VINAIGRETTE

Serves 4. *Hands-on time:* 15 minutes. *Total time:* 30 minutes.

Smooth coconut milk is your base for the exotic flavors of this oil-free vinaigrette that brightens a crunchy, colorful slaw salad. A quick sauté of salt-and-pepper-spiked shrimp adds protein to round out the meal.

INGREDIENTS:

- ½ cup light coconut milk
- ¼ cup unsalted roasted peanuts
- Zest and juice 2 limes, divided
- ½ loosely packed cup whole cilantro leaves
- ½ tsp sea salt, divided
- ½ tsp fresh ground black pepper, divided
- 1 large jalapeño pepper, seeded and minced
- 1 small head Napa cabbage (about 1 lb), halved lengthwise and sliced into ¼-inch ribbons
- 1 large red bell pepper, thinly sliced lengthwise
- 1 large carrot, peeled into ribbons, outer peel discarded
- 1 lb large shrimp, peeled and deveined (about 24 shrimp)
- 1 tsp olive oil

INSTRUCTIONS:

ONE: Prepare vinaigrette: In a blender, combine coconut milk, peanuts, zest and juice of 1 lime, cilantro, ¼ tsp salt and ¼ tsp black pepper. Blend until peanuts and cilantro are finely chopped, about 30 seconds. Set aside.

TWO: Prepare slaw: In a large bowl, toss jalapeño, cabbage, bell pepper and carrot. Set aside.

THREE: In a medium bowl, add shrimp and sprinkle with remaining ¼ tsp salt and ¼ tsp black pepper. Add oil and mix to coat. In a large sauté pan on medium-high heat, cook shrimp, tossing often, until cooked through, about 5 minutes. Add 2 Tbsp water to pan and scrape any browned bits off the bottom. Once water evaporates almost completely, remove from heat. Add zest and juice of remaining lime to shrimp and toss to coat.

FOUR: Pour vinaigrette over top of slaw and mix well. Divide among serving plates and top each with 6 shrimp.

Nutrients per serving (2½ cups slaw and 6 shrimp): Calories: 250, Total Fat: 10 g, Sat. Fat: 3 g, Monounsaturated Fat: 4 g, Polyunsaturated Fat: 3 g, Omega-3s: 580 mg, Omega-6s: 1,710 mg, Carbs: 12 g, Fiber: 4 g, Sugars: 5 g, Protein: 28 g, Sodium: 440 mg, Cholesterol: 170 mg

Salt & Pepper Shrimp over Jalapeño Slaw

Salmon &
Vegetable
Feta Farro
Salad

Roasted Salmon & Summer Vegetable Feta Farro Salad

Serves 4. Hands-on time: 25 minutes. Total time: 1 hour.

This bowlful of sweet, tender-roasted vegetables is as much a salad as any pile of cool, crisp greens. Plus, succulent salmon and farro, a chewy, nutty grain, make this colorful recipe even more nutrient-dense and satisfying.

INGREDIENTS:

- 1 cup farro
- 1 pint grape tomatoes
- 1 small head cauliflower, stemmed and cut into florets
- 2 medium yellow bell peppers, cut into ½-inch chunks
- 1 small red onion, halved and thinly sliced
- 4 cloves garlic, sliced
- 2 tsp mustard
- 3 Tbsp balsamic vinegar
- 1 Tbsp olive oil
- ½ tsp fresh ground black pepper
- 2 heads kale (about 1½ lb), tough stems trimmed, leaves torn into 2-inch pieces, rinsed and dried
- 8 oz boneless, skinless wild salmon fillet
- ½ cup crumbled low-fat feta cheese

INSTRUCTIONS:

ONE: In a medium saucepot on medium-high heat, bring farro and 2 cups water to a boil. Reduce heat to medium-low and cover. Simmer until tender, about 20 to 25 minutes. Drain, then spread farro onto a baking sheet and let cool to room temperature.

TWO: Preheat oven to 375°F. In a 9 x 13-inch glass or ceramic baking dish, toss tomatoes, cauliflower, bell peppers, onion and garlic. In a small bowl, whisk mustard, vinegar, oil and black pepper. Drizzle mustard mixture over top of vegetables and toss to coat. Cover dish with foil and transfer to lowest oven rack. Roast for 15 minutes, then remove foil and roast for an additional 15 minutes, until vegetables are soft and tender yet slightly crunchy.

THREE: On a 9 x 13-inch baking sheet, spread out kale. In a separate small glass or ceramic baking dish, place salmon. Bake kale and salmon on top oven rack for 15 minutes, until kale is crisp and salmon is cooked through. Remove from oven and break salmon into large flakes.

FOUR: Add farro and feta to roasted tomato-cauliflower mixture and stir gently to combine farro with juices from vegetables. Divide among wide, shallow bowls and top each with kale and salmon, dividing evenly.

Nutrients per serving (2 cups farro-vegetable mixture, 2 oz salmon, 1 cup kale):
Calories: 349, Total Fat: 11 g, Sat. Fat: 2 g, Monounsaturated Fat: 4 g, Polyunsaturated Fat: 2 g, Omega-3s: 1,350 mg, Omega-6s: 850 mg, Carbs: 42 g, Fiber: 9 g, Sugars: 8 g, Protein: 25 g, Sodium: 409 mg, Cholesterol: 35 mg

Spicy Beet & Carrot Salad

Serves 5. Hands-on time: 10 minutes. Total time: 50 minutes.

Light on fat and calories yet rich in flavor, fresh produce is the key to keeping you slim, trim and healthy. This salad is a simple way to get all of that goodness in one delicious dish. (And, yes, you read that right, there is tea in the dressing – trust us, it works!)

INGREDIENTS:

- Olive oil cooking spray
- 1 lb carrots, peeled and diced into ½-inch pieces
- 1 medium yellow onion, diced into ½-inch pieces
- 1 lb beets, peeled and diced into ½-inch pieces
- 1 Tbsp raw honey
- ¼ tsp chipotle chile powder
- 1 tsp Dijon mustard
- 1 Tbsp olive oil
- ½ cup regular-brewed black tea
- 2 tsp apple cider vinegar
- ⅛ tsp sea salt
- 5 cups arugula
- 2½ oz goat cheese, crumbled

INSTRUCTIONS:

ONE: Heat oven to 450°F. Mist a 9 x 13-inch roasting pan with cooking spray. On 1 side of pan, place carrots and onion; place beets on other side. Mist vegetables with cooking spray. Cover with aluminum foil and bake in oven for 20 minutes. Uncover and cook for another 20 minutes. Remove from oven.

TWO: In a small bowl, whisk together honey, chile powder, Dijon, oil, tea, vinegar and salt. In a large bowl, add beets, carrots and onion. Pour dressing over top and gently toss to coat well. To serve, place 1 cup arugula on each of 5 plates, then top with 1 cup vegetables and ½ oz goat cheese. Serve immediately.

Nutrients per serving (1 cup vegetables, 1 cup greens, ½ oz goat cheese):
Calories: 169, Total Fat: 6 g, Sat. Fat: 2.5 g, Monounsaturated Fat: 3 g, Polyunsaturated Fat: 1 g, Carbs: 25 g, Fiber: 6 g, Sugars: 16 g, Protein: 6 g, Sodium: 265 mg, Cholesterol: 6 mg

NUTRITIONAL BONUS: Each serving of this salad contains 1 cup of arugula, which provides 28% of your daily vitamin K requirement. The key role of vitamin K is to clot the blood, but it is also necessary for antioxidant activity and bone health. Studies have shown that people with higher intakes of vitamin K (from food) may be less likely to develop certain types of cancer.

Chicken Penne

WITH SUN-DRIED TOMATO & FRESH RED PEPPER SAUCE

*Serves 2. **Hands-on time:** 30 minutes. **Total time:** 45 minutes.*

Brimming with colorful produce and clean carbs, this pasta salad is the perfect summery side or satisfying entrée. A multi-tasker through and through, the leftover Red Pepper Sauce can be used as a delicious pizza topping or sauce for cooked fish with brown rice.

INGREDIENTS:

- 2 5-oz boneless, skinless chicken breasts
- 1 tsp extra-virgin olive oil
- 2 tsp low-sodium dry rub or blend of your favorite dried herbs
- 1 tsp fresh ground black pepper
- 1½ cups uncooked whole-wheat penne (or other small whole-wheat pasta)
- 1 yellow bell pepper, diced
- 2 Tbsp finely chopped fresh basil

RED PEPPER SAUCE

- 1 red bell pepper, coarsely chopped
- ½ cup sun-dried tomatoes, coarsely chopped
- 2 tomatoes, coarsely chopped
- ¼ cup unsalted raw cashews
- ¼ cup whole fresh basil leaves
- 1 clove garlic
- 1 shallot, halved
- Fresh ground black pepper, to taste

INSTRUCTIONS:

ONE: Preheat grill to medium-high. (Or alternatively, you can preheat oven to 375°F.)

TWO: Diagonally score (¼ inch deep) chicken breasts and rub with a thin coating of oil, dry rub and black pepper, dividing evenly. Grill chicken for about 7 minutes per side, until juices run clear when pierced with a fork. (Or, roast in oven for about 20 minutes.) Set aside until cool enough to handle, about 10 minutes, then chop.

THREE: Meanwhile, prepare pasta according to package directions. Rinse in cold water to remove sticky starches; drain well and set aside.

FOUR: Prepare Red Pepper Sauce: In a blender or food processor, add all sauce ingredients; blend until very smooth.

FIVE: In a large bowl, toss pasta with 1 to 1½ cups Red Pepper Sauce, yellow pepper, chicken and basil.

Nutrients per 2-cup serving: Calories: 648, Total Fat: 13 g, Sat. Fat: 2 g, Carbs: 85 g, Fiber: 14 g, Sugars: 17 g, Protein: 50 g, Sodium: 402 mg, Cholesterol: 82 mg

Salsa-Style Corn Fusilli

*Serves 8. **Hands-on time:** 30 minutes. **Total time:** 1 hour, 30 minutes (if cooking beans).*

Fresh and sweet-tart, this Mexican-inspired salad with its light, tropical and citrus flavors pairs beautifully with delicate grilled shrimp or other mild seafood.

INGREDIENTS:

- 2 cups uncooked corn fusilli pasta
- 1½ cups dry black beans, soaked overnight (TIP: To save time, swap in 1 19-oz BPA-free can black beans, drained and rinsed well.)
- 1 large tomato, diced
- 1 fresh jalapeño pepper, finely diced (and seeded, if desired)
- ¾ cup finely diced red onion
- 1 mango, peeled, pitted and diced
- 1 avocado
- Juice 2 limes
- 3 Tbsp extra-virgin olive oil
- ½ cup finely chopped fresh cilantro, leaves and tender stems
- ¼ tsp each sea salt and fresh ground black pepper

INSTRUCTIONS:

ONE: Prepare pasta according to package directions. Rinse under cold water to remove sticky starches; drain well and set aside.

TWO: Bring a large pot of water to a boil. Drain and rinse beans. Add beans to pot and boil for about 1 hour; drain and set aside to cool. (If opting for canned beans, skip this step.)

THREE: In a large bowl, add tomato, jalapeño, onion and mango. Pit, peel and dice avocado. (TIP: Prep and add last to prevent avocado from browning.) Immediately toss in lime juice.

FOUR: Add pasta and beans to bowl with vegetables and toss to combine. Add oil, cilantro, salt and pepper and mix gently. Enjoy at room temperature or chill in fridge for about 1 hour for a more refreshing flavor.

TIP: This recipe doubles as an amazing burger topper – simply omit the pasta!

Nutrients per 1-cup serving: Calories: 254, Total Fat: 12 g, Sat. Fat: 1 g, Monounsaturated Fat: 7 g, Polyunsaturated Fat: 3 g, Carbs: 33 g, Fiber: 8 g, Sugars: 5 g, Protein: 7 g, Sodium: 77 mg, Cholesterol: 0 mg

Salsa-Style
Corn Fusilli

Charred Corn
Chop Salad

Charred Corn Chop Salad
WITH CHIPOTLE CREAM DRESSING

*Serves 4. **Hands-on time:** 20 minutes. **Total time:** 1 hour.*

A confetti of vegetables over lean turkey and protein-rich beans makes this salad as filling as a belly-buster burrito.

INGREDIENTS:

- 2 cups fresh corn kernels (about 4 ears corn)
- 1 medium poblano pepper, seeded and cut into ¼-inch pieces
- 1 large sweet potato, peeled and cut into ¼-inch cubes
- 1 Tbsp olive oil
- ½ lb ground turkey breast
- 1 tsp ground cumin
- 1 15-oz BPA-free can unsalted black beans, drained and rinsed, or 1½ cups cooked black beans
- ½ cup low-fat sour cream
- ½ cup low-fat buttermilk
- ½ tsp chipotle chile powder
- 1 bunch scallions, thinly sliced, white and green parts separated
- 4 romaine hearts, halved and chopped into ¼-inch slices
- ½ cup grated low-fat cheddar cheese

INSTRUCTIONS:

ONE: Preheat oven to 450°F. In a medium bowl, toss corn, poblano and potato with oil. Spread mixture onto a 9 x 13-inch baking sheet and roast for 30 minutes, tossing with a spatula every 10 minutes, until corn and poblano begin to char and potato softens.

TWO: Meanwhile, heat a large sauté pan on high. Add turkey and cook for 10 minutes, stirring often, until browned. Add ¼ cup water to pan and scrape browned bits from the bottom. Add cumin and beans and stir to combine. Cover, reduce heat to low and keep warm until ready to serve.

THREE: Prepare dressing: In a small bowl, whisk sour cream, buttermilk, chile powder and white parts of scallions. Cover with plastic wrap and refrigerate until ready to use.

FOUR: Remove vegetables from oven and let cool slightly. Divide romaine among 4 serving plates and top each with turkey mixture and vegetables, dividing evenly. Sprinkle with remaining green parts of scallions and cheese and top with dressing, dividing evenly.

Nutrients per serving (2 cups romaine, ½ cup turkey-bean mixture, ½ cup vegetables, 3 Tbsp dressing): *Calories: 470, Total Fat: 11 g, Sat. Fat: 3.5 g, Monounsaturated Fat: 3 g, Polyunsaturated Fat: 1 g, Carbs: 61 g, Fiber: 10 g, Sugars: 13 g, Protein: 31 g, Sodium: 220 mg, Cholesterol: 40 mg*

Sweet Maine Lobster, Mango & Jicama Salad
WITH CUCUMBER VINAIGRETTE

Serves 4.

Crispy and delicate, tangy and sweet, upscale yet relaxed. Nothing says summer like this salad's winning (and sometimes contradictory) combination of tastes and textures.

INGREDIENTS:

- 2 lobsters (1 to 1¼ lb each), cooked, chilled and shelled
- 1 mango, peeled and sliced
- ¼ jicama, peeled and sliced into strips
- ½ cucumber, peeled, seeded and sliced thinly lengthwise
- 1 cup arugula
- 16 mint leaves
- 8 sprigs cilantro
- 4 Tbsp extra-virgin olive oil
- 4 Tbsp Cucumber Vinaigrette (see recipe, below)
- Sea salt, to taste

INSTRUCTIONS:

Slice lobster tail meat and arrange on a plate in a circle. In a bowl, toss claw meat with mango, jicama, cucumber, arugula, mint, cilantro, oil and Cucumber Vinaigrette. Sprinkle a touch of salt on each piece of plated lobster, and top plate with a pile of salad. Serve immediately.

Nutrients per serving: *Calories: 442, Total Fat: 17 g, Sat. Fat: 2 g, Monounsaturated Fat: 11 g, Polyunsaturated Fat: 2 g, Carbs: 21 g, Fiber: 3.5 g, Sugars: 10 g, Protein: 48 g, Sodium: 574 mg, Cholesterol: 159 mg*

Cucumber Vinaigrette

Makes about ½ cup.

To juice the cucumber, all you need to do is whirl it in the blender and give it a strain.

INGREDIENTS:

- Juice ½ cucumber (about ¼ cup)
- 1 Tbsp Sucanat
- 2 Tbsp fresh lime juice
- 1 tsp sea salt
- 1 tsp chopped jalapeño pepper

INSTRUCTIONS:

Combine all ingredients with a whisk until Sucanat is dissolved. Taste and adjust seasonings, if desired.

Nutrients per serving: *Calories: 19, Total Fat: 0 g, Sat. Fat: 0 g, Carbs: 5 g, Fiber: 0.5 g, Sugars: 4 g, Protein: 0.5 g, Sodium: 494 mg, Cholesterol: 0 mg*

Sushi Salad

Serves 4. **Hands-on time:** 20 minutes. **Total time:** 50 minutes.

This salad unrolls all of the quintessential flavors of your favorite Saturday night sushi platter and tosses them together. Crisp strips of nori soften with chewy brown rice, crunchy vegetables and plump pieces of crab. Silky avocado and a peppy wasabi vinaigrette top the deconstructed California roll on a bed of baby spinach.

INGREDIENTS:

- 1 cup short-grain brown rice
- 1 Tbsp wasabi paste
- 2 Tbsp low-sodium soy sauce
- ⅔ cup rice wine vinegar
- ½ tsp raw honey
- 1 English cucumber, diced into ¼-inch chunks
- 4 nori sheets, quartered and cut into ¼-inch strips
- 1 large carrot, peeled and thinly sliced
- 8 oz crab meat pieces (claw or jumbo lump)
- 4 cups baby spinach
- 1 avocado, pitted, peeled and sliced

TIP: If you can't find prepared wasabi paste at your local market, make your own by whisking 1 Tbsp all-natural wasabi powder with 1 Tbsp water.

INSTRUCTIONS:

ONE: In a medium saucepot, bring 2 cups water to a boil. Stir in rice, cover and reduce heat to low. Simmer for 30 minutes. Remove from heat and let sit, covered, for an additional 10 minutes. Spread rice on a baking sheet to cool to room temperature, about 15 minutes.

TWO: In a small bowl, whisk wasabi, soy sauce, vinegar and honey. Set aside.

THREE: In a large bowl, mix rice, cucumber, nori and carrot. Drizzle with wasabi-honey mixture and stir to combine. With a rubber spatula, gently fold in crab.

FOUR: Divide spinach evenly among serving bowls or plates and top each with rice-crab mixture and avocado.

Nutrients per serving (1 cup spinach, 1½ heaping cups rice-crab mixture, ¼ avocado): *Calories: 360, Total Fat: 10 g, Sat. Fat: 1.5 g, Monounsaturated Fat: 6 g, Polyunsaturated Fat: 2 g, Omega-3s: 350 mg, Omega-6s: 930 mg, Carbs: 54 g, Fiber: 9 g, Sugars: 4 g, Protein: 18 g, Sodium: 490 mg, Cholesterol: 55 mg*

NUTRITIONAL BONUS: This salad contains all the benefits of a good sushi bar. The combination of complex carbs, complete proteins and a healthy dose of vitamin B12 (69% DV) helps maintain normal metabolism and regulate energy levels.

Chile-Lime Roasted Sweet Potatoes

Serves 4. **Hands-on time:** 10 minutes. **Total time:** 35 minutes.

Earthy sweet potatoes get even sweeter with our lime and honey glaze, accented with a small amount of chile powder for added depth. Serve this simple side as a fiery companion to grilled chicken or fish.

INGREDIENTS:

- Olive oil cooking spray
- 1½ lb sweet potatoes, peeled and cut into ¾-inch chunks
- ½ tsp chile powder
- ¼ tsp sea salt
- Fresh ground black pepper, to taste
- 3 Tbsp fresh lime juice
- 1½ Tbsp raw honey
- 1 Tbsp safflower oil
- ½ large yellow onion, sliced into half-moons
- ¼ cup jarred piquillo chile peppers (packed in water), drained, or 2 small fresh red chile peppers, chopped
- ½ cup chopped fresh cilantro, optional
- Lime wedges, optional

INSTRUCTIONS:

ONE: Preheat oven to 425°F. Line a large rimmed baking sheet with foil and mist with cooking spray. Add potatoes to sheet and mist with additional cooking spray. Sprinkle with chile powder, salt and black pepper and toss to coat. Spread in a single layer and bake, turning halfway, for 20 minutes.

TWO: In a small bowl, whisk lime juice, honey and safflower oil. Remove potatoes from oven and drizzle mixture over top. Add onion and toss to coat. Spread in a single layer and bake until potatoes are tender, about 10 minutes.

THREE: Remove from oven, add chile peppers and toss to combine. If desired, top with cilantro and squeeze lime wedges over top.

Nutrients per ¾-cup serving: *Calories: 222, Total Fat: 4 g, Sat. Fat: 0 g, Carbs: 46 g, Fiber: 6 g, Sugars: 16 g, Protein: 3 g, Sodium: 220 mg, Cholesterol: 0 mg*

Chile-Lime
Roasted
Sweet
Potatoes

Chicken BLT

Chicken BLT
(Bean, Lettuce & Tomato)
WITH SMOKY TOMATO DRESSING

Serves 4. ***Hands-on time:*** *20 minutes.* ***Total time:*** *30 minutes.*

A great American sandwich classic, the BLT (bacon, lettuce and tomato) inspires this salad with its smoky, creamy flavors and cool, crunchy textures. A dash of smoked sea salt in the rich tomato dressing takes the place of bacon, while poached chicken boosts a bed of Bibb into a satisfying meal.

INGREDIENTS:

- 2 boneless, skinless chicken breasts (12 to 16 oz total)
- 2 12-oz hothouse or beefsteak tomatoes, divided
- 1 cup nonfat plain Greek yogurt
- 1 Tbsp olive oil
- 1 Tbsp white wine vinegar
- ½ tsp natural smoked sea salt
- ¼ tsp fresh ground black pepper
- ¼ cup chopped chives
- 1 large head Bibb lettuce, washed and dried well
- 1 large cucumber, peeled, quartered and sliced into ½-inch-thick pieces
- 1 15-oz BPA-free can unsalted beans (cannellini, great northern or navy), drained and rinsed, or 1½ cups cooked white beans

TIP: If smoked sea salt isn't a staple in your pantry, you may swap it for a combination of ¼ tsp smoked paprika and ½ tsp sea salt.

INSTRUCTIONS:

ONE: In a medium covered saucepan, bring 2 cups water to a boil. Add chicken and reduce heat to low. Poach, covered, until cooked through, about 15 minutes. Remove chicken and set aside until cool enough to handle, about 10 minutes. Cut into ½-inch cubes.

TWO: Prepare dressing: Quarter 1 tomato. Add to a blender with yogurt, oil, vinegar, salt and pepper and blend until smooth, about 30 seconds. Stir in chives.

THREE: Cut remaining tomato into 1-inch chunks. Divide lettuce, cucumber, beans, chicken and tomato chunks among 4 serving plates. Toss each salad with quarter of dressing.

Nutrients per serving (3 cups salad and ½ cup dressing): *Calories: 290, Total Fat: 6 g, Sat. Fat: 1 g, Monounsaturated Fat: 3 g, Polyunsaturated Fat: 1 g, Carbs: 27 g, Fiber: 6 g, Sugars: 9 g, Protein: 32 g, Sodium: 400 mg, Cholesterol: 60 mg*

Quick-Braised Kale
WITH GOJI BERRIES & CASHEWS

Serves 4. ***Hands-on time:*** *5 minutes.* ***Total time:*** *10 minutes.*

Quick-braising can be an ideal method for cooking cool-weather greens, but make sure to select sturdy varieties such as kale, collards and escarole.

INGREDIENTS:

- 2 Tbsp coconut oil
- 2 shallots, chopped into small pieces
- 1 large bunch kale, leaves chopped into small pieces, tough stems and center ribs discarded
- ⅓ cup low-sodium vegetable or chicken broth
- ¼ cup unsweetened dried goji berries
- Fresh ground white pepper, to taste
- ¼ cup chopped unsalted cashews, toasted

TIP: Unsweetened dried cranberries can be substituted for the goji berries in equal amounts.

INSTRUCTIONS:

ONE: In a large, heavy pot, heat oil on medium. Add shallots and sauté for 1 to 2 minutes, until just softened. Add kale and stir until coated in oil. Add broth, reduce heat to low, cover and cook for 5 minutes, until kale is tender but still bright green.

TWO: Add berries and stir to coat. Season with pepper. Divide mixture evenly among plates, sprinkle with cashews and serve immediately.

Nutrients per 1½-cup serving: *Calories: 180, Total Fat: 11 g, Sat. Fat: 7 g, Monounsaturated Fat: 3 g, Polyunsaturated Fat: 1 g, Carbs: 17 g, Fiber: 2 g, Sugars: 4 g, Protein: 5 g, Sodium: 55 mg, Cholesterol: 0 mg*

Nutritional Bonus:
Goji berries have definitely earned their superfood status. Ounce per ounce, they have more beta-carotene then carrots and more vitamin C than oranges. They are rich in antioxidants and even contain the eight essential amino acids necessary to make a complete protein.

Cuban Papaya Salad

Serves 4. ***Makes*** *about 6 cups.* **Hands-on time:** *40 minutes.* ***Total time:*** *45 minutes.*

All hail the papaya! This exotic fruit works well with both sweet and savory dishes – and it's a nutritional powerhouse.

INGREDIENTS:

- 2 Tbsp slivered unsalted almonds
- 1 Tbsp olive oil
- 1 boneless, skinless chicken breast (5 to 6 oz)
- Pinch each sea salt and fresh ground black pepper
- ½ cup Israeli couscous, divided
- 1 cup diced red onion (1 small), divided
- 1 cup low-sodium chicken broth or water
- 1 cup cooked black beans, rinsed and drained
- 2 packed cups fresh baby spinach
- 2 Tbsp fresh lime juice
- 1 Tbsp raw honey
- ¼ tsp red pepper flakes
- ⅛ tsp ground cumin
- 1½ cups diced papaya (see p. 70–71 for tips)
- 1 lime, cut into wedges, optional

INSTRUCTIONS:

ONE: In a large nonstick skillet on medium-high heat, toast almonds, stirring, until fragrant and beginning to brown. Remove almonds from skillet; set aside. Add oil to same skillet and heat on medium-high.

TWO: Season chicken on both sides with salt and black pepper. Add chicken to skillet and cook until center is no longer pink, 5 to 6 minutes per side. Remove chicken to a plate; allow to rest for 2 minutes, then shred with 2 forks and set aside.

THREE: Add couscous and ¾ cup onion to same skillet; stir and cook until couscous is lightly toasted and onion softens, 3 to 4 minutes. Add broth to skillet and continue to cook and stir until almost all liquid is absorbed, 4 to 5 minutes. Add beans and cook for 1 minute. Add spinach, toss and heat until spinach begins to wilt, about 1 minute more.

FOUR: Meanwhile, in a small bowl, whisk together lime juice, honey, pepper flakes and cumin.

FIVE: Add chicken, papaya and lime-honey dressing to couscous-spinach mixture in skillet; gently toss until well combined (or, if skillet is too full, toss in a large bowl). Transfer mixture from skillet to a serving bowl or platter. Top with remaining ¼ cup onion, almonds and, if desired, lime wedges. Serve warm.

Nutrients per 1½-cup serving: *Calories: 271, Total Fat: 7 g, Sat. Fat: 1 g, Monounsaturated Fat: 4 g, Polyunsaturated Fat: 1 g, Carbs: 40 g, Fiber: 7 g, Sugars: 9 g, Protein: 17 g, Sodium: 101 mg, Cholesterol: 20 mg*

Nutritional Bonus:

A little more than 1 cup of fresh papaya packs more than 300% of your daily need for vitamin C, which does wonders for your immune system. At 5.5 g per serving, papayas are loaded with fiber and they're also an excellent source of B vitamins, folate and beta-carotene which help to regulate energy levels and decrease stress, aid in the formation of DNA and RNA and strengthen eye and reproductive health, respectively.

Papaya

The velvety flesh of papaya is so versatile, you can add it to virtually any dish – sweet or savory – or simply nosh on it plain by the spoonful.

Some foods are so fresh-tasting, they can send you on a virtual vacation in just a few bites' time – and papaya is the perfect one-way ticket to a tropical state of mind.

Native to southern Mexico, papayas are now grown in every tropical region in the world. Most papayas are cultivated in Central America and Hawaii, and while there are small differences in the varieties from these regions, they all have a great deal in common. Papayas are football-shaped fruits weighing one to two pounds, and their green outer skin undergoes a dramatic and colorful transformation over time. As the fruit ripens, the skin changes in gradients from green to yellow-orange or orange-red.

Buy a papaya that has begun to ripen from its predominant green, feels heavy for its size and has skin that gives slightly when pressed gently with your thumb.

Purists find the best way to enjoy papaya is by squeezing fresh lime juice over a halved fruit and simply scooping out the sweet, tangy orange flesh with a spoon. While that method will allow you to truly taste your papaya's natural flavor (the lime juice intensifies it), the tropical fruit also lends itself well to sweet or savory salads, sorbets and shakes, and as a flavor pairing for seafood or chicken.

If for no other reason, try papaya to take advantage of its long list of health benefits. Papaya is a rich source of antioxidants, vitamin C and helpful nutrients like carotenes that may guard against colon cancer and other diseases caused by a concentration of harmful free radicals. Papaya has also been shown to potentially reduce symptoms caused by digestive problems, inflammation and heartburn. As a good source of fiber, papaya may have a positive influence on cholesterol levels, triglycerides and other blood particles that add to your risk for heart disease.

So slice up a papaya today – this tropical fruit really goes the distance when it comes to meeting your desire to serve fresh, healthful foods that enliven the taste buds.

Tip: Rinse your ripe papaya under cool running water and dry with paper towels. Papaya is ripe when most of the skin has turned from green to yellow-orange. It will be easy to slice when ripe and may smell slightly sweet on the stem end. If the papaya is green, allow it to sit on the counter at room temperature until it begins to change colors.

How to Prep Your Papaya

ONE: If serving papaya sliced or cubed, use a vegetable peeler or paring knife to remove thin strips of skin. Take care not to peel too deep so as not to waste any of the flesh.

TWO: With your large chef's knife, slice papaya in half lengthwise.

THREE: Scoop out black seeds and pale orange flesh surrounding seeds and discard. Avoid scooping too deep; you want to save as much flesh as possible!

OPTION: To enjoy papaya as a snack eaten out of hand simply skip Step 1 so the skin is left intact and follow Steps 2 and 3. Squeeze fresh lime juice over the flesh and scoop out delicious bites with a spoon.

To Add to Sweet and Savory Dishes

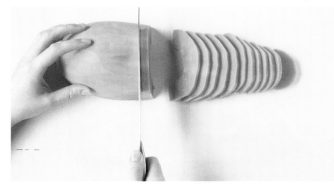

ONE: Cut each papaya half into slices, as thick or as thin as you like. Papaya slices make a nice addition to a breakfast or lunch. Serve with lime wedges for squeezing over top.

TWO: If you desire smaller pieces, cut each slice into cubes. Enjoy cubed papaya as a treat by itself, blended into a shake recipe or served in a sweet or savory salad (see Cuban Papaya Salad, p. 68).

Spinach

Here's a delicious way to prepare spinach – your ultimate nutrient booster – that steps beyond just another salad.

What
You'll
Need:

Large bowl

Medium bowl

Colander

1 large skillet or saucepan

Tongs

Cutting board

Wooden spoon

Boosting the nutrition profile of tacos, casseroles, soups, pastas and egg dishes is as easy as tossing in a few handfuls of spinach. This ultimate health food contains an excellent amount of more than 15 essential nutrients, including vitamins K and A and the mineral magnesium. Opt for vibrant green, pre-washed spinach found in bags and containers, or unwashed bunches in the fresh produce section.

Other clean alternatives are the frozen leaves or compact boxes of spinach found in the freezer aisle. Frozen spinach will save you the steps of washing, cooking, and chopping, but keep in mind it contains more sodium than fresh, and you will spend time waiting for it to thaw. Fresh requires more hands-on time, but it cooks quickly and you can control the size of the leaves and prepare it to your liking.

One of the best ways to cook fresh spinach – and other leafy greens – is by wilting (see "Your Step-by-Step Guide" at right). Wilting is similar to steaming, but it's done in a pan rather than a steamer basket. It helps to retain the bright color of greens and it's the easiest way to make a healthy vegetable side dish, since other ingredients can easily be added to the pan. Use this same method to cook chard, kale and collard or mustard greens. The greens will cook fast and you'll know they're done when they collapse and release their own liquid. Since the liquid in the pan won't evaporate, it's necessary to drain and squeeze the greens. This is especially important if you'll be using the greens in another recipe such as lasagna, dip or quiche.

Your Step-by-Step Guide to Wilting Spinach:

ONE (OPTIONAL): Some folks find the stems of spinach slightly bitter. For a milder flavor, pick through spinach, pinching off stems that are longer than ½ inch and discarding spoiled leaves.

TWO: If your spinach is not pre-washed or looks dirty, fill a large bowl with water and transfer spinach to bowl. With your hands, swish spinach around to wash thoroughly. Transfer to a colander and shake off excess water.

THREE (WILTING): Heat a large saucepan or skillet on medium. Working in batches if necessary, add spinach and cook until wilted and easily gathers into a mound with tongs, 30 seconds to 1 minute, stirring occasionally.

FOUR: Transfer to a colander placed inside a bowl to catch excess liquid and set aside until cool enough to handle, about 10 minutes.

FIVE: With your hands, gather spinach and squeeze out excess water. Transfer to a cutting board and chop coarsely.

OPTION: If mixing spinach with a hot ingredient such as cooked pasta, prepare through Step 2, then pour hot pasta cooking water over spinach to wilt.

Soups, Stews & Chilies

Coconut Curry Chili, p. 88

We at *Clean Eating* love to provide you with the comfort foods you adore, without the extra calories. Feast on savory beefy stews, hearty chilies rich in spices, and soothing soups infused with colorful veggies. Curl up with a loved one over steamy bowls of Creamy Broccoli & Pea Soup or Indian-Spiced Vegetarian Chili, whatever your taste! Make a big batch and freeze these pots of wholesome goodness to save for a chilly night.

Cauliflower & Clams in Parsley Broth

*Serves 4. **Hands-on time:** 10 minutes. **Total time:** 20 minutes.*

Thin whole-wheat pasta transforms a dish of tender cauliflower, garlicky clams and parsley-infused broth into a hearty meal. But don't be afraid to break up the elements: By skipping the spaghetti, you can take this recipe from main course to starter or tasting plate for a party. The choice is yours!

INGREDIENTS:

- 8 oz whole-wheat thin spaghetti, spaghettini or vermicelli
- 2 tsp olive oil
- ¼ cup chopped shallots
- 4 cloves garlic, minced
- 3 cups fresh cauliflower florets
- 2 cups low-sodium chicken broth
- 36 small littleneck clams (about 3¼ lb), scrubbed well
- ½ cup chopped Italian flat-leaf parsley
- Sea salt and fresh ground black pepper, to taste

NOTE: Discard clams that gape open when raw and remain open when tapped.

INSTRUCTIONS:

ONE: Cook spaghetti according to package directions; drain.

TWO: Meanwhile, in a large skillet, heat oil on medium-high. Add shallots and garlic and cook for 2 minutes, until soft. Add cauliflower and broth and bring to a simmer. Add clams, cover and cook for 5 minutes, until all clams open (discarding any clams that do not open). Add spaghetti and parsley to skillet, mix well and cook for 1 minute to heat through. Season with salt and pepper.

Nutrients per serving (9 clams and ⅔ cup spaghetti mixture): *Calories: 350, Total Fat: 5 g, Sat. Fat: 1 g, Carbs: 54 g, Fiber: 10 g, Sugars: 5 g, Protein: 27 g, Sodium: 160 mg, Cholesterol: 35 mg*

Nutritional Bonus:
If you're looking to up your iron intake, you may be surprised to learn that clams are an excellent source of this essential mineral (you'll get more than your recommended daily intake in just one serving of this dish). Clams are also a great source of low-fat protein, vitamins C and B12, and several other essential minerals.

Nutritional Bonus:
Shrimp may be small, but they contain impressive amounts of vitamin D – in fact, a single serving of this stew packs 39% of your daily requirement. The fat-soluable vitamin is key in maintaining good vascular health and promoting stong bones. And, if that weren't enough, the shrimp in this dish provide over 50% of the recipe's protein offering.

Quick & Easy Fish Stew

Quick & Easy Fish Stew

Serves 6. ***Hands-on time:*** *15 minutes.* ***Total time:*** *25 minutes.*

It's time to say good-bye to heavy cream-based chowders and hello to this slimming, savory and protein-packed stew.

INGREDIENTS:

- 3 tsp olive oil, divided
- 1 lb shell-on shrimp (24 to 30 shrimp), peeled and deveined, shells reserved
- 2½ cups low-sodium chicken broth
- 2 shallots, minced
- 1½ Tbsp brown-rice flour
- Pinch each ground cayenne pepper, sea salt and fresh ground black pepper
- 8 baby red potatoes, scrubbed well and halved
- 1 12-oz boneless, skinless cod fillet, cut into 1-inch pieces
- 1 cup low-fat milk
- 2 plum tomatoes, diced
- 2 Tbsp chopped fresh parsley for garnish

INSTRUCTIONS:

ONE: In a small saucepan, heat ½ tsp oil on medium. Add shrimp shells and sauté, stirring occasionally, until pink, about 2 minutes. Add broth and bring to a boil; reduce heat to medium-low and simmer for 5 minutes. Drain over top of a large bowl, reserving broth; discard shells.

TWO: In a large sauté pan with a tight-fitting lid, heat remaining 2½ tsp oil on medium-high. Add shallots and sauté, stirring occasionally, until soft and translucent, about 3 minutes. Stir in flour, cayenne, salt and black pepper; cook for 2 minutes. Gradually add reserved broth, whisking constantly. Add potatoes and bring to a boil; reduce heat to a simmer, cover and cook for 4 more minutes. Add cod, cover and simmer for 5 minutes. Add shrimp, cover and simmer until cod is opaque and shrimp is pink, 5 to 6 minutes. Add milk and cook until heated through, about 2 to 3 minutes; add tomatoes. Spoon into serving bowls and garnish with parsley, dividing evenly.

Nutrients per 1-cup serving: Calories: 225, Total Fat: 5 g, Sat. Fat: 1 g, Omega-3s: 510 mg, Omega-6s: 450 mg, Carbs: 14 g, Fiber: 1 g, Sugars: 4 g, Protein: 30 g, Sodium: 216 mg, Cholesterol: 142 mg

Roasted Butternut Squash & Pear Soup

Serves 6. ***Hands-on time:*** *10 minutes.* ***Total time:*** *35 minutes.*

What better way to indulge in autumn's bounty than with a hearty butternut squash soup?

INGREDIENTS:

- 2 firm pears (such as Anjou), peeled, cored and chopped into 1-inch chunks
- 1 small butternut squash, peeled, seeded and chopped into 1-inch chunks
- 3 tsp olive oil, divided
- 1 small yellow onion, finely diced
- Pinch each sea salt and fresh ground black pepper
- 3 cups low-sodium chicken or vegetable broth
- ¼ cup low-fat plain yogurt for garnish, optional
- 1 Tbsp pumpkin seeds for garnish, optional
- Pinch fresh grated or ground nutmeg for garnish, optional

INSTRUCTIONS:

ONE: Preheat oven to 400°F. In a roasting pan, combine pears and squash. Drizzle with 1½ tsp oil, toss to coat, then spread out to cover bottom of pan, allowing for some overlap. Roast in oven, uncovered, until squash begins to brown and soften, about 20 minutes. Remove from oven and set aside.

TWO: Meanwhile, in a large saucepan, heat remaining 1½ tsp oil on medium. Add onion and sprinkle with salt and pepper. Sauté until onion is softened and golden in color, 3 to 4 minutes. Add pear-squash mixture and broth and bring to a boil. Reduce heat to low and simmer for 15 minutes.

THREE: Using a hand blender or upright blender, purée mixture until smooth, about 45 to 60 seconds. (**NOTE:** If using an upright blender, work in small, cooled batches to avoid scalding. Then return to saucepan on low until reheated.) Garnish each serving with yogurt, pumpkin seeds and nutmeg, if desired.

Nutrients per ¾-cup serving: Calories: 120, Total Fat: 4.5 g, Sat. Fat: 1 g, Carbs: 17 g, Fiber: 3 g, Sugars: 8 g, Protein: 4 g, Sodium: 65 mg, Cholesterol: 0 mg

NUTRITIONAL BONUS: Just ½ cup of cubed butternut squash has a full day's supply of beta-carotene, an antioxidant that may reduce your risk of heart disease, cancer and diabetes. Foods high in carotenoids – including carrots and sweet potatoes – are easily spotted by their brilliant hue, as beta-carotene is an orange plant pigment.

Super-Fast French Onion Soup

Serves 4. **Hands-on time:** *13 minutes.* **Total time:** *30 minutes.*

Rich broth, caramelized onions, melted cheese – it's a team made in comfort-food heaven! As beef broth is one of the main components of this soup, be sure to use a good-quality one.

INGREDIENTS:

- 1 tsp olive oil
- 1 tsp organic unsalted butter
- 3 large red onions, peeled and thinly sliced
- 2 cloves garlic, minced
- 1 tsp dried thyme leaves
- Pinch each sea salt and fresh ground black pepper
- 2 tsp balsamic vinegar
- 4 cups low-sodium beef broth
- 1 tsp Worcestershire sauce
- 4 slices whole-wheat baguette (½ inch each)
- 2 oz low-fat Swiss cheese, grated

INSTRUCTIONS:

ONE: In a large saucepan, heat oil and butter on medium. Add onions, garlic, thyme, salt and pepper; stir with a large wooden spoon to coat. Sauté, stirring occasionally, until onions begin to soften, 2 to 3 minutes. Stir in vinegar and reduce heat to medium-low. Cover and cook, stirring occasionally, until onions are limp and begin sticking to bottom of pan, 10 to 12 minutes. Add broth and Worcestershire sauce and stir, using spoon to scrape up any browned bits from bottom of pan. Increase heat to medium and bring to a simmer; reduce heat to low and continue simmering for 10 minutes.

TWO: Meanwhile, place a rack in top third of oven; preheat broiler to high and let heat for 5 minutes. Place baguette on a cookie sheet or broiler pan and broil until lightly toasted, flipping once to toast both sides, about 1 minute total. Remove from oven and sprinkle cheese on bread, dividing evenly. Return to oven and broil until cheese is melted, 45 to 60 seconds. Divide soup among serving bowls and place 1 baguette slice in center of each bowl. Serve immediately.

Nutrients per serving (1 cup soup and 1 baguette slice): *Calories: 207, Total Fat: 5 g, Sat. Fat: 2 g, Carbs: 27 g, Fiber: 4 g, Sugars: 7 g, Protein: 10 g, Sodium: 277 mg, Cholesterol: 7 mg*

NUTRITIONAL BONUS: This soup calls for red onions, which have a higher concentration of flavonoids than typical cooking onions. Studies have shown that flavonoids can help reduce the risk of heart disease, cancer and diabetes. To maximize the health benefits, don't over-peel your onions when removing the outer layer.

Lentil & Sweet Potato Stew

Serves 8. **Hands-on time:** *12 minutes.* **Total time:** *30 minutes.*

When Tosca Reno, *Clean Eating* columnist and author of *The Eat-Clean Diet®* series, tells us to "Color up!" she's talking about choosing produce in a rainbow of colors. One look at the varied hues in this stew and you'll see exactly what she means.

INGREDIENTS:

- 2 tsp olive oil
- 1 yellow onion, finely diced
- 1 stalk celery, diced
- 1 carrot, peeled and finely diced
- 2 cloves garlic, minced
- Pinch each sea salt and fresh ground black pepper
- 2 cups dry green lentils, picked over
- 1 large sweet potato, peeled and cubed
- 1 bay leaf
- 4 cups low-sodium vegetable broth
- 2 plum tomatoes, seeded and diced
- ¼ cup chopped fresh Italian parsley

INSTRUCTIONS:

In a large, heavy-bottomed pot, heat oil on medium. Add onion, celery, carrot and garlic and sauté, stirring occasionally, until softened, 3 to 4 minutes. Add salt, pepper, lentils, potato, bay leaf, broth and 2 cups water; stir to combine. Bring to a simmer and cook until lentils and potatoes are tender, 12 to 15 minutes. Remove from heat and stir in tomatoes and parsley. Remove bay leaf and divide stew among serving bowls.

Nutrients per 1-cup serving: *Calories: 199, Total Fat: 2 g, Sat. Fat: 0 g, Carbs: 35 g, Fiber: 9 g, Sugars: 4 g, Protein: 11 g, Sodium: 114 mg, Cholesterol: 0 mg*

NUTRITIONAL BONUS: Adding sweet potato to this stew does more than give it color; it also ups the feel-full fiber content and provides you with potassium, which aids skeletal, heart and muscular functioning.

Kale Barley Soup

Makes 10 cups. ***Hands-on time:*** *15 minutes.* ***Total time:*** *30 minutes.*

If you're looking for ways to incorporate more greens into your diet, stop right here. This nutrient-packed soup is heavy on kale and light on calories – only 110 per serving!

INGREDIENTS:

- 1 Tbsp olive oil
- 1 yellow onion, chopped
- 4 carrots, peeled, halved lengthwise and sliced into half-moons
- 2 cloves garlic, minced
- 1 plum tomato, chopped
- 2 cups cooked barley
- 1 tsp ground cumin
- ¼ tsp ground turmeric
- ¼ tsp sea salt
- ½ tsp ground black pepper
- 1 bunch kale, chopped (about 6 cups)

INSTRUCTIONS:

In a large skillet or stockpot, heat oil on medium. Add onion and sauté, stirring occasionally, for about 3 minutes, until translucent. Add carrots and sauté until soft, about 5 minutes. Add garlic, tomato, barley, cumin, turmeric, salt and pepper; stir to combine. Reduce heat to medium-low. Add 4 cups water, cover and simmer for 10 minutes. Add kale, cover and cook until kale turns bright green, about 5 minutes.

Nutrients per 1-cup serving: Calories: 110, Total Fat: 2.5 g, Sat. Fat: 0 g, Carbs: 21 g, Fiber: 5 g, Sugars: 2 g, Protein: 3 g, Sodium: 85 mg, Cholesterol: 0 mg

Leek, Potato & Cheddar Soup

Leek, Potato & Cheddar Soup

Serves 6. **Hands-on time:** 10 minutes. **Total time:** 30 minutes.

If you'd like to add a bit more color and texture to this puréed soup, garnish it with 2 Tbsp chopped fresh Italian parsley or an additional sprinkling of nutmeg.

INGREDIENTS:

- 2 tsp olive oil
- 3 large leeks, white and light green parts only, rinsed and finely sliced into semicircles
- Pinch each sea salt and fresh ground black pepper
- 3 Yukon gold potatoes, peeled and diced
- 4 cups low-sodium chicken broth
- 2 cups low-fat milk
- Pinch ground nutmeg
- ½ cup grated low-fat sharp cheddar cheese

INSTRUCTIONS:

ONE: In a large saucepan, heat oil on medium-high. Add leeks, salt and pepper and cook, stirring frequently, until very soft, about 5 minutes. Add potatoes and broth and bring to a boil. Reduce heat to medium-low and simmer until potatoes soften, 8 to 10 minutes. Add milk and nutmeg, stir and cook until heated through, about 3 minutes.

TWO: Using a ladle or large spoon, carefully remove 2 cups soup and transfer to an upright blender; purée until smooth, about 2 minutes. Return purée to saucepan, add cheese and stir just until cheese melts. Ladle into serving bowls, dividing evenly.

Nutrients per 1-cup serving: *Calories: 202, Total Fat: 4 g, Sat. Fat: 1 g, Carbs: 32 g, Fiber: 2 g, Sugars: 7 g, Protein: 11 g, Sodium: 176 mg, Cholesterol: 6 mg*

Nutritional Bonus:

The milder-tasting relative of garlic and onions, the leek is a great alternative for those seeking the nutritional benefits that the allium family of vegetables provide – without the strong flavor. Leeks contain free-radical-fighting polyphenols, as well as the energy-producing and immune-boosting combo of iron and vitamin C.

Pork & Beans Chili

Serves 8. **Hands-on time:** 20 minutes. **Total time:** 2 hours, 30 minutes.

In the mood for a one-pot meal and can't decide between chili or Boston baked beans? You're in luck because this recipe combines the best of both meals, as well as a whopping dose of feel-good fiber.

INGREDIENTS:

- 1 Tbsp spelt flour
- 1½ Tbsp chile powder
- 1 tsp ground cayenne pepper
- ¼ tsp each sea salt and fresh ground black pepper
- 2 tsp ground cumin
- 2¼ lb pork loin, trimmed of visible fat and cut into 1-inch chunks
- 3 tsp olive oil, divided
- 1 yellow onion, diced
- 2 cloves garlic, minced
- 2 cups cooked red kidney beans or BPA-free canned red kidney beans, drained and rinsed well
- 2 cups cooked pinto beans or BPA-free canned pinto beans, drained and rinsed well
- 2 cups boxed diced tomatoes with juices
- 1 cup low-sodium chicken broth
- ½ cup nonfat plain Greek yogurt, optional
- Chopped fresh cilantro leaves for garnish, optional

INSTRUCTIONS:

ONE: In a large zip-top bag, combine flour, chile powder, cayenne, salt, black pepper and cumin. Add pork, seal bag and shake to coat. In a large stockpot, heat 2 tsp oil on medium-high. Working in batches if necessary, add pork and cook until browned on all sides, turning with tongs. Transfer pork to a medium bowl and set aside.

TWO: Heat remaining 1 tsp oil in pot on medium-high. Add onion and garlic and cook, stirring occasionally, until onion softens, 2 to 3 minutes. Return pork to pot and add beans, tomatoes with juices and broth, scraping up any browned bits from bottom of pot with a wooden spoon. Reduce heat to medium-low and simmer until pork is very tender, 1½ to 2 hours. Divide among serving bowls and, if desired, garnish with yogurt and cilantro, dividing evenly.

Nutrients per 1½-cup serving: *Calories: 306, Total Fat: 5 g, Sat. Fat: 1 g, Carbs: 27 g, Fiber: 10 g, Sugars: 3 g, Protein: 36 g, Sodium: 178 mg, Cholesterol: 83 mg*

Classic Beef Stew

Serves 4. **Hands-on time:** *40 minutes.* **Total time:** *3 hours.*

The ultimate one-pot comfort food gets the *Clean Eating* treatment!

INGREDIENTS:

- 1¼ lb top round roast, trimmed of fat and cut into 1-inch chunks
- 1 tsp smoked paprika
- ½ scant tsp sea salt, divided
- ¼ tsp ground cayenne pepper
- Fresh ground black pepper, to taste
- 1 Tbsp safflower oil, divided
- ½ large white onion, chopped
- Large pinch dried thyme
- Large pinch dried rosemary
- 2 Tbsp low-sodium tomato paste
- 3 cloves garlic, chopped
- 2 Tbsp white whole-wheat flour
- 4 Tbsp balsamic vinegar, divided
- 2½ cups low-sodium vegetable broth
- 2 dried bay leaves
- 2 carrots, peeled and cut into ½-inch pieces (about 1 cup)
- 6 oz Yukon gold or redskin potatoes, scrubbed and cut into ¾-inch chunks (about 1½ cups)
- 5 oz celery root, peeled and cut into ¾-inch chunks (about 1 cup)
- Olive oil cooking spray
- 2 large portobello mushroom caps, cut into 1-inch chunks
- ¾ cup frozen peas

INSTRUCTIONS:

ONE: Pat beef dry and sprinkle with paprika, all but 1 pinch salt, cayenne and black pepper. In a large, heavy pot, heat ½ Tbsp oil on medium-high. Add half of beef and cook, undisturbed, for 2 to 3 minutes, until bottom is browned; flip beef and repeat on opposite side. Transfer to a large plate and repeat with remaining ½ Tbsp oil and beef; set aside.

TWO: Add onion to pot and cook until soft and lightly browned, about 6 minutes. Reduce heat to medium-low and add thyme, rosemary, tomato paste and garlic; mix well. Return beef and accumulated juices to pot. Sprinkle with flour and cook for 1 minute, stirring constantly. Add 2 Tbsp vinegar and simmer for 1 minute, until slightly reduced. Add broth and bay leaves, cover and increase heat to medium-high. Once mixture begins to simmer, reduce heat, adjusting as needed to maintain a slow simmer. Cover and cook for 1 hour and 15 minutes, stirring 2 to 3 times.

THREE: Add carrots, cover and simmer for 30 minutes. Add potatoes, cover and simmer for 10 minutes. Add celery root, cover and simmer until vegetables and beef are tender, 20 to 30 minutes.

FOUR: Meanwhile, coat a large skillet with cooking spray and heat on medium-high. Add mushrooms, remaining 2 Tbsp vinegar, remaining salt and black pepper. Cook, stirring frequently, until mushrooms begin to soften, 3 to 5 minutes. Reduce heat to medium-low and cook until vinegar is almost completely reduced, about 3 minutes.

FIVE: Add peas to pot and return to a simmer; cook until just heated through, 1 to 2 minutes. Stir in mushrooms and remove from heat. Remove bay leaves and serve immediately.

Nutrients per 1½-cup serving: *Calories: 386, Total Fat: 10 g, Sat. Fat: 2 g, Carbs: 32 g, Fiber: 5 g, Sugars: 6 g, Protein: 35 g, Sodium: 510 mg, Cholesterol: 91 mg*

Split Pea, Ham & Barley Soup

Serves 4. **Hands-on time:** *25 minutes.* **Total time:** *35 minutes.*

Hearty barley, split peas and ham give this classic soup a comforting appeal that will stick to your ribs long after you've scraped the final spoonful from your bowl. Refrigerate leftover soup for three to four days or keep frozen for up to three months. If it gets a bit too thick upon standing, simply stir in additional broth or water while reheating.

INGREDIENTS:

- ¾ cup dry yellow split peas
- 1 tsp extra-virgin olive oil
- 1 Spanish onion, chopped
- 28 oz low-sodium chicken broth
- 4 carrots, peeled and chopped
- 2 tsp dried sage
- 1 cup quick-cooking pearl barley
- ½ lb low-sodium, nitrate-free, lean cooked ham, cut into ½-inch cubes
- 4 green onions, green parts only, minced

INSTRUCTIONS:

ONE: In a medium pot, bring 2 cups water to a boil on high heat. Add peas and reduce heat to medium-low; simmer, uncovered, for 20 minutes. Drain and set aside.

TWO: In a large stockpot, heat oil on medium for 1 minute. Add Spanish onion and cook, stirring occasionally, for 5 minutes. Stir in broth, ½ cup water, carrots, sage and barley. Bring to a boil on high heat; reduce heat to medium-low and simmer for 10 more minutes.

THREE: To stockpot, add ham and peas, stir and cook for an additional 2 minutes, until heated through. Garnish with green onions and serve immediately.

Nutrients per 1½-cup serving: *Calories: 460, Total Fat: 5 g, Sat. Fat: 0.5 g, Carbs: 77 g, Fiber: 22 g, Sugars: 9 g, Protein: 28 g, Sodium: 590 mg, Cholesterol: 25 mg*

Nutritional Bonus:

Split peas are jam-packed with soluble fiber, a substance which, when mixed with liquid, turns into a gel that helps you feel full – without all the added calories! Soluble fiber also helps to move cholesterol out of your body and it stabilizes blood sugar levels.

Split Pea, Ham & Barley Soup

Creamy
Broccoli &
Pea Soup

Creamy Broccoli & Pea Soup
WITH CARAMELIZED SHALLOTS

Serves 4. **Hands-on time:** *30 minutes.* **Total time:** *45 minutes.*

Sweet, bright peas add a punch of color to this smooth fall favorite. For a quick and stunning garnish, we've topped each warming bowl with creamy yogurt, caramelized shallots and aromatic chives.

INGREDIENTS:

- 1½ Tbsp olive oil, divided
- 1 large yellow onion, chopped
- Sea salt and fresh ground black pepper, to taste
- 3 cloves garlic, chopped
- 1 tsp ground ginger
- ½ tsp dried thyme
- Pinch red pepper flakes, optional
- 4 cups low-sodium chicken broth
- 1¼ lb broccoli crowns, thick stems trimmed and separated into small florets
- 1 cup thinly sliced shallots (5 to 7 shallots)
- 2 cups frozen peas
- Juice ½ lemon
- ¾ cup nonfat plain Greek yogurt
- 1½ Tbsp chopped fresh chives or mint

INSTRUCTIONS:

ONE: In a large saucepan or Dutch oven, heat ¾ Tbsp oil on medium-high. Add onion, salt and black pepper and sauté, stirring occasionally, until tender, about 8 minutes. Add garlic, ginger, thyme and pepper flakes and sauté, stirring frequently, for 2 minutes. Add broth and increase heat to high. Cover and bring to a boil. Add broccoli, reduce heat to medium and cover. Simmer until broccoli is very tender, 15 to 18 minutes.

TWO: Meanwhile, in a small skillet, heat remaining ¾ Tbsp oil on low. Add shallots and season with additional salt and black pepper. Sauté, stirring occasionally, until very soft, light brown and caramelized, about 8 minutes.

THREE: Add peas to saucepan. Cover and simmer for 3 minutes. Stir in lemon juice and remove from heat.

FOUR: With an immersion blender, purée soup until smooth. (Alternatively, working in batches, carefully transfer soup to an upright blender. Remove plastic stopper from lid and cover loosely with a towel to allow steam to escape. Purée until smooth and return to saucepan.) If necessary, reheat soup on medium-low before serving. Top each serving with yogurt, shallots and chives.

Nutrients per 1¼-cup serving: Calories: 259, Total Fat: 7 g, Sat. Fat: 1 g, Monounsaturated Fat: 4 g, Polyunsaturated Fat: 1 g, Carbs: 35 g, Fiber: 9 g, Sugars: 9 g, Protein: 19 g, Sodium: 249 mg, Cholesterol: 0 mg

Herbed Kale & Potato Soup
WITH BEEF RIBBONS

Serves 4. **Hands-on time:** *20 minutes.* **Total time:** *40 minutes.*

Our hearty greens and roots soup is inspired by a classic Portuguese dish called caldo verde (green broth). We've axed the traditional fatty linguiça sausage yet managed to keep the savory flavor intact by opting for thinly cut ribbons of sirloin beef, seasoned to perfection with dried herbs and fresh garlic.

INGREDIENTS:

- 2 eggs, shell-on
- ½ tsp extra-virgin olive oil
- 4 cloves garlic, chopped
- 2½ cups low-sodium chicken broth
- 1 Tbsp dried oregano
- 1 Tbsp dried thyme
- ½ tsp fresh ground black pepper
- ½ lb carrots, peeled and chopped
- 1 lb redskin potatoes, scrubbed well and cut into ½-inch cubes
- ½ lb beets, peeled and cut into ½-inch cubes
- ½ lb beef sirloin, cut into ¼-inch-thick ribbons
- 1 bunch kale, tough stems removed, leaves coarsely chopped

INSTRUCTIONS:

ONE: In a medium pot, add eggs and enough cold water to cover. Place on high heat, cover and bring just to a boil. Reduce heat to medium and cook for 10 minutes. Immediately remove from heat and fill pot with cold water to prevent eggs from cooking further. Drain water and refill pot with cold water. Set aside until cool enough to handle, about 5 minutes.

TWO: In a large stockpot, heat oil on medium-low for 1 minute. Add garlic and sauté, stirring occasionally, for 3 minutes or until fragrant and soft. Add broth and 2½ cups water. Stir in oregano, thyme and pepper, increase heat to high and bring to a boil. Add carrots, potatoes and beets, reduce heat to medium-high and simmer for 5 minutes (reduce heat further if soup begins to boil).

THREE: Meanwhile, remove and discard shells from eggs. Halve or chop eggs and set aside.

FOUR: Add beef and kale to stockpot and simmer for 5 minutes, until beef is cooked through. Remove from heat and divide among serving bowls. Garnish each with egg half or 2 Tbsp chopped egg.

Nutrients per serving (2 cups soup and ½ egg): Calories: 310, Total Fat: 9 g, Sat. Fat: 3 g, Monounsaturated Fat: 3 g, Polyunsaturated Fat: 1 g, Carbs: 38 g, Fiber: 7 g, Sugars: 8 g, Protein: 22 g, Sodium: 226 mg, Cholesterol: 133 mg

NUTRITIONAL BONUS: The combination of carrots and kale in this hearty soup means just 1 bowl gives you a whopping 596% of your daily vitamin K requirement. Vitamin K is essential for the strengthening and maintenance of healthy bones and assists your body in the absorption and movement of calcium.

Coconut Curry Chili

*Serves 4. Makes 10 cups. **Hands-on time:** 10 minutes. **Total time:** 27 minutes.*

The perfect Meatless Monday meal! The addition of red curry paste and coconut milk puts a Thai twist on this comfort-food favorite, and the bulgur is sure to keep you slim yet satisfied.

INGREDIENTS:

- 1½ tsp red curry paste
- 1 tsp ground cumin
- 4 cups low-sodium vegetable broth, divided
- ½ cup uncooked bulgur
- ½ medium sweet potato, peeled and cubed (about 2 cups)
- 1 large green bell pepper, chopped (about 2 cups)
- 3 cups cooked kidney beans or BPA-free canned kidney beans, drained and rinsed well
- ½ cup light coconut milk
- 2 cups jarred or boxed tomato purée (aka passata)
- 2 scallions, chopped
- Fresh ground black pepper, to taste

INSTRUCTIONS:

ONE: In a 4-qt pot, add curry paste, cumin and a bit of broth. Mash mixture and stir until paste is no longer in lumps. Add remaining broth, bulgur, potato and bell pepper. Set over high heat and bring mixture to a boil. Cover tightly, reduce heat to medium-low and cook for 10 minutes.

TWO: Add beans, coconut milk and tomato purée to pot and stir. Cook, uncovered, for 7 minutes, until bulgur is tender and chili is thick. Stir in scallions and black pepper and serve.

Nutrients per 2½-cup serving: Calories: 340, Total Fat: 4 g, Sat. Fat: 1.5 g, Carbs: 65 g, Fiber: 16 g, Sugars: 10 g, Protein: 17 g, Sodium: 412 mg, Cholesterol: 0 mg

For a photo of this recipe, see page 74.

Hearty Country Soup

*Serves 6. **Hands-on time:** 20 minutes. **Total time:** 5 hours, 50 minutes.*

Wouldn't it be nice to come home to a simmering bowl of hearty and nutritious soup after your long day? Don't worry, with this recipe, a few ingredients and a slow cooker, all of your dinner dreams can come true!

INGREDIENTS:

- Olive oil cooking spray
- 2½ Tbsp olive oil, divided
- 12 oz extra-lean chuck roast, cut into bite-size pieces
- 4 oz fresh green beans, cut into 1-inch pieces
- 2 green bell peppers, coarsely chopped
- 10 oz grape tomatoes, halved
- 3 Tbsp low-sodium tomato paste
- 2 Tbsp balsamic vinegar
- 2 cloves garlic, minced
- 1 packet stevia
- ¾ tsp coarsely ground black pepper
- 2 oz dry whole-grain rotini or elbow macaroni pasta
- 2 cups coarsely chopped green cabbage
- ¼ cup chopped fresh Italian parsley
- 2 Tbsp chopped fresh oregano
- 1 tsp chopped fresh thyme
- 1¼ tsp sea salt

INSTRUCTIONS:

ONE: Coat a 3- to 3½-qt slow cooker with cooking spray. In a large nonstick skillet, heat 1 tsp oil on medium-high. Add roast and cook, stirring occasionally, until browned, about 3 minutes. Transfer to slow cooker and add beans, bell peppers, tomatoes, tomato paste, vinegar, garlic, stevia, black pepper and 4 cups water; stir to combine. Cover and cook until roast is tender, 5 hours on high or 10 hours on low.

TWO: Stir in pasta, cabbage, parsley, oregano, thyme, salt and remaining oil; cover and cook for 30 more minutes on high.

Nutrients per 1-cup serving: Calories: 213, Total Fat: 9 g, Sat. Fat: 2 g, Monounsaturated Fat: 5.5 g, Polyunsaturated Fat: 1 g, Carbs: 18 g, Fiber: 5 g, Sugars: 5 g, Protein: 16 g, Sodium: 465 mg, Cholesterol: 25 mg

Hearty
Country
Soup

Spicy
Corn
Chowder

Spicy Corn Chowder

Serves 6. **Hands-on time:** *10 minutes.* **Total time:** *30 minutes.*

After a day of browsing the farmers' markets, what better way to put your newly purchased produce to use than in this chowder? It's the perfect meal to spice up a chilly summer evening.

INGREDIENTS:

- 2 tsp olive oil
- 1 yellow onion, finely diced
- 1 celery stalk, diced
- 1 carrot, peeled and diced
- 1 red bell pepper, diced
- ¼ tsp ground cayenne pepper
- Pinch each sea salt and fresh ground black pepper
- 8 baby red potatoes, scrubbed well and halved
- 4 cups low-sodium chicken broth
- 2 cups fresh or frozen corn kernels (thawed, if frozen)
- 1½ cups low-fat milk
- 2 Tbsp chopped fresh chives for garnish, optional

INSTRUCTIONS:

In a large saucepan, heat oil on medium-high. Add onion, celery and carrot and sauté, stirring occasionally, until slightly softened, 2 to 3 minutes. Add red pepper, cayenne, salt and black pepper and cook, stirring occasionally, for 2 minutes. Add potatoes, broth and corn; bring to a boil. Reduce heat to medium-low and simmer until potatoes are tender, 12 to 15 minutes. Add milk, stir to combine and cook until heated through, 2 to 3 minutes. Ladle soup into serving bowls, dividing evenly. If desired, garnish with chives.

Nutrients per 1-cup serving: Calories: 144, Total Fat: 3 g, Sat. Fat: 1 g, Carbs: 24 g, Fiber: 2 g, Sugars: 7 g, Protein: 6 g, Sodium: 471 mg, Cholesterol: 7 mg

Nutritional Bonus:
Typically corn does not have a reputation for being healthful, perhaps because it is commonly eaten from a butter-slathered cob. But fear not – the star ingredient of this chowder is a good source of fiber, folate, vitamin C, manganese and niacin.

Mole Chicken Chili

Serves 8. **Hands-on time:** *18 minutes.* **Total time:** *50 minutes.*

Unsweetened cocoa powder adds not only a warm richness to this chili, but also a host of nutritional benefits.

INGREDIENTS:

- 2 tsp olive oil
- 1 large yellow onion, diced
- 1 clove garlic, minced
- 2 lb ground chicken breast
- 1 tsp chipotle chile powder
- 1 tsp ancho chile powder
- 1 tsp ground cumin
- 1 tsp ground cinnamon
- ½ tsp paprika
- ½ tsp ground cloves
- 1 red bell pepper, diced
- 1 green bell pepper, diced
- 28 oz boxed diced tomatoes with juices
- 1 cup low-sodium chicken broth
- 2 cups cooked red kidney beans or BPA-free canned red kidney beans, drained and rinsed well
- 2 Tbsp unsweetened cocoa powder

INSTRUCTIONS:

In a large stockpot, heat oil on medium-high. Add onion and garlic and cook, stirring frequently, until garlic is fragrant and onion softens, 2 to 3 minutes. Add chicken, breaking up with a wooden spoon, and sprinkle with chipotle chile powder, ancho chile powder, cumin, cinnamon, paprika and cloves. Cook, stirring frequently, until chicken is well browned, 5 to 7 minutes. Add both bell peppers and stir constantly for 1 minute. Add tomatoes, broth, beans and cocoa powder, stirring to combine. Bring to a simmer; reduce heat to medium-low and cook until chicken is tender, about 30 minutes.

Nutrients per 1-cup serving: Calories: 255, Total Fat: 10 g, Sat. Fat: 3 g, Monounsaturated Fat: 5 g, Polyunsaturated Fat: 2 g, Carbs: 18 g, Fiber: 7 g, Sugars: 4 g, Protein: 24 g, Sodium: 113 mg, Cholesterol: 86 mg

NUTRITIONAL BONUS: Cocoa powder is loaded with flavonoids, plant pigments and antioxidants that fight disease-causing free radicals. In fact, studies show that the antioxidant concentration of cocoa powder is 2 times stronger than that of red wine and green tea, and 4 times that of black tea.

Indian-Spiced Vegetarian Chili

*Serves 8. **Hands-on time:** 15 minutes. **Total time:** 55 minutes.*

When shopping for the pumpkin in this recipe, avoid the standard field variety made famous by Halloween. Instead, look for smaller Cinderella, Baby Bear, Long Island Cheese and Sugar Pie pumpkins.

INGREDIENTS:

- 2 tsp olive oil
- 1 yellow onion, peeled and diced
- 1 clove garlic, minced
- ½ tsp ground ginger
- ½ tsp ground cardamom
- 1 tsp ground coriander
- 1 tsp ground turmeric
- 1 tsp ground cumin
- 2 tsp curry powder
- ¼ tsp sea salt
- 1 eggplant, diced (about 2 cups)
- 2 cups peeled and diced pumpkin
- 2 cups cooked chickpeas (aka garbanzo beans) or BPA-free canned chickpeas, drained and rinsed well
- 28 oz boxed diced tomatoes with juices
- Fresh cilantro leaves for garnish, optional

INSTRUCTIONS:

In a large stockpot, heat oil on medium-high. Add onion and garlic and cook, stirring, until garlic is fragrant and onion softens, about 2 minutes. Add ginger, cardamom, coriander, turmeric, cumin, curry powder and salt; reduce heat to medium-low and stir until onion is coated and very soft, about 4 minutes. Add eggplant, pumpkin and chickpeas and cook, stirring frequently, until pumpkin is softened slightly, about 5 minutes. Add tomatoes with juices and 1 cup water; stir gently and simmer until thickened, 25 to 30 minutes. Ladle into serving bowls and garnish with cilantro, if desired.

Nutrients per 1⅛-cup serving: Calories: 132, Total Fat: 3 g, Sat. Fat: 0.5 g, Carbs: 23 g, Fiber: 7 g, Sugars: 8 g, Protein: 6 g, Sodium: 102 mg, Cholesterol: 0 mg

NUTRITIONAL BONUS: The pumpkin in this chili is an excellent source of beta-carotene, which your body converts into vitamin A. This fat-soluble vitamin plays a key role in maintaining good vision, as well as keeping your immune system and skin healthy.

NEW!

Creamy Carrot & Cauliflower Soup
WITH HERBES DE PROVENCE

*Serves 6. **Hands-on time:** 30 minutes. **Total time:** 1 hour.*

A staple in French Mediterranean cooking, herbes de Provence is a mixture that often includes thyme, rosemary, marjoram, fennel and lavender. The fragrant blend perks up the sweet earthiness of this brilliant creamed soup.

INGREDIENTS:

- 1 Tbsp olive oil
- 1 large white onion, chopped
- 4 cloves garlic, finely chopped
- 2 tsp herbes de Provence
- 4 cups low-sodium chicken broth
- 2 lb carrots, peeled and chopped into ½-inch pieces
- 1 head cauliflower (about 2 lb), trimmed and broken into small florets
- 1 Tbsp white wine vinegar
- Sea salt and fresh ground black pepper, to taste
- 2 Tbsp chopped fresh parsley, optional

INSTRUCTIONS:

ONE: In a large saucepan or Dutch oven, heat oil on medium. Add onion and sauté, stirring occasionally, until light brown, about 8 minutes. Add garlic and herbes de Provence and sauté, stirring frequently, for 2 minutes. Add broth and 2 cups water. Cover, increase heat to high and bring to a boil. Add carrots and cauliflower. Reduce heat to medium, cover and simmer until carrots and cauliflower are very tender, about 30 minutes. Remove from heat.

TWO: With an immersion blender, purée soup until smooth. (Alternatively, working in batches, carefully transfer soup to an upright blender. Remove plastic stopper from lid and cover loosely with a towel to allow steam to escape. Purée until smooth and return to saucepan.)

THREE: If soup is too thick, add up to 1 cup water to reach desired consistency; if necessary, reheat soup on medium-low. Stir in vinegar, salt and pepper. If desired, garnish with parsley.

MAKE-AHEAD: Soup may be made up to 2 days ahead. Cool, then cover and refrigerate.

Nutrients per 1½-cup serving: Calories: 159, Total Fat: 4 g, Sat. Fat: 1 g, Monounsaturated Fat: 2 g, Polyunsaturated Fat: 1 g, Carbs: 27 g, Fiber: 8 g, Sugars: 11.5 g, Protein: 8 g, Sodium: 220 mg, Cholesterol: 0 mg

Creamy
Carrot &
Cauliflower
Soup

Foods That Help Protect

While no food can cure or prevent any disease, there's scientific evidence supporting the health benefits of some foods and their ability to reduce certain health risks. Here's part of what we know.

Shocked as you may be to hear it, your dinner plate may hold the (tasty) materials that help you reduce your risk of developing cancer. So much of what is done both to fight and treat cancer seems to be happening in a test tube – an artificial environment, or as they call it, in vitro – and I don't know about you, but that makes me feel pretty far removed from boosting my own immunity against this multifaceted disease. Indeed, the laboratory is a crucial component in the crusade to end an illness that until the turn of the century was relatively rare, but you can strengthen your body's defenses against it by choosing certain foods reputed to assist in this defense.

Is the Mediterranean diet any better than the standard North American diet when it comes to defense against disease?

The Lyon Diet Heart Study, conducted approximately 20 years ago, examined the effect of consuming a Mediterranean diet primarily for its positive effect on reducing the risk of a second heart attack. The diet, rich in plant-based foods containing immune-boosting nutrients and antioxidants, focused on the consumption of natural, unprocessed foods, including plenty of olive and canola oil (but no butter), fresh fish, whole grains, fresh fruit, loads of vegetables and legumes, more poultry, and less beef and pork. The groundbreaking Lyon study observed a 50 to 70 percent reduction in recurrent heart disease, a staggering number to be sure.

Though subsequent research has addressed some of the original study's limitations, one thing has remained quite clear – even emphasized: The Mediterranean diet confers cardiovascular health benefits, period. But there's more.

When we eat this way we also tend to eat more raw foods and fiber, which are both beneficial in fighting free radicals in the body and potentially reducing the risk of cancer, as originally observed in the Lyon study. A 2008 study published in the *British Journal of Cancer* revealed that the Mediterranean diet in fact showed reductions of up to 12 percent in cancer incidence (more than 25,000 people participated).

Does green tea have any effect against cancer? I drink two cups a day. Am I doing myself any good?

The lowly green tea leaf doesn't look like much, but each leaf contains special molecules called catechins, which seem to be able to zone in on assorted steps that cells take on the way toward turning cancerous. Epigallocatechin gallate (EGCG) is one of the more prevalent catechins in green tea, and according to Richard Béliveau, PhD and Denis Gingras, PhD, writing in *Cooking with Foods that*

Tosca Reno, *Clean Eating* columnist and author of *The Eat-Clean Diet®* series, discusses the protective benefits of certain foods.

My mother keeps telling me Brussels sprouts are good for me because they may protect against cancer. I don't like them because they smell! Do I have to eat them?

Brussels sprouts belong to a family that sports many other strong-smelling vegetables. Called crucifers, these vegetables – including broccoli, kale, cauliflower, curly kale, Brussels sprouts and cabbage – possess a strong odor and pungent flavor. That strong smell you react to is an indication of how beneficial the Brussels sprout is to your health.

The vegetables in this family are high in glucosinolate, a phytochemical with the ability to protect against toxic substances that can change cellular DNA, making those cells more susceptible to developing tumors. Glucosinolates speed up the elimination process so that toxic substances don't linger in the body, which lessens the time they need to negatively affect cells. Eating two cups of these strong-smelling vegetables at least three times a week is recommended. But you don't only have to eat sprouts: Try broccoli or kale, too.

I have heard that chocolate is really good for me because it's supposed to protect against cancer. My favorite is a Kit Kat bar. How many can I eat?

You are partly correct: Chocolate is a nutritious and delicious food, but your choice of chocolate is weak. It's better to reach for 70 percent cocoa or more when selecting a dark chocolate, and restrict yourself to two squares per day. The reason dark chocolate is so beneficial to your health is because it contains cocoa. Loaded with the polyphenol procyanidins, cocoa may protect against heart disease as well as cancer. The most recent studies show that when lab animals are given dark chocolate, tumor growth slows down. The research on cocoa and its effect in cancer protection, however, is in the early stages, but so far the results are promising. So at present, it can't hurt to eat chocolate, as long as you are careful to choose good-quality high-cocoa chocolate and enjoy it in moderation. Kit Kats just won't cut it.

Fight Cancer (McClelland & Stewart, 2007), they say that EGCG "may block certain mechanisms used by cancer cells to reproduce and invade surrounding tissue: It is able to prevent the formation of a new network of blood vessels by angiogenesis." This means that blood vessels that might otherwise feed a tumor may be unable to grow.

The best green teas to drink for this purpose are Japanese teas, which contain more catechins than Chinese varieties. According to the National Cancer Institute, some studies suggest that assorted polyphenols in green tea may also help in the fight against cancer, although we do not yet know how this happens. Drink two to five cups of plain green tea per day.

Snacks, Starters, Dips & Spreads

Poblano & Mushroom
Queso Fundido, p. 113

Coming up with tasty new snack ideas is tough. Luckily, *Clean Eating* is here to help you think outside the box! Spoon some Caramelized Onion & White Bean Spread onto whole-grain crackers for a satisfying munch. Entertaining friends? Start them off with mouthwatering Cream Cheese & Shrimp-Stuffed Mushrooms. These low-fat mini-meals are quick to whip up as a tease for your guests' taste buds, or to satisfy your own cravings if you're all alone!

Stuffed Potatoes
WITH ROASTED VEGGIES

Serves 4. **Hands-on time:** *10 minutes.* **Total time:** *3 hours, 10 minutes.*

Better than fatty bacon and sour cream-filled potato skins, this snack will fill you up without the extra calories. Fresh herbs, spices and veggies add a dose of antioxidants as an added bonus!

INGREDIENTS:

• Olive oil cooking spray
• 1 green bell pepper, cut into 1-inch pieces
• 1 yellow onion, cut into 8 wedges
• 1 cup frozen corn kernels
• 1 carrot, scrubbed well and thinly sliced
• ⅛ tsp ground cayenne pepper
• 1 Tbsp safflower oil
• 4 6-oz Yukon gold potatoes, scrubbed well
• ¼ cup fresh Italian parsley, chopped
• 1 clove garlic, minced
• ¼ tsp each sea salt and coarsely ground black pepper
• ½ cup shredded low-fat sharp cheddar cheese
• ¼ cup crumbled low-fat blue cheese

INSTRUCTIONS:

ONE: Coat a 6-qt slow cooker with cooking spray. Add bell pepper, onion, corn, carrot, cayenne and oil; stir to combine. Using a fork, pierce each potato in several spots, wrap in foil and place over top of pepper-corn mixture. Cover and cook until potatoes are tender when pierced with a fork, 3 hours on high or 6 hours on low.

TWO: Remove potatoes and set aside for 5 to 10 minutes. Add parsley, garlic, salt and black pepper to pepper-corn mixture and stir to combine.

THREE: In a small bowl, add cheddar and blue cheese and toss gently until well blended. Remove potatoes from foil and cut each in half lengthwise.

TIP: Use a clean towel to prevent fingers from burning, or let potatoes cool for an additional 5 to 10 minutes before handling.) Fluff flesh with a fork, sprinkle with cheese mixture and top with pepper-corn mixture, dividing evenly.

Nutrients per stuffed potato: Calories: 275, Total Fat: 7 g, Sat. Fat: 2 g, Monounsaturated Fat: 3 g, Polyunsaturated Fat: 1 g, Carbs: 45 g, Fiber: 5 g, Sugars: 5 g, Protein: 10.5 g, Sodium: 230 mg, Cholesterol: 7 mg

Nutritional Bonus:
Strike gold! Yukon gold potatoes offer great flavor and moist flesh, which means you'll feel less inclined to pile on fattening condiments. Once considered simply a dietary source of starch, potatoes are now being credited for their bevy of nutrients. Potatoes possess varying quantities of most macronutrients, vitamins and minerals (including fiber, if you consume the skin).

Stuffed Potatoes

Eggplant Parmesan

Eggplant Parmesan
WITH CHUNKY TOMATO SAUCE

Serves 4. *Hands-on time:* 15 minutes. *Total time:* 15 minutes.

We've taken this traditional Italian dish and stripped out the extra calories you don't need – but kept all the flavors!

INGREDIENTS:

- 2 Tbsp olive oil, divided
- 1 yellow onion, chopped
- 2 cloves garlic, minced
- ½ tsp dried basil
- 28 oz boxed diced tomatoes with juices
- 1 tsp balsamic vinegar
- ½ tsp raw honey
- 2 egg whites
- 1 cup whole-wheat panko bread crumbs
- ¼ cup grated low-fat Parmesan cheese
- 1 Tbsp chopped fresh parsley, plus additional for garnish
- 1 Italian eggplant (about 1 lb), peeled and sliced into ⅓-inch-thick rounds
- ½ cup shredded part-skim mozzarella cheese

INSTRUCTIONS:

ONE: In a medium saucepan, heat 1 tsp oil on medium-high. Add onion, garlic and basil and cook until fragrant, about 1 minute. Add tomatoes, ½ cup water, vinegar and honey; bring to a boil. Reduce heat to a simmer, cover and cook for 10 minutes, stirring occasionally. Spread 1 cup tomato mixture on the bottom of an 8-cup baking dish. Set remaining mixture aside and keep warm.

TWO: In a small bowl, beat egg whites; set aside. In a separate small bowl, combine panko, Parmesan and parsley. Dip eggplant slices, 1 at a time, into egg mixture, then panko mixture, turning and pressing to coat both sides.

THREE: Heat remaining oil in 2 large nonstick skillets on medium-high, dividing evenly. Add eggplant slices and cook, turning once or twice, until golden and crispy on the outside and tender on the inside, 6 to 8 minutes. (Alternatively, cook eggplant slices in 1 skillet in 2 batches, dividing oil between batches.)

FOUR: Preheat broiler to high. Transfer eggplant to baking dish with tomato mixture, overlapping slices slightly to cover the bottom. Sprinkle with mozzarella. Broil until cheese is bubbly and melted, about 1 minute. Serve with remaining tomato mixture and garnish with additional parsley.

Nutrients per serving (4 to 5 eggplant slices and 1 cup tomato mixture): *Calories: 283, Total Fat: 11 g, Sat. Fat: 3 g, Monounsaturated Fat: 6 g, Polyunsaturated Fat: 1 g, Carbs: 33 g, Fiber: 8 g, Sugars: 11 g, Protein: 13 g, Sodium: 293 mg, Cholesterol: 13 mg*

Chinese Dumplings

Serves 4. *Hands-on time:* 45 minutes. *Total time:* 1 hour, 30 minutes.

Better than your local Chinese take out! Enjoy these dumplings without the added deep-fried fats.

INGREDIENTS:

- 1½ cups whole-wheat pastry flour
- 8 oz ground turkey breast
- ½ Tbsp rice vinegar
- 1 green onion, finely chopped
- ¾ cup finely shredded Chinese cabbage

PANTRY STAPLES:

- Pinch sea salt
- ½ Tbsp low-sodium soy sauce
- 1 tsp fresh ginger, minced
- 1 clove garlic, minced

INSTRUCTIONS:

ONE: In a small bowl, combine flour and salt. Gradually add about ¾ cup cold water, stirring with a wooden spoon to form a smooth dough. Knead into a small ball, about 1 minute; cover and set aside for 30 minutes to let dough rest.

TWO: Meanwhile, prepare filling: In a medium bowl, combine turkey, soy sauce, vinegar, onion, cabbage, ginger and garlic. Mix thoroughly and set aside at room temperature.

THREE: Prepare dumplings: Divide dough into 16 equal portions. Using a rolling pin, roll each portion into a circle approximately 3 inches in diameter. Place 1 Tbsp filling in center of each circle; wet edges with water, fold dough over into a half-moon shape and pinch edges to seal. Repeat with remaining dough and filling.

FOUR: Fill a 7 or 8-qt pot halfway with water; bring to a boil. Add half of dumplings and stir gently to prevent dumplings from sticking to each other. Once water returns to a boil, add 1 cup cold water, cover and return to a boil. Add an additional 1 cup cold water, cover and return to a boil. Drain; repeat with remaining dumplings. Allow 15 to 20 minutes per batch.

Nutrients per 4 dumplings: *Calories: 267, Total Fat: 7 g, Sat. Fat: 2 g, Monounsaturated Fat: 2 g, Polyunsaturated Fat: 2 g, Carbs: 35 g, Fiber: 6 g, Sugars: 0.25 g, Protein: 15 g, Sodium: 185 mg, Cholesterol: 46 mg*

Samosas

Serves 6. *Makes* 12 samosas. *Hands-on time:* 15 minutes. *Total time:* 40 minutes.

Baked, not fried – that's how we like our samosas! Snack on the tasty flavors of India with the added benefit of vitamin A from sweet potatoes.

INGREDIENTS:

- 1½ lb sweet potatoes, peeled and cut into 1-inch chunks
- 2 cups cauliflower florets and stems, cut into 1-inch pieces
- 1 Tbsp olive oil, divided
- 1 medium onion, finely chopped
- ⅜ tsp sea salt, divided
- 1 cup frozen peas, thawed
- 3 Tbsp cilantro, finely chopped
- 2 tsp curry powder
- 2 tsp garam masala
- ¼ tsp ground cayenne pepper
- 12 sheets frozen whole-wheat phyllo dough, thawed
- Olive oil cooking spray

INSTRUCTIONS:

ONE: Preheat oven to 400°F. Bring a 3-qt saucepot of water to a boil on high heat. Add sweet potatoes and cook for 5 minutes. Add cauliflower and cook for 10 minutes, until vegetables are soft. Drain and set aside.

TWO: Meanwhile, in a small sauté pan, heat 1 tsp oil on medium-high. Add onion and sprinkle with ⅛ tsp salt. Cook, stirring frequently, for 5 minutes or until soft and slightly brown. Set aside.

THREE: With a potato masher, mash potato-cauliflower mixture until smooth. Mix in onion, peas, cilantro, remaining ¼ tsp salt, curry powder, garam masala and cayenne.

FOUR: Assemble samosas: Working quickly, place 1 phyllo sheet on a cutting board and mist with cooking spray. Fold in half lengthwise and mist with cooking spray. Place ⅓ cup potato-caulilfower mixture at 1 corner. Fold corner over filling to opposite side, making a triangle. Fold triangle up to meet straight side, then across again. Continue folding over triangle until you reach end of phyllo sheet. Repeat steps with remaining phyllo sheets and potato-cauliflower mixture.

FIVE: Mist a baking sheet with cooking spray and place samosas on sheet. Brush tops of samosas with remaining 2 tsp oil. Bake for 15 minutes or until tops are golden brown.

Nutrients per 2 samosas: Calories: 269, Total Fat: 5 g, Sat. Fat: 1 g, Monounsaturated Fat: 3 g, Polyunsaturated Fat: 1 g Carbs: 50 g, Fiber: 7 g, Sugars: 7 g, Protein: 6 g, Sodium: 257 mg, Cholesterol: 0 mg

Indian-Style Lentil & Cauliflower Biryani

Serves 4. *Hands-on time:* 15 minutes. *Total time:* 15 minutes.

Here's a way to spice up any old cauliflower dish, and the lentils add a dose of protein to satisfy your hunger. Quick to make, you can serve it as a side dish or as a meal all on its own.

INGREDIENTS:

- 1 Tbsp safflower or olive oil
- 1 yellow onion, chopped
- 1 carrot, peeled and diced
- 3 cloves garlic, minced
- 1 tsp garam masala
- 1 tsp ground coriander
- 1 tsp dried mint
- ½ tsp ground turmeric
- 2 cups cauliflower florets, chopped
- 2 cups low-sodium vegetable broth
- 1 cup quick-cooking brown rice
- ¼ cup dried unsweetened currants or small raisins
- 1 cup frozen peas, thawed
- 1 cup BPA-free canned lentils, drained and rinsed well
- ⅓ cup sliced unsalted almonds, toasted
- 3 Tbsp fresh cilantro or parsley, chopped
- ½ cup low-fat plain yogurt, optional

INSTRUCTIONS:

ONE: In a large shallow saucepan, heat oil on medium-high. Add onion, carrot, garlic, garam masala, coriander, mint and turmeric; cook until onion softens, stirring occasionally, about 2 minutes.

TWO: Stir in cauliflower, broth, rice and currants; cover and simmer for 7 minutes. Stir in peas and lentils; cover and simmer until liquid is absorbed, about 4 minutes. Stir in almonds and cilantro. If desired, serve with a dollop of yogurt.

Nutrients per 1¾-cup serving: Calories: 393, Total Fat: 9 g, Sat. Fat: 1 g, Monounsaturated Fat: 6 g, Polyunsaturated Fat: 2 g, Carbs: 66 g, Fiber: 12 g, Sugars: 12 g, Protein: 13 g, Sodium: 174 mg, Cholesterol: 0 mg

NUTRITIONAL BONUS: One of the first foods to be cultivated, there's a reason lentils have withstood the test of time. These inexpensive little gems are not only a great source of low-fat protein, but they are also high in brain-boosting folic acid, blood-boosting iron and cholesterol-fighting dietary fiber.

Lentil & Cauliflower Biryani

THE BEST OF CLEAN EATING 3

Sweetened
Vanilla
Berry Parfait

Sweetened Vanilla Berry Parfait

Serves 4. **Hands-on time:** *5 minutes.* **Total Time:** *35 minutes*

Creamy yogurt enriched with fresh berries, vanilla, honey and mint makes the perfect snack – or even dessert!

INGREDIENTS:

- 3 cups low-fat plain yogurt
- 2 tsp raw honey
- ½ tsp pure vanilla extract
- ¼ cup chopped fresh mint, plus additional for garnish
- 1 cup blueberries
- 1⅓ cups strawberries, hulled and quartered
- 1⅓ cups blackberries

INSTRUCTIONS:

ONE: Dampen a cheesecloth with water and wring out excess liquid. Line a colander with cheesecloth and set on top of a large bowl to catch draining liquid. Spoon yogurt into colander and strain in refrigerator for 20 to 30 minutes or until yogurt is thickened and reduced to 2¾ cups. Transfer yogurt to a small bowl, discarding strained liquid. Stir in honey, vanilla and mint.

TWO: Layer ingredients evenly in each of 4 glass sundae cups in the following order: ¼ cup blueberries, ⅓ cup yogurt mixture, ⅓ cup strawberries, ⅓ cup yogurt mixture and ⅓ cup blackberries. Garnish with additional mint.

Nutrients per parfait: Calories: 180, Total Fat: 3 g, Sat. Fat: 2 g, Carbs: 29 g, Fiber: 5 g, Sugars: 23 g, Protein: 11 g, Sodium: 121 mg, Cholesterol: 10 mg

Nutritional Bonus:
The berries in this parfait are a clean eater's best friend – not only are they nutrient dense, but their fiber content will keep you full and their sweetness will satisfy your craving for a treat.

Fresh Beets
WITH HORSERADISH SOUR CREAM

Serves 4. **Hands-on time:** *10 minutes.* **Total time:** *2 hours, 10 minutes.*

With the powerful health benefits of beets, it's an added bonus that they taste so good! The Horseradish Sour Cream gives this dish a tasty kick.

INGREDIENTS:

- 1 lb red beets, trimmed, peeled and cut into ½-inch wedges
- ⅓ cup low-fat sour cream
- 1 Tbsp skim milk
- 1 Tbsp prepared horseradish
- 1 tsp Dijon mustard
- ¼ tsp dried tarragon
- ¼ tsp sea salt
- 2 Tbsp finely chopped green onion, divided

TIP: To prevent your fingers from staining, peel beets under cold running water.

INSTRUCTIONS:

ONE: In a 3 to 3½-qt slow cooker, add beets and 3 cups water. Cover and cook until just tender, 2 hours on high or 4 hours on low.

TWO: Meanwhile, prepare Horseradish Sour Cream: In a small bowl, whisk sour cream, milk, horseradish, Dijon, tarragon, salt and all but 2 tsp onion. Refrigerate, covered, until needed. (Horseradish Sour Cream can be made up to 24 hours ahead.)

THREE: Drain beets well. Divide among plates and serve with Horseradish Sour Cream on the side. Sprinkle sauce with remaining 2 tsp onion, dividing evenly.

Nutrients per serving (1 cup beets and 2 Tbsp Horseradish Sour Cream):
Calories: 72, Total Fat: 2 g, Sat. Fat: 1 g, Carbs: 11 g, Fiber: 3 g, Sugars: 8 g, Protein: 3 g, Sodium: 249 mg, Cholesterol: 7 mg

Spicy Scalloped Sweet Potatoes

Serves 4. ***Hands-on time:*** *10 minutes.* ***Total time:*** *40 minutes.*

Full of antioxidants *and* flavor, this side dish will complement any meal.

INGREDIENTS:

- 1 large sweet potato, peeled and sliced into ¼-inch-thick rounds, divided
- 2 Tbsp olive oil
- 2 Tbsp whole-wheat flour
- 1 cup skim milk
- ½ tsp sea salt
- 1 tsp fresh ground black pepper
- 1 tsp chile powder
- 1 tsp ground cumin
- 1 tsp red pepper flakes
- ½ cup shredded low-fat cheddar cheese

INSTRUCTIONS:

ONE: Preheat oven to 400°F.

TWO: In a 10-inch square baking dish, spread half of potato slices in an even layer, overlapping slightly if needed.

THREE: In a medium skillet, heat oil on medium-high. Sprinkle in flour and whisk until combined (mixture will resemble a paste). Gradually whisk in milk until lumps smooth out and mixture begins to thicken. Add salt, black pepper, chile powder, cumin and pepper flakes; stir to combine. Add cheese and stir until completely melted, about 2 minutes. Pour three-quarters of chile-cheese sauce over potatoes. Layer remaining potatoes over top, overlapping slightly if needed. Top with remaining chile-cheese sauce.

FOUR: Transfer to oven and bake for 30 to 35 minutes, uncovered, until browned and bubbly. Remove from oven and let rest for 5 minutes before serving.

Nutrients per 4.4-oz serving: Calories: 157, Total Fat: 8.5 g, Sat. Fat: 1.5 g, Monounsaturated Fat: 6 g, Polyunsaturated Fat: 1 g, Carbs: 14 g, Fiber: 2 g, Sugars: 4.5 g, Protein: 7 g, Sodium: 384 mg, Cholesterol: 4 mg

NUTRITIONAL BONUS: Thanks to the beta-carotene (vitamin A) content, apparent by their orange hue, sweet potatoes may help stabilize blood sugar levels, boost metabolism and help to fight chronic diseases.

Moroccan Cocktail Meatballs
WITH LEMON YOGURT SAUCE

Serves 9. ***Hands-on time:*** *20 minutes.* ***Total time:*** *35 minutes.*

A blend of lamb and turkey ensures these party-starters are both moist and lean, while a sprinkling of dried herbs and spices inexpensively adds a depth of enticing flavor. For easy entertaining, prep and refrigerate the meatballs up to 24 hours ahead, then remove meatballs from the refrigerator to cook in the oven before serving.

INGREDIENTS:

- Olive oil cooking spray
- 1¼ lb lean ground lamb and/or turkey
- 1 large egg
- ⅓ cup dried unsweetened currants
- ¼ cup fine whole-wheat bread crumbs
- 1½ tsp dried mint
- 1¼ tsp ground cumin
- 1¼ tsp chile powder
- 1 tsp onion powder
- ½ tsp ground cinnamon
- ½ tsp sea salt
- ¼ tsp fresh ground black pepper
- ¼ tsp ground cayenne pepper, or to taste
- Fresh mint and/or parsley for garnish, optional

SAUCE

- Juice 1 lemon
- 1 small clove garlic, finely chopped
- 1 cup nonfat plain Greek yogurt
- 3 Tbsp tahini
- 2 Tbsp chopped fresh mint or 1 Tbsp dried mint

INSTRUCTIONS:

ONE: Preheat oven to 375°F. Line a large rimmed baking sheet with foil and mist with cooking spray.

TWO: In a large bowl, gently mix lamb and/or turkey, egg, currants, bread crumbs, dried mint, cumin, chile powder, onion powder, cinnamon, salt, black pepper and cayenne until thoroughly combined. Form into 1-inch balls and transfer to baking sheet. Bake until cooked through, 18 to 22 minutes.

THREE: Meanwhile, in a small bowl, combine sauce ingredients. Serve meatballs with sauce. If desired, garnish with fresh mint.

Nutrients per serving (4 meatballs and 2 Tbsp sauce): Calories: 198, Total Fat: 11 g, Sat. Fat: 4 g, Monounsaturated Fat: 1 g, Polyunsaturated Fat: 1 g, Carbs: 10 g, Fiber: 1 g, Sugars: 5 g, Protein: 16.5 g, Sodium: 214 mg, Cholesterol: 65 mg

Moroccan
Cocktail
Meatballs

Buckwheat Blinis
WITH APPLE CHUTNEY & COTTAGE CHEESE WHIP

Serves 12. **Hands-on time:** *1 hour.* **Total time:** *1 hour.*

This traditional Eastern European pancake can be made into thin crepes or fluffy pancakes. Buttermilk adds an extra-creamy touch to our whipped cottage cheese topping, and the peppered apple chutney adds a slightly spicy finishing touch.

INGREDIENTS:

- ¾ cup low-fat cottage cheese
- 2 Tbsp plus 1¾ cups low-fat buttermilk, divided
- ¾ cup buckwheat flour
- ¾ cup whole-wheat pastry flour
- 1 tsp baking powder
- ¾ tsp baking soda
- ½ tsp sea salt
- ½ tsp dried thyme
- 2 large eggs
- Olive oil cooking spray

CHUTNEY

- 2 apples, any variety, cored and cut into ⅓-inch dice
- 2 jalapeño peppers, seeded and finely chopped
- ½ large white onion, finely chopped
- Juice ½ lemon
- ½ cup unsweetened Sultana raisins
- 2 Tbsp fresh ginger, peeled and finely chopped
- 1½ Tbsp raw honey
- 1 tsp apple cider vinegar
- ½ tsp dried thyme
- Pinch sea salt and fresh ground black pepper
- 2 Tbsp fresh mint, chopped, plus additional for garnish

INSTRUCTIONS:

ONE: Prepare chutney: In a large nonstick skillet, combine apples, jalapeños, onion, lemon juice, raisins, ginger, honey, vinegar, thyme, pinch salt and pepper and ½ cup water. Heat on medium-high and cook, stirring occasionally, until beginning to simmer. Cover and reduce heat to low. Cook, stirring occasionally, until apples are very tender, 20 to 25 minutes; if mixture becomes too dry, add an additional 2 to 4 Tbsp water.

MAKE AHEAD: Chutney can be made up to 2 days ahead. Cover and refrigerate. Serve chilled, warm or at room temperature.

TWO: Meanwhile, in a food processor, pulse cottage cheese until almost smooth, about 1 minute. While pulsing, add 2 Tbsp buttermilk and continue to pulse, stopping to scrape down sides of bowl, until smooth and creamy, about 1 minute. Transfer to a small bowl, cover and refrigerate until ready to serve.

THREE: Preheat oven to 200°F. In a large bowl, whisk flours, baking powder, baking soda, ½ tsp salt and thyme. In a medium bowl, whisk eggs. Stir in remaining 1¾ cups buttermilk until combined. Add to flour mixture and stir until just moistened.

FOUR: Heat a large skillet or griddle on medium and mist with cooking spray. Working in batches, add batter to skillet to form 2 to 2½-inch rounds. Cook until bubbles form and edges are set, about 2 minutes. Flip and cook until golden brown, 1 to 2 minutes. Loosely wrap cooked blinis in foil, place on a baking sheet and transfer to oven to keep warm while remaining blinis cook.

TIP: If blinis brown too quickly, reduce heat to medium-low.

FIVE: When ready to serve, stir mint into chutney. Top blinis with cottage cheese mixture and chutney. Garnish with additional mint.

TIP: Blinis are best eaten warm, but will keep at room temperature for up to 1 hour.

Nutrients per serving (4 blinis, 4 tsp cottage cheese mixture, 8 tsp chutney):
Calories: 136, Total Fat: 2 g, Sat. Fat: 1 g, Carbs: 26 g, Fiber: 3.5 g, Sugars: 12 g, Protein: 6 g, Sodium: 264 mg, Cholesterol: 37 mg

Nutritional Bonus:
Although many are aware of ginger's stomach-calming qualities, they may not know that this potent root is also packed with powerful phyto-nutrients called gingerols. These inflammation-fighters may help reduce your risk of Alzheimer's disease, diabetes, cardiovascular disease and some types of cancer.

Spicy Moroccan Steamed Mussels

*Serves 4. **Hands-on time:** 15 minutes. **Total time:** 15 minutes.*

With mussels, broth is the key to taste, and the aromatic flavors of North Africa accent the ocean flavor of quick-cooking mussels in this hearty one-pot meal. Yukon gold potatoes add appealing color and buttery richness, but quartered red bliss or diced all-purpose potatoes make a fine substitute.

INGREDIENTS:

- 2 Tbsp extra-virgin olive oil
- 1 Tbsp fresh garlic, chopped
- 1 Tbsp paprika
- 1 Tbsp ground coriander
- 2 tsp ground cumin
- 2 cups low-sodium tomato juice
- ½ tsp red pepper flakes (or to taste)
- ¾ lb Yukon gold potatoes, peeled and cubed
- 1 2-lb bag cultivated mussels
- 2 Tbsp chopped fresh cilantro or Italian parsley, optional

INSTRUCTIONS:

ONE: In a large pot, combine oil, garlic, paprika, coriander and cumin. Cook on medium heat, stirring frequently, until sizzling and aromatic, about 1 minute. Add tomato juice, red pepper flakes and 2 cups water; bring to a boil. Add potatoes and return to a boil. Reduce heat to a simmer and cook until potatoes are almost tender when pierced, about 10 minutes.

TWO: Meanwhile, fill a large bowl with cold water. Place mussels in bowl and rinse. Tap any mussels that have gaped open slightly. If they close, they're alive and safe to cook. Discard any mussels that remain open (indicating that they're no longer alive) and any that have broken shells. Drain.

THREE: Increase heat to high and add mussels to pot. Cover and cook for about 5 minutes, shaking pot several times. Remove lid and discard any mussels that remain closed. Add cilantro or parsley, if desired, and toss to combine. Serve immediately.

Nutrients per serving: Calories: 243, Total Fat: 9 g, Sat. Fat: 1 g, Monounsaturated Fat: 6 g, Polyunsaturated Fat: 1 g, Carbs: 26 g, Fiber: 3 g, Sugars: 5 g, Protein: 13 g, Sodium: 335 mg, Cholesterol: 24 mg

NUTRITIONAL BONUS: Mussels are rich in protein and minerals and low in fat and cholesterol. A 3-oz portion of steamed mussel meat contains 146 calories, 20 g of protein, 4 g of fat, 28 mg of calcium, 6 mg of iron and 314 mg of sodium. One pound of mussels in the shell will yield about ¼ lb of mussel meat. Mussels are also an excellent source of selenium and vitamin B12.

Cream Cheese & Shrimp-Stuffed Mushrooms

*Serves 8. **Hands-on time:** 15 minutes. **Total time:** 30 minutes.*

At just over 30 calories a pop, these indulgent cream-stuffed mushrooms are a perennial crowd-pleaser. The best part? They only take 15 minutes to make!

INGREDIENTS:

- Olive oil cooking spray
- 24 white button or baby Portobello mushrooms, stemmed
- ½ lb small cooked shrimp, tails removed, chopped
- 4 oz Neufchâtel (⅓-less-fat) cream cheese
- 1 large shallot, finely chopped (about ¼ cup)
- 2 Tbsp fresh parsley, chopped
- 1 tsp fresh thyme, plus additional for garnish
- ⅛ tsp fresh ground black pepper
- Pinch ground cayenne pepper, or to taste
- ¼ cup grated Parmigiano-Reggiano cheese
- 2 Tbsp fine whole-wheat bread crumbs
- 1½ tsp seafood seasoning

INSTRUCTIONS:

ONE: Preheat oven to 350°F and mist a large baking sheet with cooking spray. Arrange mushrooms stem side up on sheet.

TWO: In a medium bowl, combine shrimp, Neufchâtel, shallot, parsley, thyme, black pepper and cayenne. Spoon mixture into mushrooms, dividing evenly.

THREE: In a small bowl, combine Parmigiano-Reggiano, bread crumbs and seafood seasoning. Sprinkle over mushrooms.

MAKE AHEAD: Prepare through this step up to 4 hours ahead; cover with plastic wrap and refrigerate.

FOUR: Bake until mushrooms are fork-tender and topping is lightly browned, 15 to 20 minutes. Garnish with additional thyme.

Nutrients per serving (3 mushrooms): Calories: 108, Total Fat: 5 g, Sat. Fat: 3 g, Monounsaturated Fat: 1 g, Polyunsaturated Fat: 0 g, Carbs: 4 g, Fiber: 0 g, Sugars: 2 g, Protein: 11 g, Sodium: 337 mg, Cholesterol: 71 mg

Cream Cheese & Shrimp-Stuffed Mushrooms

Caramelized
Onion & White
Bean Spread

Caramelized Onion & White Bean Spread

Serves 6. **Hands-on time:** 20 minutes. **Total time:** 20 minutes.

Serve our ultra-creamy, chunky onion and bean dip to treasured guests for an elegant appetizer, or simply enjoy it on your own for an afternoon snack. For a decadent touch, drizzle with extra-virgin olive oil before serving with crispy crackers or a warm whole-grain baguette.

INGREDIENTS:

- 1 Tbsp olive oil
- 1 small red onion, chopped
- ⅛ tsp sea salt
- Fresh ground black pepper, to taste
- 1 15-oz BPA-free can cannellini beans, drained and rinsed
- ¼ cup low-sodium chicken broth
- 1 tsp fresh rosemary, chopped
- 2 to 3 whole leaves or 1 Tbsp chopped fresh basil, optional
- Whole-grain bread or crackers, as desired

INSTRUCTIONS:

ONE: In a large skillet, heat oil on medium-low. Add onion, salt and pepper and sauté, stirring occasionally, until onion is very tender, light brown and caramelized, 15 to 20 minutes.

TWO: In a food processor, purée beans and broth until smooth. Add onions and process into a slightly chunky purée. Add rosemary and additional black pepper and pulse to combine. Transfer to a serving bowl. If desired, garnish with basil. Serve at room temperature or chilled with bread or whole-grain crackers.

MAKE AHEAD: This spread can be made up to 4 hours ahead; cover and refrigerate.

Nutrients per ¼-cup serving: *Calories: 81, Total Fat: 3 g, Sat. Fat: 0 g, Carbs: 10.5 g, Fiber: 3 g, Sugars: 1 g, Protein: 4 g, Sodium: 65 mg, Cholesterol: 0 mg*

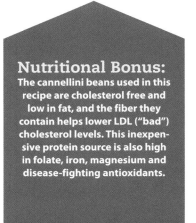

Nutritional Bonus:
The cannellini beans used in this recipe are cholesterol free and low in fat, and the fiber they contain helps lower LDL ("bad") cholesterol levels. This inexpensive protein source is also high in folate, iron, magnesium and disease-fighting antioxidants.

Poblano & Mushroom Queso Fundido

Serves 10. **Makes** about 3⅓ cups. **Hands-on time:** 35 minutes. **Total time:** 55 minutes.

We've lightened up the traditionally rich Mexican appetizer Queso Fundido (Spanish for "cheese fondue") with Greek yogurt and low-fat cream cheese.

INGREDIENTS:

- 2 poblano peppers
- 1 red bell pepper
- 2 cups shredded part-skim mozzarella cheese
- ½ cup nonfat plain Greek yogurt
- ½ cup low-fat cream cheese, softened
- 2 Tbsp fresh lime juice, divided
- ⅛ tsp ground cayenne pepper
- ½ tsp sea salt, divided
- Olive oil cooking spray
- ¾ cup thinly sliced white onions
- 1 cup thinly sliced cremini mushrooms
- 12 small corn tortillas
- ½ tsp ground cumin
- ¼ tsp fresh ground black pepper
- 2 Tbsp fresh cilantro, chopped

INSTRUCTIONS:

ONE: Preheat oven to 450°F. Place poblano and bell peppers on a parchment-lined baking tray and roast in center of oven for 20 minutes, turning once, until lightly charred and tender. Transfer peppers to a large bowl. Cover tightly with plastic wrap. Allow to steam for 10 minutes.

TWO: Meanwhile, combine mozzarella, yogurt, cream cheese, 1 Tbsp lime juice, cayenne and ¼ tsp salt in a food processor. Purée until combined and almost smooth. Transfer to a mixing bowl and set aside.

THREE: Heat a large frying pan on medium-high and mist with cooking spray. Add onions and mushrooms. Cook, stirring frequently, until onions are translucent. Add to cheese mixture.

FOUR: Carefully remove cover from peppers and set peppers aside until cool enough to handle, about 5 minutes. Remove skin, core and seeds from peppers and slice into thin strips. Add peppers to cheese mixture and fold in with a spatula until combined. Transfer mixture to an 8 x 8-inch oven-safe casserole dish and set aside.

FIVE: Cut each tortilla into 6 triangles and place in large mixing bowl. Mist with cooking spray, toss and mist again. Then toss with remaining 1 Tbsp lime juice, cumin, black pepper and remaining ¼ tsp salt. Arrange chips in a single layer on 2 parchment-lined baking sheets (chips may overlap slightly). Bake in oven for 12 to 15 minutes, until crisp and golden brown, stirring 3 times and removing chips as they become brown and crispy. Transfer to a bowl and let cool.

SIX: Place casserole dish into oven and bake for 15 to 18 minutes, until hot and bubbly. Remove from oven, stir to loosen top and sprinkle with cilantro.

Nutrients per serving (about ⅓ cup dip and 7 chips): *Calories: 178, Total Fat: 7 g, Sat. Fat: 4 g, Monounsaturated Fat: 2 g, Polyunsaturated Fat: 0.5 g, Carbs: 20 g, Fiber: 2 g, Sugars: 2 g, Protein: 12 g, Sodium: 281 mg, Cholesterol: 21 mg*

For a photo of this recipe, see page 96.

Jarlsberg Soufflés
WITH MUSTARD GREENS & ROASTED RED PEPPERS

*Serves 4. **Hands-on time:** 30 minutes. **Total time:** 1 hour.*

The key to a flawless soufflé is perfectly hand-whipped egg whites. These savory appetizers will give you plenty of practice, plus they pack a flavor punch with a hit of Jarlsberg cheese.

INGREDIENTS:

- 1 tsp plus 2 Tbsp olive oil buttery spread, divided
- 2 Tbsp finely grated low-fat Parmesan cheese
- 6 oz mustard greens, tough stems removed
- 2 Tbsp white whole-wheat flour
- 1¼ cups 1% milk
- ¼ tsp plus ⅛ tsp sea salt, divided
- ⅛ tsp fresh grated nutmeg
- Pinch fresh ground white pepper
- 1 egg yolk
- ½ cup finely grated low-fat Jarlsberg cheese
- 4 oz jarred roasted red peppers packed in water, liquid discarded, finely chopped
- 6 egg whites, room temperature
- ¼ tsp cream of tartar

INSTRUCTIONS:

ONE: Lightly coat the inside of 4 straight-sided 1-cup ramekins with 1 tsp buttery spread, dividing evenly. Spoon ½ Tbsp Parmesan into each ramekin; tilt to coat bottoms and sides of ramekins with cheese.

TWO: Fill a large pot with 2 to 3 inches of water and fit with a steamer basket. Bring to a boil on high heat. Place greens in basket and steam for 5 minutes or until wilted. Transfer greens to a colander to cool. Once cooled, use your hands or a rubber spatula to push greens up against the sides of colander, squeezing out excess water; transfer to a cutting board and finely chop. Set aside.

THREE: Preheat oven to 375°F. In a medium saucepan, melt remaining 2 Tbsp buttery spread on medium-low. Add flour and cook, stirring constantly, for 1 minute, until mixture is clumpy and paste-like. Gradually add milk, whisking between additions until mixture is smooth. Once all milk has been added, increase heat to medium and bring to a simmer. Cook, whisking frequently, for about 8 minutes or until thick. Stir in ¼ tsp salt, nutmeg and white pepper; remove from heat.

FOUR: In a small bowl, use a fork to combine egg yolk and Jarlsberg. Gradually add 1 cup milk mixture to bowl and stir until combined and warmed. Add Jarlsberg mixture to remaining milk mixture and stir to combine. Once cheese melts, add greens and red peppers. Set aside.

FIVE: In a large stainless steel or copper bowl, add egg whites, remaining ⅛ tsp salt and cream of tartar. Begin slowly beating with cleaned whisk, gradually increasing speed as mixture turns foamy, until soft peaks form, about 10 minutes. (**TIP:** Take frequent breaks if your arm gets tired, or take turns with a helper.)

SIX: Stir a quarter of egg white mixture into greens mixture until combined. Gently fold in remaining egg white mixture. Divide batter among 4 ramekins, filling to just below rims. Bake on middle rack in oven for 20 to 25 minutes, until tops are lofty, browned and dry, but soufflés still jiggle when lightly shaken. (NOTE: Do not open oven door during first 15 minutes or soufflés may collapse.) Serve immediately, as soufflés deflate quickly.

Nutrients per soufflé: *Calories: 190, Total Fat: 9 g, Sat. Fat: 3.5 g, Monounsaturated Fat: 2 g, Polyunsaturated Fat: 1.5 g, Carbs: 11 g, Fiber: 2 g, Sugars: 5 g, Protein: 16 g, Sodium: 550 mg, Cholesterol: 65 mg*

Spicy Chicken Wings
WITH BLUE CHEESE DIP

*Serves 4. **Hands-on time:** 10 minutes. **Total time:** 1 hour (including marinating time).*

Whether you're hosting a party or a big game, these wings are sure to keep everyone satisfied.

INGREDIENTS:

- 12 bone-in, skin-on chicken wings (about 2 lb), trimmed of visible fat
- 4 Tbsp hot sauce
- ¼ cup low-fat cottage cheese
- ¼ cup low-fat plain yogurt
- 1 Tbsp crumbled low-fat blue cheese

PANTRY STAPLES:

- 2 Tbsp extra-virgin olive oil
- 1 Tbsp paprika
- ¼ tsp ground cayenne pepper
- ⅛ tsp fresh ground black pepper
- ¼ tsp sea salt, divided
- Pinch fresh ground white pepper
- Olive oil cooking spray

INSTRUCTIONS:

ONE: Place chicken wings in a large resealable plastic bag. In a small bowl, stir together oil, hot sauce, paprika, cayenne, black pepper and ⅛ tsp salt. Pour mixture into bag with chicken, seal and set aside to marinate at room temperature for 30 minutes.

TWO: Prepare dip: In a small bowl, blend cottage cheese, yogurt, blue cheese, remaining ⅛ tsp salt and white pepper with a fork. Refrigerate until serving.

THREE: Preheat oven to 425°F. Line a baking sheet with foil and lightly coat with cooking spray. Remove chicken from bag, discarding marinade. Arrange chicken on sheet in a single layer and bake for 15 minutes. Flip chicken and bake for 15 more minutes or until chicken starts to brown. Serve with dip, removing chicken skin before eating, if desired.

Nutrients per serving (3 skinless wings and ¼ cup dip): *Calories: 203, Total Fat: 13 g, Sat. Fat: 2 g, Monounsaturated Fat: 6 g, Polyunsaturated Fat: 1 g, Carbs: 3 g, Fiber: 1 g, Sugars: 2 g, Protein: 23 g, Sodium: 605 mg, Cholesterol: 53 mg*

Nutritional Bonus:
Olive oil contains monoun-saturated fatty acids (MUFAs) and polyunsaturated fatty acids (PUFAs), healthy fats that help reduce your risk of heart disease. MUFAs also play a role in stabilizing blood sugar, mak-ing them particularly helpful for those with type 2 diabetes.

Spicy
Chicken
Wings

Beef Jerky

You can make better-than-purchased beef jerky with basic kitchen materials. All you need is an oven, flavorful spices and a few hours to spare.

What You'll Need:

Cutting board

Chef's knife

Gallon-size heavy-duty zip-top bag

Rimmed baking sheet

Paper towels

12-inch wooden skewers

Gas or electric oven

Aluminum foil or foil pan

Small kitchen towel or wooden spoon

Cooling racks

Airtight containers

Dehydrating foods predates kitchens, grocery stores and cooking in general. No longer a means of survival, dehydration is a prehistoric preservation method that's still popular today. The technique probably stuck around because it's fairly simple and works well for everything from meats and fruits to vegetables and seeds. Plus, it's fun!

Spicy Oven-Dried Beef Jerky

Makes *12 oz (about 50 pieces).*
Hands-on time: *1 hour.* **Total time:** *10 hours.*

INGREDIENTS:

- 2 lb eye of round beef roast, flank steak or London broil, trimmed of visible fat
- ⅔ cup low-sodium soy sauce
- ⅔ cup low-sodium Worcestershire sauce
- 1 Tbsp raw honey
- 2 tsp fresh ground black pepper
- 1 tsp onion powder
- 1 tsp garlic powder
- 1 tsp red pepper flakes
- 1 tsp smoked paprika or liquid smoke, optional

INSTRUCTIONS:

ONE: If using a large roast or steak, slice beef into 2 or 3 equal pieces. Wrap beef in plastic wrap and place in freezer for about 1 hour to ease slicing. Remove from freezer and transfer to a cutting board. Using only the tip of a chef's knife, slice beef along the grain into equal ⅛-inch-thick strips.

TWO: Meanwhile, prepare marinade: In a 2-cup measure, whisk remaining ingredients and, if desired, paprika, until smooth.

THREE: Transfer beef to a large, heavy-duty zip-top bag. Pour marinade into bag, seal tightly and turn to coat beef. Lay flat in refrigerator and marinate for 3 to 6 hours, turning bag 1 to 2 times (**NOTE:** Do not exceed 6 hours).

FOUR: Line a large baking sheet with 2 sheets paper towel. Remove beef from bag, shaking or gently wringing each strip to remove excess marinade. Transfer to baking sheet and cover with additional 2 sheets paper towel. Press down through towel to flatten strips and absorb as much marinade as possible. Remove oven racks and place a foil drip pan in bottom of oven, or line bottom with foil. Preheat oven to lowest setting, 140 to 170°F.

FIVE: Thread skewers through 1 end of strips, leaving 1 inch between each strip. Lay skewers horizontally across 1 oven rack. Transfer rack to highest position in oven, allowing strips to hang without touching oven walls. Close oven, propping door open a crack with a small, dry, rolled-up dish towel or a wooden spoon. (**NOTE:** This is necessary to allow moisture to escape from the oven; the oven temperature is low enough that this is not a fire danger.) Cook for 5 hours.

SIX: Check strips for doneness; remove dry, hard and darkened pieces from skewers and place on a cooling rack. Cook remaining strips for 1 to 2 hours, checking often for doneness. Transfer to cooling racks. When strips are fully cooled, transfer to airtight containers and store upright at room temperature for up to 2 months (**NOTE:** Do not pack strips tightly). Discard strips that show signs of spoilage (mold or unpleasant odor) over time.

Nutrients per serving (2 large strips):
Calories: 27, Total Fat: 1 g, Sat. Fat: 0 g, Carbs: 1 g, Fiber: 0 g, Sugars: 1 g, Protein: 4 g, Sodium: 92 mg, Cholesterol: 8 mg

Your Step-by-Step Guide to Homemade Beef Jerky:

ONE: Trim any fat from a lean cut of beef, and slice beef along the grain into ⅛-inch-thick strips.

TWO: Prepare marinade and transfer with beef to a large, heavy-duty zip-top bag.

THREE: Line a baking sheet with 2 sheets paper towel. Preheat oven to lowest setting.

FOUR: Thread skewers through 1 end of strips, leaving 1 inch between each strip.

FIVE: Lay skewers horizontally across oven rack. Place rack in highest position, allowing strips to hang without touching sides of oven.

SIX: Close oven, propping door open a crack with a small, dry, rolled-up dish towel or a wooden spoon to release moisture. Cook for 5 hours.

SEVEN: Check beef for doneness; remove dry, hard and darkened pieces from skewers and place on a cooling rack.

Cheeseburger Pizza, p. 143

Main Courses: Beef, Pork & Lamb

Are you a grill connoisseur or a meatball lover? *Clean Eating* offers you pages of delicious lean red meat recipes to satisfy all tastes. Your kids will love melt-in-your-mouth Lamburgers or classic Spaghetti and Meatballs – and so will you! For date night, impress your significant other when you serve Herbed Steak Rolls with Goat Cheese & Capers. Or create a succulent Bison Stroganoff for a full family feast and enjoy a gourmet dinner like no other.

Lamburgers
WITH TZATZIKI & FRESH MINT

Serves 4. **Hands-on time:** *25 minutes.* **Total time:** *40 minutes.*

Tzatziki (pronounced za-DZEE-kee) is a Greek sauce made with yogurt, cucumber, garlic and fresh dill or mint. It adds summery freshness to this sandwich, but also works equally well as a dip or draped over a just-grilled fish fillet or chicken breast.

INGREDIENTS:

- ½ cup nonfat plain Greek yogurt
- ¼ cucumber, peeled, halved lengthwise, seeded and cut into chunks
- 2 Tbsp fresh dill, coarsely chopped
- 1 Tbsp fresh lemon juice
- ½ small shallot, coarsely chopped
- 1 clove garlic
- 8 oz 95% lean ground beef
- 4 oz ground lamb, preferably lean
- ½ tsp each sea salt and fresh ground black pepper
- High-heat cooking oil (such as sunflower, safflower, peanut or grape seed oil), as needed
- 2 whole-wheat pitas, cut in half to make 4 pita pockets
- 1 cup loosely packed fresh mint leaves
- 4 romaine lettuce leaves, torn in half crosswise

INSTRUCTIONS:

ONE: Prepare tzatziki: In a food processor, combine yogurt, cucumber, dill, lemon juice, shallot and garlic. Pulse to make a chunky sauce; set aside. (Tzatziki can be made 1 day ahead; cover and store in refrigerator.)

TWO: In a large bowl, combine beef, lamb, salt and pepper and mix gently. With dampened hands, shape mixture into 4 patties, about 4 inches long and ½-inch thick.

THREE: Heat grill to medium-high and lightly oil grate. Grill patties to desired doneness, about 3 minutes per side for medium and 3½ minutes per side for medium-well. During final minute of grilling, toast both sides of pitas lightly on grill.

FOUR: Place 1 lamburger in each pita pocket. Add mint, lettuce and 2 to 3 Tbsp tzatziki to each.

Nutrients per burger: *Calories: 201, Total Fat: 9 g, Sat. Fat: 3.5 g, Monounsaturated Fat: 3.5 g, Polyunsaturated Fat: 1 g, Omega-3s: 160 mg, Omega-6s: 560 mg, Carbs: 11 g, Fiber: 2 g, Sugars: 1 g, Protein: 19 g, Sodium: 372 mg, Cholesterol: 51 mg*

Nutritional Bonus:
Including ground lamb in these burgers not only adds to their Greek-inspired flavor – it adds nutritional value. Compared to beef, lamb has slightly higher levels of vitamin B12 and selenium, plus over 10 times the omega-3 fatty acids.

Lamburgers

Spiced Eggplant & Beef Stir-Fry

Spiced Eggplant & Beef Stir-Fry

Serves 4. **Hands-on time:** 30 minutes. **Total time:** 30 minutes.

Since baby eggplants have a much smaller diameter than standard eggplants, you can simply slice the baby variety into rounds before sautéing them. But if you can't track down the small nightshade vegetables (whose family also includes tomatoes, sweet peppers and potatoes), you can easily use full-size eggplants and cut the rounds into quarters before adding them to your pan.

INGREDIENTS:

- 1 Tbsp extra-virgin olive oil, divided
- 1 large yellow onion, chopped
- 1 red bell pepper, cut into ½-inch strips
- 2 tsp ground cumin
- 2 tsp ground coriander
- 1 Tbsp sweet paprika
- ¾ tsp sea salt
- 2 Roma tomatoes, chopped
- 4 cloves garlic, chopped
- 1 lb baby eggplant, cut into ½-inch rounds
- 1 yellow squash, cut into ½-inch rounds
- ½ lb extra-lean ground sirloin
- ¼ cup minced radish tops, rinsed well and patted dry, optional

INSTRUCTIONS:

ONE: In a large nonstick pan, heat 1 tsp oil on medium for 1 minute. Add onion and pepper and sauté for 5 minutes, stirring occasionally.

TWO: Meanwhile, in a small bowl, blend cumin, coriander, paprika and salt. Set spice blend aside.

THREE: Stir tomatoes and garlic into onion mixture on stovetop and cook for another 2 minutes. Add remaining 2 tsp oil and stir in eggplant and squash. Cover pan and cook for 5 minutes. Scoop mixture into a large bowl and set aside.

FOUR: Place same pan back on medium heat and add sirloin. Cook for 2 minutes, stirring constantly. Add reserved spice blend and cook for 1 minute longer. Remove pan from heat and return vegetables to pan, mixing well, for 1 minute or until heated through. Divide stir-fry mixture among 4 bowls or plates, garnishing with radish tops, if desired.

Nutrients per 1½-cup serving: Calories: 168, Total Fat: 7 g, Sat. Fat: 2 g, Monounsaturated Fat: 3 g, Polyunsaturated Fat: 2 g, Carbs: 16 g, Fiber: 6 g, Sugars: 7 g, Protein: 14 g, Sodium: 406 mg, Cholesterol: 38 mg

Potato, Pork & Spinach Salad
WITH GARLICKY CORN ON THE COB

Serves 4. **Hands-on time:** 30 minutes. **Total time:** 30 minutes.

Traditional German-style potato salad is made with bacon, but you can now opt for a cleaner and quicker version by using lean pork tenderloin instead. And, lighten up yet another summertime staple by skipping the butter and brushing your ears of corn with garlic-infused oil – a pleasant surprise for your taste buds!

INGREDIENTS:

- 1 clove garlic, crushed or minced
- 3 tsp extra-virgin olive oil, divided
- ½ lb redskin potatoes, scrubbed and cut into ½-inch cubes
- 4 ears corn, shucked
- 10 oz curly spinach
- ½ lb pork tenderloin, trimmed of visible fat, cut into ½-inch cubes
- 1 tsp dried sage
- ½ tsp sea salt
- Sweet paprika, to taste, optional

INSTRUCTIONS:

ONE: In a small bowl, mix garlic and 2 tsp oil. Set aside.

TWO: Fill a medium pot halfway with water and bring to a boil on high heat. Reduce to a simmer, add potatoes and cook for 8 minutes or until potatoes have reached desired tenderness. (Pierce with a sharp knife tip to test.) Drain and place in a large bowl.

THREE: Fill a large pot halfway with water and bring to a boil on high heat. Add corn, cover and cook for 3 minutes. Remove corn with tongs and set in a colander over a bowl or sink to drain and cool. To same empty pot, add ¼ cup water and spinach. Heat on medium and cook spinach for 5 minutes or until leaves are wilted, turning leaves often to prevent scorching. Drain well, then add spinach to potatoes.

FOUR: In a large nonstick skillet, heat remaining 1 tsp oil on medium for 1 minute. Add pork and sage and cook for 5 minutes or until thickest cube of tenderloin is opaque and cooked through, flipping after 2 minutes. Add pork and pan drippings to potato-spinach mixture. Season with salt and stir to combine.

FIVE: Using a pastry brush, apply garlic-oil mixture to corn. If desired, sprinkle each ear with paprika before serving alongside potato-pork salad.

Nutrients per serving (6 oz salad and 1 ear corn): Calories: 320, Total Fat: 6 g, Sat. Fat: 1 g, Monounsaturated Fat: 3 g, Polyunsaturated Fat: 1 g, Carbs: 49 g, Fiber: 7 g, Sugars: 7 g, Protein: 19 g, Sodium: 400 mg, Cholesterol: 35 mg

NUTRITIONAL BONUS: Like most grains, corn is rich in B vitamins such as thiamin and folate. The latter is crucial for heart health. Folate lowers levels of homocysteine, an amino acid found naturally in the blood, but an excess of which can damage blood vessels and increase your risk of heart attack and stroke.

Lamb Osso Bucco
WITH HERBED COUSCOUS

*Serves 6. **Hands-on time:** 30 minutes. **Total time:** 2 hours, 30 minutes.*

Texas Chef Mark Paul shares his Austin-style recipe, prizing local food and seasonality. Give it a try!

INGREDIENTS:

- 2 Tbsp grape seed oil
- 1 cup whole-wheat flour
- 8 pieces lamb foreshank, each cross-cut into 2-inch-thick pieces and tied around middle with butcher's twine (5 oz each, including bone; ask butcher to cut across the shank)
- 1 to 1½ tsp kosher salt
- ½ tsp fresh ground black pepper, divided
- 1 cup yellow onion, finely chopped
- ⅔ cup peeled and finely chopped carrots
- ⅔ cup celery, finely chopped
- ¼ tsp garlic, finely chopped
- 1 cup red wine
- 1½ cups low-sodium veal or lamb stock (or low-sodium chicken broth)
- 1½ cups boxed or jarred coarsely chopped Italian-style tomatoes with juices

- 1 tsp fresh thyme, chopped
- 4 leaves fresh basil, optional
- 2 bay leaves
- 2 to 3 sprigs fresh parsley

HERBED COUSCOUS
- 1 Tbsp olive oil
- ½ cup diced sweet onion
- 3 cups low-sodium chicken broth
- ¼ cup unsweetened golden raisins
- ½ tsp fresh thyme, chopped
- ½ tsp fresh rosemary, chopped
- ½ tsp fresh marjoram, chopped
- ½ tsp fresh mint, minced
- 2 cups couscous
- 2 Tbsp organic butter, softened
- 1 Tbsp fresh parsley, chopped
- Kosher salt and fresh ground black pepper, to taste

INSTRUCTIONS:

ONE: Preheat oven to 350°F.

TWO: In a heavy Dutch oven or roasting pan with a tight-fitting lid, heat grape seed oil on medium-high. (**NOTE:** Use a Dutch oven that's just large enough to hold the lamb pieces in a single layer.) On a wide plate, spread flour. Season lamb with salt and ¼ tsp pepper, then dredge each piece in flour, shaking off any excess. Add lamb to Dutch oven and brown on all sides for 8 to 10 minutes; transfer lamb to a clean plate, uncovered.

THREE: Reduce heat to medium and add onion, carrots and celery. Cook for 6 minutes, stirring frequently, until vegetables brown and soften slightly. Add garlic when vegetables are nearly softened. Add wine and bring to a boil; boil briskly for about 3 minutes, using a wooden spoon to scrape up any browned bits from bottom of Dutch oven. Add stock and return to a boil. Add tomatoes and their juices, thyme, basil, bay leaves, parsley and remaining ¼ tsp pepper. Simmer for 1 minute on medium; remove from heat.

FOUR: Skim any fat from top of vegetable-wine mixture. Place pieces of lamb side by side in Dutch oven among vegetables and liquid. (**NOTE:** The liquid should come up to the top of the pieces but shouldn't cover lamb. If necessary, add a bit of additional stock or water.) Place Dutch oven on medium heat and bring to a simmer. Cover pot tightly and transfer to middle rack in oven. Cook for about 2 hours, checking lamb every 30 minutes and basting as needed so exposed areas do not dry out.

TIP: USDA guidelines suggest a minimum internal temperature of 145°F for lamb. Temperatures during a braise will actually exceed that level, but when braised correctly, meats will remain cooked through without any loss of moisture.

FIVE: Meanwhile, prepare herbed couscous: In a medium saucepan, heat olive oil on medium. Add onion and cook, stirring frequently, until soft. Stir in broth and raisins and bring to a boil. Add thyme, rosemary, marjoram and mint; immediately stir in couscous. Cover and remove from heat; let sit for 10 minutes, until liquid is absorbed. Fluff with a fork; stir in butter and parsley. Season with salt and pepper.

SIX: Divide couscous among serving plates. Remove string from lamb shanks and arrange over top of couscous, dividing evenly. Remove and discard bay leaves. Top lamb with vegetable-sauce mixture, dividing evenly, and serve.

Nutrients per serving (4 to 4½ oz lamb, ½ cup couscous, ¼ cup vegetable-sauce mixture): *Calories: 650, Total Fat: 19 g, Sat. Fat: 6 g, Monounsaturated Fat: 5 g, Polyunsaturated Fat: 4 g, Carbs: 19 g, Fiber: 10 g, Sugars: 10 g, Protein: 53 g, Sodium: 520 mg, Cholesterol: 135 mg*

Nutritional Bonus:
When you are shopping for this recipe, try to opt for organic grass-fed lamb. The meat from grass-fed animals contains more heart-healthy omega-3 fatty acids, vitamin E and beta-carotene than meat from grain- or corn-fed animals.

Lamb Osso
Bucco

Ginger-
Garlic Pork

Ginger-Garlic Pork
WITH STICKY EGGPLANT RICE

Serves 4. **Hands-on time:** *25 minutes.* **Total time:** *1 hour, 15 minutes (plus marinating time).*

This simple *CE* marinade is all it takes to turn mild pork into a mouth-watering, Asian-inspired treat for your senses. Roasted eggplant takes on sweet, earthy undertones in our sushi-style rice.

INGREDIENTS:

- 1¼ lb pork tenderloin, trimmed
- ¾ cup short-grain brown rice
- 2 cloves garlic, finely chopped
- 1 1-inch piece fresh ginger, peeled and minced
- ¼ tsp plus ⅛ tsp sea salt, divided
- 1 tsp dark sesame oil
- Olive oil cooking spray
- 2 lb eggplant, preferably Japanese variety, cut into 1½-inch chunks
- Fresh ground black pepper, to taste

- ½ packed cup fresh cilantro, chopped, plus additional for garnish
- Lime wedges for garnish, optional

MARINADE

- 5 cloves garlic, finely chopped
- 1 3-inch piece fresh ginger, peeled and minced
- 1½ cups 100% orange juice
- ¼ cup low-sodium soy sauce
- 2 Tbsp raw honey
- 1 Tbsp white miso paste
- 1 tsp Sriracha or hot sauce

INSTRUCTIONS:

ONE: In a medium bowl, whisk marinade ingredients until thoroughly combined. In a large heavy-duty zip-top bag, add pork and 1½ cups marinade, massaging bag to coat. Refrigerate for 4 hours, or overnight. Cover and refrigerate remaining marinade.

TWO: In a small saucepan, bring 1½ cups water to a boil. Stir in rice, 2 cloves garlic, 1-inch piece ginger and ¼ tsp salt and return to a boil. Reduce heat to low, cover and simmer until tender, about 50 minutes. Remove from heat and let rest, covered, for 10 minutes. Drizzle with sesame oil and fluff with a fork. Transfer to a large bowl.

THREE: Meanwhile, arrange 1 oven rack in upper third and 1 rack in lower third of oven. Preheat oven to 375°F. Line a large rimmed baking sheet with foil and mist with cooking spray. Add eggplant, drizzle with remaining marinade and toss well to coat. Spread in a single layer and sprinkle with pepper, to taste. Transfer to upper oven rack and bake for 10 minutes. Remove from oven and stir well. Return to oven and bake until tender and lightly browned, 8 to 10 minutes; maintain oven heat at 375°F. Transfer to a small bowl and set aside.

FOUR: Line same baking sheet with a new sheet of foil and mist with cooking spray. Remove pork from bag and pat dry with paper towel; discard marinade. Transfer pork to sheet and sprinkle with remaining ⅛ tsp salt and ¼ tsp pepper. Bake on lower rack at 375°F until an instant-read thermometer registers 155°F when inserted in center of pork, 22 to 27 minutes. Remove from oven and let rest for 10 minutes. Cut into ½-inch-thick slices. Gently fold eggplant and cilantro into rice. To serve, garnish pork and rice mixture with additional cilantro and serve with lime.

Nutrients per serving (4 oz pork and 1 cup rice mixture): *Calories: 399, Total Fat: 8 g, Sat. Fat: 2 g, Monounsaturated Fat: 3 g, Polyunsaturated Fat: 2 g, Carbs: 50 g, Fiber: 10 g, Sugars: 11 g, Protein: 35 g, Sodium: 421 mg, Cholesterol: 92 mg*

Skinny Shepherd's Pie

Serves 8. **Hands-on time:** *20 minutes.* **Total time:** *50 minutes.*

CE's shepherd's pie packs in a hearty taste without the fat. Bison, a highly nutrient-dense protein, has a greater concentration of iron as well as omega-3 fatty acids than ground beef. Opt for grass-fed and free-range bison for maximum omega-3s and beefy flavor!

INGREDIENTS:

- 2 Yukon gold potatoes, scrubbed well and quartered
- 2 cups cauliflower florets
- 1 tsp each sea salt and fresh ground black pepper
- ½ cup skim milk
- Olive oil cooking spray
- 1 yellow onion, diced
- 3 cloves garlic, minced
- 1 lb ground bison
- 1 cup sliced carrots (peeled, halved lengthwise and sliced into half-moons)
- 2 Tbsp olive oil
- 2 Tbsp whole-wheat flour
- 1 cup low-sodium beef broth
- 1 Tbsp low-sodium Worcestershire sauce
- 1 Tbsp fresh thyme
- 1 cup frozen peas

INSTRUCTIONS:

ONE: Preheat oven to 375°F.

TWO: Bring a large pot of water to a boil on high heat. Add potatoes and cook for 8 minutes. Add cauliflower and cook for an additional 7 minutes or until potatoes are fork-tender. Drain and transfer to a large bowl; add salt, pepper and milk and mash with a potato masher until smooth. Set aside.

THREE: Heat a large skillet on medium-high and mist with cooking spray. Add onion, garlic, bison and carrots and cook for 8 minutes or until no pink remains, stirring often and using a wooden spoon to break up bison.

FOUR: Meanwhile, in a medium skillet, heat oil on medium. Sprinkle in flour and whisk until no lumps remain, about 1 minute. Gradually add broth, whisking constantly, until mixture is smooth and begins to thicken. Add Worcestershire sauce and thyme, whisking to combine.

FIVE: In a 10 x 15-inch casserole dish, add bison mixture, broth mixture and peas; stir to combine. Spread mixture in an even layer, then top with potato-cauliflower mixture in an even layer. Run a fork over top in a crosshatch pattern or use the back of a spatula or spoon to create a swirl texture. Mist top with cooking spray, transfer to oven and bake until filling is bubbling and top is golden brown, about 30 minutes. Let rest for 5 minutes before serving.

Nutrients per 1-cup serving: *Calories: 191, Total Fat: 5 g, Sat. Fat: 1 g, Carbs: 19 g, Fiber: 3 g, Sugars: 3.5 g, Protein: 16 g, Sodium: 332 mg, Cholesterol: 41 mg*

Pork Burgers
WITH ASIAN PEAR SLAW & GORGONZOLA

*Serves 4. **Hands-on time:** 35 minutes. **Total time:** 35 minutes.*

The most popular variety of Asian pear available in the US is the Japanese Nijisseki, although Asian pears are also grown in China and Korea. The ones you're likely to find most often in supermarkets hail from California and Chile. More like an apple than a pear, this juicy, crisp fruit remains firm when ripe.

INGREDIENTS:

- ¼ cup nonfat plain Greek yogurt
- 1 Tbsp raw honey
- 2 tsp apple cider vinegar
- 1 tsp ground mustard
- 2 Asian pears, cored and sliced into matchsticks
- ¼ head red cabbage, cored and thinly sliced (about 1 cup)
- ¼ packed cup fresh parsley, chopped
- Fresh ground black pepper, to taste
- 1 lb lean ground pork
- 2 tsp mild chile powder
- ½ tsp dried thyme
- Olive oil cooking spray, optional
- 4 whole-wheat hamburger buns
- ½ cup baby spinach leaves
- 1¾ oz gorgonzola cheese, sliced

INSTRUCTIONS:

ONE: Prepare slaw: In a large bowl, whisk yogurt, honey, vinegar and mustard. Wrap pears in a double layer of paper towel and squeeze gently to remove as much moisture as possible. Add pears to bowl, discarding paper towel. Add cabbage and parsley, stir gently and season with pepper.

TWO: Preheat a grill or broiler to high. In a separate large bowl, combine pork, chile powder, thyme and a few grinds of pepper. Shape mixture into 4 equal patties, about ¹⁄₂ inch thick each. Grill or broil (if broiling, place patties on a broiler pan misted with cooking spray and cook about 8 to 10 inches from heat), turning once, until centers are no longer pink and juice runs clear, about 10 minutes.

THREE: To serve, fill each bun with spinach, patties, cheese and slaw, dividing evenly.

Nutrients per burger: Calories: 347, Total Fat: 9 g, Sat. Fat: 4 g, Monounsaturated Fat: 1.5 g, Polyunsaturated Fat: 1.5 g, Carbs: 36 g, Fiber: 6 g, Sugars: 13 g, Protein: 33 g, Sodium: 473 mg, Cholesterol: 84 mg

NUTRITIONAL BONUS: Just like the standard variety, Asian pears are a very good source of fiber, helping to bring this meal's tally to 6 g per serving. Factor in the red cabbage, which is also a great source of fiber, not to mention iron, potassium and vitamins A and C, and this Asian Pear Slaw makes for a filling, energy-boosting and antioxidant-rich burger topper.

TIP: Since Asian pears contain a lot of water, our slaw is best prepared just before serving.

Spice-Crusted Lamb Chops
WITH BABY POTATOES

*Serves 4. **Hands-on time:** 10 minutes. **Total time:** 25 minutes.*

Our coated chops partner well with an Argentinean Malbec. This varietal is well-oaked and tinged with chocolate and tobacco flavors, which complement the nutty, slightly gamey taste of lamb chops.

INGREDIENTS:

- 1 Tbsp shelled unsalted pistachios
- 1 Tbsp unsweetened shredded coconut
- 2 tsp toasted sesame seeds
- 1 tsp cumin seeds
- 1 tsp fennel seeds
- ¼ tsp coarse sea salt
- ¼ tsp black peppercorns
- 4 4-oz lamb loin chops, about 1 inch thick
- Olive oil cooking spray
- 1 lb small potatoes (such as Yukon Gold), scrubbed well and halved
- 2 tsp pumpkin seed oil
- 1 Tbsp chives, chopped
- Fine sea salt and fresh ground black pepper, to taste

INSTRUCTIONS:

ONE: In a coffee grinder, spice grinder or mortar with pestle, grind pistachios, coconut, sesame seeds, cumin, fennel, coarse salt and peppercorns until well ground. Transfer spice mixture to a large plate and shake gently to cover surface with mixture.

TWO: Place lamb chops on a cutting board or in a baking dish and coat both sides of lamb with cooking spray. Dredge each lamb chop in spice mixture.

THREE: Arrange broiler rack on second position in oven and set broiler to high. Place lamb chops on a foil-lined baking sheet and broil for 6 to 7 minutes per side or until lamb chops are light pink in center. Remove lamb chops and let sit for 5 minutes before serving.

NOTE: Lamb chops will continue cooking after being removed from oven.

FOUR: Meanwhile, set a steamer basket in a pot and add enough water to reach bottom portion of basket. Bring water to a boil, add potatoes, cover and reduce heat to medium. Steam until tender when pierced with a sharp knife, about 8 minutes. Transfer potatoes to a large serving bowl and toss with oil, chives, fine salt and ground black pepper. Serve lamb chops with potatoes on the side.

Nutrients per serving (1 lamb chop and 3 potatoes): Calories: 340, Total Fat: 19 g, Sat. Fat: 7 g, Monounsaturated Fat: 7 g, Polyunsaturated Fat: 2 g, Carbs: 22 g, Fiber: 3 g, Sugars: 1 g, Protein: 20 g, Sodium: 210 mg, Cholesterol: 65 mg

Baby Potatoes

Spice-Crusted Lamb Chops

Nutritional Bonus:
Thanks to the avocado and whole-wheat pasta, this dish supplies 95% of your daily need for manganese. This essential mineral helps you metabolize proteins and carbohydrates and aids your body in digesting nutrients such as thiamin (vitamin B1) and ascorbic acid (vitamin C).

Guacamole Fettucine

Guacamole Fettucine

WITH SAUTÉED BEEF STRIPS

Serves 4. *Hands-on time:* 25 minutes. *Total time:* 25 minutes.

You're undoubtedly accustomed to serving mashed avocado with chips and salsa (homemade guacamole ring a bell?). But the fruit's creamy texture is also perfect for tossing with whole-wheat noodles, especially when smooth Greek yogurt is added to the mix. Simply think of this dish as a pasta-inspired twist on tacos!

INGREDIENTS:

- 8 oz whole-wheat fettucine
- 1 avocado, peeled and pitted
- 1 Tbsp fresh lime juice
- ¼ cup 2% plain Greek yogurt
- ¼ tsp sea salt
- ½ lb sirloin beef, trimmed of visible fat and cut into ½-inch-thick strips
- 4 cloves garlic, chopped
- ⅓ lb Roma tomatoes, chopped
- ¼ cup minced cilantro for garnish, optional

INSTRUCTIONS:

ONE: Fill a large pot halfway with water and bring to a boil. Prepare fettucine according to package directions. Drain well and set aside.

TWO: In a large bowl, add avocado and mash into a smooth cream using a fork. Stir in lime juice, yogurt and salt. Set aside.

THREE: In a large nonstick skillet on medium heat, sauté beef for 2 minutes. Add garlic and cook for 5 more minutes or until strips are cooked through, turning occasionally. Drain beef and garlic in a fine-mesh strainer, then transfer to bowl with avocado mixture. Add fettucine and toss.

FOUR: Divide fettucine mixture among 4 plates, then top each with a quarter of tomatoes and garnish with cilantro, if desired.

Nutrients per 2-cup serving: Calories: 365, Total Fat: 10 g, Sat. Fat: 2 g, Monounsaturated Fat: 6 g, Polyunsaturated Fat: 1.5 g, Carbs: 50 g, Fiber: 4 g, Sugars: 3.5 g, Protein: 22 g, Sodium: 168 mg, Cholesterol: 30 mg

Bison Stroganoff

Serves 4. *Hands-on time:* 15 minutes. *Total time:* 30 minutes.

We've cleaned up this famed Russian comfort food without skimping on its well-known succulent flavor. Grass-fed bison, along with a low-cal cream sauce made with Greek yogurt, leans out this dish for guilt-free enjoyment. Plus, this easy-to-make masterpiece is family ready in as little as 30 minutes!

INGREDIENTS:

- 4 tsp olive oil, divided
- 1 lb bison tenderloin (or beef tenderloin), sliced into thin, bite-size strips (about 1 inch long x ¼ inch thick)
- ⅛ tsp each sea salt and fresh ground black pepper, plus additional to taste
- 2 cups sliced baby portobello or button mushrooms
- 1 cup red onion, chopped
- 2 cloves garlic, minced
- 10 cups baby spinach leaves
- 1 cup nonfat plain Greek yogurt
- ⅓ cup evaporated milk
- 2 tsp Dijon mustard

INSTRUCTIONS:

ONE: In a large nonstick skillet, heat 2 tsp oil on high. Add bison and sauté for 2 minutes, stirring occasionally. Season with salt and pepper, transfer to a large bowl and cover to keep warm.

TWO: Reduce heat to medium-high; add remaining 2 tsp oil. Once oil is hot, add mushrooms and onion and sauté until golden, about 8 minutes. Add garlic and spinach, several handfuls at a time, until greens are just wilted, about 1 minute. Reduce heat to low.

THREE: Meanwhile, in a small bowl, whisk yogurt, milk and Dijon. Slowly add mixture to skillet and heat until warm, about 2 minutes. (**NOTE:** Avoid letting mixture simmer, as this causes yogurt to curdle.) Stir in bison and any accompanying juices until just hot throughout. Season with additional salt and pepper and serve.

Nutrients per 1-cup serving: Calories: 280, Total Fat: 8 g, Sat. Fat: 1.5 g, Monounsaturated Fat: 5 g, Polyunsaturated Fat: 1 g, Carbs: 18 g, Fiber: 4 g, Sugars: 7 g, Protein: 34 g, Sodium: 360 mg, Cholesterol: 80 mg

Nutritional Bonus:

A leaner alternative to beef, bison is an excellent source of lean protein for your caloric buck – a ¼-lb serving contains a mere 128 calories and 3 g of total fat, yet 24 g of protein.

Balsamic Rosemary Steak
WITH BLUE CHEESE & ARUGULA

Serves 4. Hands-on time: 15 minutes. Total time: 40 minutes (plus marinating time).

While sweet-tart balsamic vinegar and pungent rosemary nicely complement the earthy qualities of this steak, don't be afraid to experiment. Try this dish with chicken or lamb chops and you've easily multiplied one recipe into three!

INGREDIENTS:

- 1 lb top sirloin steak, about ¾-inch thick, trimmed of visible fat
- 1 cup Balsamic Rosemary Marinade (see recipe, p. 234)
- High-heat cooking oil (such as sunflower, safflower, peanut or grape seed oil), as needed
- 3 oz arugula (about 6 cups)
- ¼ cup crumbled blue cheese

INSTRUCTIONS:

ONE: Place steak in a large zip-top bag. Add Balsamic Rosemary Marinade and seal, squeezing out as much air as possible. Refrigerate for 2 to 6 hours, turning occasionally.

TWO: Heat grill to medium-high and lightly oil grate. Remove steak from marinade and pat dry with paper towel. Grill steak to desired doneness, about 4 minutes per side for medium-rare or 5 minutes per side for medium. Remove from grill, transfer to a plate and loosely cover with foil. Let rest for 5 minutes.

THREE: Cut steak diagonally into thin slices. Arrange arugula on 4 plates and top with steak, dividing evenly. Drizzle with any steak juices accumulated on plate, sprinkle with cheese and serve.

Nutrients per serving (about 3½ oz steak, ¾ oz arugula, 1 Tbsp cheese): *Calories: 272, Total Fat: 14 g, Sat. Fat: 4 g, Monounsaturated Fat: 8 g, Polyunsaturated Fat: 1 g, Carbs: 8 g, Fiber: 0.5 g, Sugars: 6 g, Protein: 27 g, Sodium: 388 mg, Cholesterol: 86 mg*

NUTRITIONAL BONUS: Serving this steak on a bed of arugula is a great way to boost its nutritional heft. The greens add fiber, vitamins and minerals, and are especially rich in vitamin K. Also known as phylloquinone, fat-soluble vitamin K helps transport all-important calcium, making it critical for both bone growth and blood coagulation.

Braised Beef
WITH CARAMELIZED ONIONS & GREENS CHIFFONADE

Serves 4. Hands-on time: 30 minutes. Total time: 2 hours, 30 minutes.

Turnips stand in as a less-starchy substitute for potatoes, while caramelized onions add a rich depth of flavor with the help of a little healthy fat. Don't be afraid to tweak the dish to your liking: If you'd prefer a more stew-like meal, add more broth. In search of a flavorful gravy? Simply reduce the cooking liquid and serve over top!

INGREDIENTS:

- 16 oz lean beef stew meat
- ¼ tsp sea salt, plus additional to taste
- ½ tsp fresh ground black pepper, plus additional to taste
- 1 Tbsp olive oil
- 1 yellow onion, halved lengthwise and thinly sliced lengthwise
- 3½ cups low-sodium beef broth, divided
- 4 medium carrots, peeled and halved (if small) or sliced ½-inch thick on the diagonal
- 1 large turnip, cubed
- 5 cloves garlic, chopped
- 1 large rosemary sprig
- 1 small bunch turnip greens
- Sprinkling of chopped flat-leaf parsley for garnish

TIP: If you have a hard time finding turnip greens, substitute chard.

INSTRUCTIONS:

ONE: Pat beef dry with paper towel and season with salt and pepper. In a large Dutch oven or heavy pot, heat oil on medium-high. Working in batches, sear beef in pot, browning well on all sides, for about 8 minutes.
NOTE: By working in batches you'll avoid overcrowding.) Transfer to a plate and cover to keep warm.

TWO: Reduce heat to low, add onion to Dutch oven and cook for 15 to 20 minutes, until caramelized and golden, stirring occasionally. Stir in ½ cup broth and increase heat to bring to a boil, scraping browned bits from bottom of Dutch oven with a wooden spoon.

THREE: Stir in carrots, turnip, garlic, rosemary, beef and remaining 3 cups broth. Return to a boil; reduce heat to low and simmer, partially covered, for 2 hours, until beef is very tender.

FOUR: About 5 minutes before beef is done, prepare greens chiffonade: Wash greens well and remove and discard stems. Stack greens and thinly slice crosswise into strips, about ¼ inch thick.

FIVE: Remove rosemary and discard. Stir in greens and season with additional salt and pepper. Garnish with parsley and serve immediately.

Nutrients per serving (3 oz beef and 2 cups vegetable-broth mixture): *Calories: 310, Total Fat: 12 g, Sat. Fat: 3.5 g, Monounsaturated Fat: 6 g, Polyunsaturated Fat: 1 g, Carbs: 19 g, Fiber: 5 g, Sugars: 8 g, Protein: 32 g, Sodium: 370 mg, Cholesterol: 65 mg*

Braised Beef

Mediterranean Meatballs
WITH CHUNKY TOMATO SAUCE & COUSCOUS

*Serves 8. **Hands-on time:** 1 hour. **Total time:** 1 hour, 20 minutes.*

This hearty crowd-pleaser calls on simple pantry spices to add layers of flavor to thick, patty-like meatballs, which are first seared to lock in juiciness, then baked to perfection in a rich veggie tomato sauce.

INGREDIENTS:

- 2 lb extra-lean ground beef and/or lamb (TIP: For less fat and more flavor, try 1½ lb beef and ½ lb lamb)
- 2 large eggs
- ½ cup fine whole-wheat bread crumbs
- ⅓ cup chopped fresh parsley, plus additional for garnish
- ¼ packed cup sun-dried tomatoes (dry-packed), chopped
- 2 tsp ground allspice
- 1 tsp dried oregano
- 1 tsp onion powder
- 1 tsp sea salt, divided
- ½ tsp garlic powder
- ½ tsp fresh ground black pepper, plus additional to taste
- Olive oil cooking spray

- 2 cups whole-wheat couscous
- 5 scallions, white and light green parts only, sliced
- 18 Kalamata olives, pitted and roughly chopped, optional

SAUCE

- 1½ tsp olive oil
- 1 large carrot, peeled and cut into ¼-inch dice
- 1 stalk celery, cut into ¼-inch dice
- ½ large white onion, chopped
- ½ tsp whole fennel seeds
- 3 cloves garlic, chopped
- 43 oz boxed or jarred unsalted diced tomatoes
- 1 dried bay leaf
- 1 tsp dried oregano
- Pinch sea salt
- ¼ tsp red pepper flakes, optional

INSTRUCTIONS:

ONE: Prepare sauce: In a medium saucepan, heat oil on medium. Add carrot, celery, onion and fennel. Cover and cook, stirring occasionally, until onions are translucent and all vegetables are soft but not brown, about 10 minutes. Uncover, add garlic and sauté, stirring frequently, for 1 minute. Add diced tomatoes. Stir in remaining sauce ingredients, bring to a simmer and cover. Cook, stirring occasionally, until sauce thickens and vegetables are very tender, 20 to 25 minutes; reduce heat as necessary if mixture sticks to pan.

MAKE AHEAD: Prepare sauce up to 1 day ahead; cover and refrigerate. Reheat before serving.)

TWO: Meanwhile, prepare meatballs: Preheat oven to 400°F. In a large bowl, mix beef and/or lamb, eggs, bread crumbs, parsley, sun-dried tomatoes, allspice, oregano, onion powder, ¾ tsp salt, garlic powder and black pepper until just combined. Form into 16 thick ⅓-cup patties.

MAKE AHEAD: Prepare meatballs up to 1 day ahead; cover and refrigerate. Cook meatballs before serving.

THREE: Heat a large nonstick skillet on medium-high and mist with cooking spray. Working in batches, add meatballs and cook, turning once, until well browned, about 4 minutes. Transfer to a 2-qt baking dish. Pour sauce over top of meatballs, discarding bay leaf. Bake until meatballs are cooked through, 30 to 35 minutes.

FOUR: Meanwhile, in a separate medium saucepan, bring 2 cups water to a boil. Add remaining ¼ tsp salt and black pepper, to taste. Stir in couscous. Cover, remove from heat and set aside for 5 minutes. Fluff with a fork and stir in scallions. Cover and set aside for 2 more minutes. To serve, top couscous with meatballs and sauce. If desired, garnish with olives and additional parsley.

Nutrients per serving (2 meatballs, ⅓ cup sauce, ¾ cup couscous mixture):
Calories: 367, Total Fat: 7 g, Sat. Fat: 5 g, Monounsaturated Fat: 1 g, Polyunsaturated Fat: 0 g, Carbs: 37 g, Fiber: 7 g, Sugars: 7 g, Protein: 33 g, Sodium: 533 mg, Cholesterol: 122 mg

Nutritional Bonus:
Although the olives in this recipe are optional, if you decide to include them you will adding a dose of heart-healthy monounsaturated fats to this meal, as well as free-radical-fighting vitamins E and A. Olives are also a good source of iron, copper and dietary fiber.

Spaghetti & Meatballs
WITH FRESH TOMATO SAUCE

Serves 8. *Makes* 32 to 34 meatballs. *Hands-on time:* 30 minutes.
Total time: 1 hour, 5 minutes.

This classic Italian recipe will become your standard go-to for pasta night! Adding fresh basil gives you a kick of flavonoids, which help protect cells and chromosomes from radiation damage.

INGREDIENTS:

- 1 lb lean ground venison (or extra-lean ground beef)
- ⅓ cup fresh whole-wheat bread crumbs
- ¼ cup nonfat plain Greek yogurt
- ¼ cup fresh parsley, finely chopped
- 1 egg white
- 1 small yellow onion, minced
- ¼ cup grated low-fat Parmesan cheese
- 3 cloves garlic, minced
- ½ tsp sea salt
- ½ tsp fresh ground black pepper
- 12 oz Kamut spaghetti

SAUCE

- 2 Tbsp extra-virgin olive oil
- 1 yellow onion, chopped
- 2 cloves garlic, minced
- 3 large vine-ripe tomatoes, chopped, juices reserved
- 1¼ packed cups fresh basil, thinly sliced, divided
- Sea salt and fresh ground black pepper, to taste
- ¼ cup grated low-fat Parmesan cheese, optional

INSTRUCTIONS:

ONE: Preheat oven to 400°F. Line a baking sheet with parchment paper. In a large bowl, combine venison, bread crumbs, yogurt, parsley, egg white, onion, Parmesan, garlic, salt and pepper. Shape mixture into 32 to 34 walnut-sized balls. Transfer to baking sheet and bake until browned, about 15 minutes.

TWO: Meanwhile, cook spaghetti according to package directions. Reserve ½ cup pasta cooking water; drain and transfer spaghetti to a separate large bowl.

THREE: Prepare sauce: In a large skillet, heat oil on medium. Add onion and garlic and cook until softened and golden, about 5 minutes. Stir in tomatoes and reserved juices, half of basil and reserved pasta cooking water; simmer until tomatoes break down to form a sauce, about 5 minutes. Add meatballs and cook for 2 minutes.

FOUR: Scrape into bowl with spaghetti. Add remaining basil and season with salt and pepper, tossing to coat. If desired, sprinkle with Parmesan before serving.

Nutrients per serving (1½ cups spaghetti and 4 meatballs): *Calories: 333, Total Fat: 7 g, Sat. Fat: 2 g, Monounsaturated Fat: 3 g, Polyunsaturated Fat: 1 g, Carbs: 42 g, Fiber: 7 g, Sugars: 7 g, Protein: 25 g, Sodium: 301 mg, Cholesterol: 50 mg*

NEW!

Slow-Cooker Brisket
WITH SWEET POTATOES & CITRUSY PEPPER SALSA

Serves 8 to 10. *Hands-on time:* 50 minutes. *Total time:* 4 hours, 50 minutes.

You'll seal in the brisket's natural melt-in-your-mouth tenderness by slow-cooking the lean cut in tart juices, which then thicken into a rich, zero-effort sauce. A fresh tomato, olive and herb salsa adds a vibrant finishing touch.

INGREDIENTS:

- 1 Tbsp olive oil
- 4- to 5-lb flat or first-cut brisket, trimmed of visible fat and cut into 3 equal pieces
- ½ tsp sea salt
- ¾ tsp fresh ground black pepper
- 2½ lb sweet potatoes, peeled and cut into 2-inch chunks
- 1 large yellow onion, chopped
- 4 cloves garlic, minced
- 1½ cups low-sodium chicken broth
- 1 dried bay leaf
- 1 cup 100% orange juice
- ⅓ cup red wine vinegar
- 3 Tbsp double-concentrated low-sodium tomato paste or 6 Tbsp regular low-sodium tomato paste

- 1 tsp ground coriander
- 1 tsp paprika, preferably smoked
- 1 tsp dried thyme

SALSA

- 18 Kalamata and/or green olives, pitted and chopped
- 2 large vine tomatoes, chopped
- 1 jalapeño chile pepper, seeded and finely chopped
- 1 shallot, finely chopped
- Zest 1 orange, plus 2 Tbsp juice
- 6 Tbsp chopped fresh parsley and/or mint, divided

INSTRUCTIONS:

ONE: In a large, heavy pot or Dutch oven, heat oil on medium-high. Season brisket with salt and black pepper. Working in batches, add brisket to pot and cook until browned all over, about 2 minutes per side. Transfer to a 5- to 6-qt slow cooker and top with potatoes.

TWO: Reduce heat to medium-low. Add onion and sauté, stirring frequently, until lightly browned, about 8 minutes. Add garlic and sauté for 1 more minute. Add broth and increase heat to high. Bring to a simmer, scraping up browned bits from bottom of pot. Stir in bay leaf, 1 cup orange juice, vinegar, tomato paste, coriander, paprika and thyme and return to a simmer. Add to slow cooker, cover and cook for 4 hours on high or 8 hours on low.

THREE: Prepare salsa: In a medium bowl, combine olives, tomatoes, jalapeño, shallot and orange zest and 2 Tbsp juice. Stir well to combine and fold in 3 Tbsp parsley and/or mint.

FOUR: Remove brisket from slow cooker and cut against the grain into ¼-inch-thick slices. Remove bay leaf from potato-broth mixture. To serve, top brisket and potato-broth mixture with salsa and garnish with remaining 3 Tbsp parsley and/or mint.

Nutrients per serving (4 oz brisket, ½ cup potatoes, ¼ cup salsa): *Calories: 511, Total Fat: 13 g, Sat. Fat: 4 g, Monounsaturated Fat: 7 g, Polyunsaturated Fat: 1 g, Carbs: 42 g, Fiber: 6 g, Sugars: 13 g, Protein: 54 g, Sodium: 538 mg, Cholesterol: 93 mg*

Slow-Cooker
Brisket

Fusion
Mango Sushi
Hand Rolls

Fusion Mango Sushi Hand Rolls
WITH STIR-FRIED PORK

Serves 4. Hands-on time: *40 minutes.* **Total time:** *1 hour, 25 minutes.*

To check for ripeness, try sniffing a mango at its stem end – it should smell fragrant and sweet. And, if you've never worked with the nori (edible seaweed sheets) called for in these fusion-style sushi rolls, there's nothing to it: Simply cut and roll. Find it, along with rice vinegar and short-grain brown sushi rice, in the Asian section of most supermarkets or at Asian grocery stores.

INGREDIENTS:

- ⅓ cup short-grain brown rice (sushi rice)
- ⅛ tsp sea salt
- 3 tsp unseasoned rice vinegar, divided
- 1½ Tbsp low-sodium soy sauce
- 2 Tbsp raw honey
- 1 clove garlic, finely chopped
- ½ tsp ground ginger
- Dash ground cayenne pepper, or to taste
- ½ lb pork tenderloin
- 1 Tbsp safflower oil
- 6 sheets nori
- 1 mango, peeled and thinly sliced
- Cilantro leaves for garnish, optional

INSTRUCTIONS:

ONE: In a small saucepan, bring ⅔ cup water to a boil. Add rice and salt, cover and reduce to a simmer on low heat until rice absorbs water and becomes tender, about 40 minutes. Remove from heat and keep covered for 10 minutes. Transfer rice to a bowl and sprinkle with 1 tsp vinegar. Mix gently and spread rice out in a thin layer on a baking sheet to cool. (May be made up to 2 hours in advance; cover with plastic wrap and keep at room temperature.)

TWO: In a small bowl, whisk together remaining 2 tsp vinegar, soy sauce, honey, garlic, ginger and cayenne. Slice pork ¼-inch thick, then cut into 2-inch strips. Heat oil in a large skillet on medium-high. Add pork and cook, stirring occasionally, until center is no longer pink, 4 to 5 minutes. Add soy sauce mixture and cook, stirring constantly, until reduced by two thirds, about 2 minutes.

THREE: Cut nori in half to form 12 rectangles and have a small bowl of water nearby. Place a piece of nori on a clean work surface, shiny side down, dip your fingertips in water (to prevent rice from sticking) and place about 3 Tbsp rice near 1 of the short ends on a slight diagonal. Make a small indentation in the rice with your finger and place 1 strip (or 2, if small) pork and 1 slice mango on rice. Add cilantro, if desired. Fold lower corner of nori over, tucking it over and around filling. Continue rolling nori into a cone shape. With wet fingertips, lightly crush a few grains of rice and use to "glue" the end of the nori around the cone. Repeat with remaining ingredients, making a total of 12 rolls. Serve immediately or cover and refrigerate for up to 2 hours. Bring to room temperature before serving.

Nutrients per 3 hand rolls: Calories: 239, Total Fat: 5 g, Sat. Fat: 1 g, Carbs: 33 g, Fiber: 2 g, Sugars: 16 g, Protein: 15 g, Sodium: 294 mg, Cholesterol: 37 mg

Beefy Zucchini Rolls
WITH FRESH MARINARA & SWEET POTATO FRIES

Serves 4. Hands-on time: *45 minutes.* **Total time:** *45 minutes.*

Combine fresh basil with tomatoes and you have not only a flavorful marinara sauce, but also a pairing that's light and summery. Keep the Fresh Marinara recipe on hand for a quick pasta or protein topper.

INGREDIENTS:

- 1 lb sweet potatoes, peeled, quartered and cut into ¼-inch strips
- 3 tsp extra-virgin olive oil, divided
- ¾ tsp sea salt, divided
- ½ large yellow onion, chopped
- 1 lb stem tomatoes (on-the-vine tomatoes), chopped
- 4 cloves garlic, chopped
- 1 bunch fresh basil (about 2 loosely packed cups), chopped
- 2 zucchini, rinsed and ends trimmed
- ½ lb extra-lean ground sirloin

INSTRUCTIONS:

ONE: Preheat oven to 425°F. Line 2 baking sheets with parchment paper and set aside. In a large bowl, add potatoes and toss gently with 2 tsp oil and ½ tsp salt. Spread on baking sheets and bake for 15 minutes. Turn potatoes over and bake for another 10 minutes or until they begin turning golden brown.

TWO: Meanwhile, prepare Fresh Marinara: In a large nonstick skillet, heat remaining 1 tsp oil on medium for 1 minute. Add onion and sauté for 3 minutes or until translucent. Add tomatoes, garlic and basil; cover skillet. Simmer for 10 minutes, reducing heat to medium-low if marinara starts to boil. Remove from heat.

THREE: Using a sharp chef's knife, trim a thin lengthwise slice off zucchini to create a flat surface. Place zucchini cut side down and carefully cut lengthwise into thin, even slices. (Each zucchini should yield about 8 uniform slices. The outer-most slices won't be useful since they're curved and uneven.)

FOUR: Fill a shallow saucepan halfway with water. Bring to a boil, then reduce heat to medium-low and slip zucchini into saucepan. Simmer gently for 2 minutes, then drain. Fill a large bowl or refill saucepan with cool water and add zucchini. Soak for 5 minutes, drain and set aside.

FIVE: Heat a separate large nonstick skillet on medium. Add sirloin and cook for 5 minutes, stirring often, or until meat is cooked through. Stir in remaining ¼ tsp salt. Drain pan drippings and transfer sirloin to a bowl.

SIX: Top 1 end of each zucchini slice with 1 heaping Tbsp sirloin. Gently roll up. Plate, top with Fresh Marinara and serve with a side of fries, dividing evenly.

TIP: If possible, choose zucchini that are straight, not curved, to make slicing easier.

Nutrients per serving (4 rolls, ½ cup marinara, ½ cup fries): Calories: 250, Total Fat: 7 g, Sat. Fat: 2 g, Monounsaturated Fat: 4 g, Polyunsaturated Fat: 1 g, Carbs: 33 g, Fiber: 6 g, Sugars: 10 g, Protein: 16 g, Sodium: 480 mg, Cholesterol: 30 mg

Steak Salad

Serves 4. *Hands-on time:* 20 minutes. *Total time:* 30 minutes.

Use a lean cut of grass-fed beef to make this leafy dish savory and full of wholesome nutrients.

INGREDIENTS:

- 4 cups iceberg lettuce, chopped
- 4 cups arugula, chopped
- 4 cups romaine lettuce, chopped
- 2 cups thinly sliced mushrooms
- 1 medium red bell pepper, sliced into thin strips
- 1 cucumber, peeled and thinly sliced
- ½ medium red onion, thinly sliced
- Olive oil cooking spray
- 10 oz beef tenderloin, trimmed of visible fat and cut into 3-inch-long strips, (⅛-inch thick and ½-inch wide)
- 4 Tbsp peeled and chopped avocado

BLACK PEPPERCORN YOGURT DRESSING

- ½ cup nonfat plain Greek yogurt
- ½ cup low-fat buttermilk
- 1 tsp whole black peppercorns, crushed or ground
- 2 cloves garlic, crushed
- 2 tsp apple cider vinegar
- ¼ tsp sea salt

INSTRUCTIONS:

ONE: Set oven to broil on low. In a large bowl, combine iceberg, arugula and romaine lettuces. Divide greens among 4 plates. Arrange ½ cup mushrooms and quarter of each red pepper, cucumber and onion on each plate of greens.

TWO: Prepare Black Peppercorn Yogurt Dressing: In a small bowl, whisk together yogurt, buttermilk, peppercorns, garlic and vinegar until smooth and incorporated. Season with salt and whisk again.

THREE: Mist a small baking pan or stone with cooking spray. Place beef strips on pan and broil for 6 minutes, turning once after 3 minutes. Divide beef among salads (about 2½ oz each). Drizzle each with ¼ cup Black Peppercorn Yogurt Dressing and sprinkle 1 Tbsp avocado over top.

Nutrients per salad: *Calories: 187, Total Fat: 5 g, Sat. Fat: 2 g, Monounsaturated Fat: 2 g, Polyunsaturated Fat: 0.5 g Carbs: 15 g, Fiber: 5 g, Sugars: 8 g, Protein: 22 g, Sodium: 220 mg, Cholesterol: 39 mg*

Pork Chops
WITH PEPPERS, ONIONS & OLIVES

Serves 4. *Hands-on time:* 20 minutes. *Total time:* 35 minutes.

A classic pan-seared chop complemented by a vegetable sauté gets a distinctly Mediterranean flair thanks to tender peppers and briny olives. To vary the dish, try replacing the chops with chicken, halibut or deli-fresh sausages.

INGREDIENTS:

- 4 5-oz boneless pork loin chops, about ¾ inch thick, trimmed of visible fat
- ½ tsp each fine sea salt and fresh ground black pepper
- 1 Tbsp olive oil
- ½ green bell pepper, cut into ¼-inch slices
- ½ red bell pepper, cut into ¼-inch slices
- ½ yellow bell pepper, cut into ¼-inch slices
- ½ red onion, cut into ¼-inch slices
- 1 Tbsp no-salt-added tomato paste
- 8 to 12 pitted Kalamata olives, drained and rinsed
- ½ cup low-sodium chicken broth

INSTRUCTIONS:

ONE: Season both side of chops with salt and black pepper. In a large skillet or sauté pan (not nonstick), heat oil on medium. Add chops and cook for 5 minutes per side or until cooked through (or 150°F on an instant-read thermometer). Transfer chops to serving plates and let rest for 5 minutes.

TWO: Return skillet to medium heat. Add bell peppers and cook, stirring occasionally, for 2 minutes. Add onion and cook, stirring occasionally, until both peppers and onion are tender, about 3 minutes. Add tomato paste and cook, stirring, for 30 seconds. Add olives and broth and deglaze pan by scraping up any browned bits from bottom of skillet with a heatproof spoon or spatula. Cook, stirring occasionally, until broth is reduced to a thin layer, about 2 minutes. To serve, top pork with pepper-onion mixture, dividing evenly.

Nutrients per serving (1 chop and 1/2 cup pepper-onion mixture): *Calories: 204, Total Fat: 9 g, Sat. Fat: 2 g, Monounsaturated Fat: 5 g, Polyunsaturated Fat: 1 g, Carbs: 6 g, Fiber: 1 g, Sugars: 2 g, Protein: 31 g, Sodium: 452 mg, Cholesterol: 92 mg*

Nutritional Bonus:
In this dish, the trio of bell peppers offers a bevy of vitamins: Yellow has the most collagen-forming vitamin C; red packs vitamin A to help with night vision; and green's vitamin K helps ensure that your body is making the most of calcium for bone density.

Pork Chops

Beef Tacos

Beef Tacos
(TACOS DE CARNE ASADA)

Serves 4.

Aarón Sánchez of Food Network's *Heat Seekers* has created this spicy Latin dish exclusively for *CE*. Enjoy healthy Mexican cooking complete with a kick of jalapeño heat and a lively salsa recipe.

INGREDIENTS:

- 1 16-oz flank steak, trimmed of visible fat
- 1 cup pickled jalapeño pepper, carrot and onion mixture with juices
- Pinch each sea salt and fresh ground black pepper
- 1 Tbsp safflower oil, plus additional as needed
- 8 corn tortillas
- ¼ cup coarsely chopped white onion
- ¼ cup fresh cilantro leaves

SALSA DE ARBOL

- 4 dried chiles de arbol, stemmed
- 1 lb plum tomatoes, halved
- ½ white onion, chopped
- 1 clove garlic, minced
- 1 tsp dried oregano, preferably Mexican
- Juice ½ lime
- Pinch organic evaporated cane juice
- Kosher salt, to taste
- Chopped fresh cilantro for garnish, optional

INSTRUCTIONS:

ONE: Prepare Salsa de Arbol: In a small pot, bring ½ cup water to a boil. In a skillet or saucepan on medium-low, toast chiles for 2 minutes, shaking skillet, then remove from heat. Pour boiling water over top of chiles, cover and let soak for 15 minutes.

TWO: Preheat a grill or grill pan to high. Grill tomatoes, turning until charred on all sides. Transfer tomatoes to a food processor. Add chiles and any remaining water from skillet, onion, garlic, oregano, lime juice, cane juice and salt; pulse until chunky. Set aside for about 1 hour, covered, at room temperature. Garnish with cilantro, if desired.

THREE: Meanwhile, top steak with pickled vegetables, cover and marinate at room temperature for 1 hour, turning once.

FOUR: Preheat grill or a broiler to high. Uncover steak and discard pickled vegetables. Season both sides of steak with salt and black pepper and place on grill or under broiler. Cook, turning once, for 5 to 6 minutes per side for medium rare, 7 to 8 minutes per side for medium. Transfer to a cutting board; allow steak to rest for 5 to 10 minutes before slicing into ¼-inch strips.

FIVE: In a small saucepan, heat oil on medium. Add 1 tortilla and cook, turning once, for 30 seconds per side. Repeat with remaining tortillas (add additional oil if using thick tortillas). Place tortillas on a work surface, place steak in center of tortillas and top with onion and cilantro, dividing evenly. Sprinkle Salsa de Arbol over each taco, dividing evenly, and serve.

Nutrients per 2 tacos: *Calories: 400, Total Fat: 11 g, Sat. Fat: 3 g, Monounsaturated Fat: 5 g, Polyunsaturated Fat: 2 g, Carbs: 41 g, Fiber: 5 g, Sugars: 4 g, Protein: 31 g, Sodium: 370 mg, Cholesterol: 35 mg*

Cheeseburger Pizza

*Serves 12. **Hands-on time:** 15 minutes. **Total time:** 35 minutes.*

Two favorites come together in this quick and lightened-up dish that's sure to please a crowd. Feel free to add other cheeseburger-inspired toppings before baking: a few pickled hot peppers, sliced and pitted green or black olives or even slices of dill pickle. But be sure to drain and rinse any of these jarred condiments first to keep sodium levels in check.

INGREDIENTS:

- 8 oz extra-lean ground beef
- 1 small onion, chopped
- ½ tsp Italian seasoning
- Sea salt and fresh ground black pepper, to taste
- 14½ oz no-salt-added diced tomatoes, drained
- 3 Tbsp Dijon mustard
- 2 thin whole-wheat pizza crusts
- 1 cup low-fat ricotta cheese
- 1 cup grated part-skim mozzarella cheese
- 1½ cups baby arugula or baby spinach

INSTRUCTIONS:

ONE: Preheat oven to 450°F. Preheat a nonstick skillet on medium-high. Add beef, onion, Italian seasoning, salt and pepper and cook for about 5 minutes, breaking up beef with a spoon until no longer pink. Stir in tomatoes and Dijon. Set aside.

TWO: Place each crust on an individual pizza pan (or place both on 1 large rimless baking sheet). Divide ricotta among pizza crusts, spreading evenly. Top with beef mixture and sprinkle with mozzarella, dividing evenly.

THREE: Bake for 10 minutes or until cheese melts. Remove pizzas from oven and sprinkle each with arugula, dividing evenly. Let rest for 1 minute before slicing and serving.

Nutrients per serving (⅙ of pizza): *Calories: 200, Total Fat: 6 g, Sat. Fat: 3 g, Monounsaturated Fat: 1.5 g, Polyunsaturated Fat: 0.25 g, Carbs: 26 g, Fiber: 5 g, Sugars: 4 g, Protein: 14 g, Sodium: 313 mg, Cholesterol: 23 mg*

For a photo of this recipe, see page 118.

Steak

WITH MIXED MUSHROOM SAUTÉ

Serves 4. **Hands-on time:** *20 minutes.* **Total time:** *35 minutes.*

You can put together your own combination of preferred mushrooms or look for already-combined sampler packages at your local market. And don't be afraid to break up this recipe: Try the sautéed side over top of pan-seared chicken, polenta or even pizza.

INGREDIENTS:

- 1 Tbsp olive oil
- 4 5-oz top loin steaks, about ¾ inch thick, trimmed of visible fat
- ½ tsp fine sea salt
- ½ tsp fresh ground black pepper
- 4 cloves garlic, smashed
- 1 lb mixed mushrooms (Blend to try: white, Portobello, shiitake, chanterelle and trumpet), cleaned, trimmed and cut into ¼-inch slices
- 1 Tbsp chopped fresh thyme, plus additional sprigs for garnish
- ½ cup low-sodium beef broth
- 1 tsp low-sodium soy sauce

INSTRUCTIONS:

ONE: In a large skillet or sauté pan (not nonstick), heat oil on medium-high. Season both sides of steaks with salt and pepper. Add steaks to skillet and cook to desired doneness, about 3½ minutes per side for medium-rare and 4 minutes per side for medium. Transfer steaks to serving plates and let rest for 5 minutes.

TWO: Meanwhile, place same skillet on medium heat. Add garlic and cook, stirring, for 30 seconds. Add mushrooms, 1 variety at a time, leaving 1 minute between additions. Add thyme and cook, stirring occasionally, until mushrooms are tender, 3 to 6 minutes, depending on the varieties of mushrooms used. Add broth and soy sauce, deglazing pan by scraping up any browned bits from bottom of skillet with a heatproof spoon or spatula. Cook, stirring occasionally, until liquid is reduced to a thin layer, 1 to 2 minutes.

THREE: Serve steaks with mushroom mixture over top, dividing evenly, and garnish with additional thyme sprigs.

TIP: Cooking times for mushrooms differ based on the variety. For best results, add the sturdiest, most meaty mushrooms first, such as Portobello and trumpet. Cook for 1 minute, then add the more delicate varieties, such as white or button mushrooms, leaving 1 minute between each addition.

Nutrients per serving (1 steak and ½ cup mushrooms): *Calories: 254, Total Fat: 10 g, Sat. Fat: 3 g, Monounsaturated Fat: 5 g, Polyunsaturated Fat: 1 g, Carbs: 5 g, Fiber: 1 g, Sugars: 2 g, Protein: 36 g, Sodium: 367 mg, Cholesterol: 59 mg*

Herbed Steak Rolls

WITH GOAT CHEESE & CAPERS

Serves 4. **Hands-on time:** *15 minutes.* **Total time:** *20 minutes.*

These steak rolls are a breeze to prepare on a busy weeknight and yet elegant enough for weekend entertaining.

INGREDIENTS:

- 8 oz whole-wheat penne pasta
- 4 oz soft goat cheese
- 2 Tbsp fresh chives, chopped
- 2 Tbsp fresh parsley, chopped
- 2 Tbsp fresh basil, chopped
- 1 Tbsp capers, drained
- 4 4-oz extra-lean sirloin steaks, pounded to ¼-inch thickness
- ¼ tsp each sea salt and fresh ground black pepper
- 1 tsp olive oil
- 1 red bell pepper, chopped
- 1 cup snow or snap peas, trimmed

INSTRUCTIONS:

ONE: Cook penne according to package directions; drain.

TWO: Meanwhile, in a small bowl, combine cheese, chives, parsley, basil and capers; stir with the back of a spoon until herbs and capers blend into cheese.

THREE: Place steaks on a flat work surface. Spread cheese mixture on top of steaks, dividing evenly. Starting from shorter ends of steaks, roll each steak up like a jelly roll and secure with wooden toothpicks. Season outside of steak rolls with salt and black pepper.

FOUR: In a large skillet, heat oil on medium-high. Add steak rolls and cook for 3 minutes, turning frequently, until browned on all sides. Cover loosely with foil and cook to desired doneness, 2 to 3 more minutes – slighty pink for medium and no longer pink for medium-well. Remove foil, add penne, bell pepper and peas to skillet and stir to coat penne with pan juices. Cook for 1 minute to heat through.

Nutrients per serving (1 steak roll and 1½ cups penne mixture): *Calories: 470, Total Fat: 13 g, Sat. Fat: 7 g, Monounsaturated Fat: 4 g, Polyunsaturated Fat: 0.5 g, Carbs: 46 g, Fiber: 6 g, Sugars: 4 g, Protein: 38 g, Sodium: 360 mg, Cholesterol: 60 mg*

Thai Pork & Papaya on Couscous

*Serves 4. **Hands-on time:** 20 minutes. **Total time:** 20 minutes.*

Don't throw away those papaya seeds! Not only do they make for an attractive garnish, but they also have a peppery, fresh flavor. In fact, in many Southeast Asian regions, papaya seeds are dried, ground and used similarly to the way Westerners cook with peppercorns.

INGREDIENTS:

- 7.6 oz whole-wheat couscous
- 1 tsp extra-virgin olive oil
- 2 tsp low-sodium soy sauce
- ½ tsp ground ginger
- 3 cloves garlic, minced
- ½ lb pork tenderloin, sliced into ½-inch x 2-inch strips
- Juice 1 lime
- ¼ cup minced cilantro
- 1 lb Hawaiian papaya, peeled, halved, seeds removed and reserved, flesh cut into ½-inch cubes

INSTRUCTIONS:

ONE: In a medium saucepan, bring 1½ cups water to a boil. Stir in couscous, cover tightly and remove from heat. Let sit for 5 minutes, then uncover and fluff with a fork. Set aside.

TWO: In a large nonstick skillet, heat oil on medium for 1 minute. Add soy sauce, ginger, garlic and pork and cook for 3 to 4 minutes, occasionally flipping pork strips with a spatula until meat is cooked through. Remove skillet from heat and stir in lime juice and cilantro.

THREE: Place 1 cup couscous onto each of 4 plates. Top each with 2 oz pork mixture, ½ cup papaya and 1 Tbsp skillet juices. Garnish with reserved papaya seeds, if desired.

Nutrients per serving (1 cup couscous, 2 oz pork mixture, ½ cup papaya): Calories: 328, Total Fat: 3.5 g, Sat. Fat: 1 g, Carbs: 57 g, Fiber: 9 g, Sugars: 7 g, Protein: 21 g, Sodium: 134 mg, Cholesterol: 37 mg

NUTRITIONAL BONUS: Papain, an enzyme found in papaya, is so effective at breaking down protein that it's used as both a digestive aid and a meat tenderizer. While many supplements include the enzyme, your best bet may be instead to enjoy a fresh, raw papaya.

Your (Easiest-Ever) Guide To Roasting

Turn to roasting for its laid-back, no-fuss attitude and the added benefit of rich, caramelized results. We know life is busy, so we're giving you a valuable shortcut to mealtime.

Are you ready to learn about one of the easiest cooking methods ever? Introducing: Roasting. You simply put food in a pan, put the pan in the oven and walk away, letting the heat do its job. And what a job it does!

Roasting is a slow, dry cooking method, making it best for foods that need more cooking time than a quick sauté allows or when you'd like to add delicious caramelized flavors through browning. Therefore, thick cuts of relatively tender meat are ideal for roasting. (Thick cuts of tough meat – a chuck roast, for example – need a wet cooking method, such as braising, to break down their sinews and make them tender.) But roasting can also work for smaller fare (think chicken breasts, fish fillets or sliced vegetables) as long as the heat is high enough to generate that browning on the outside before the food becomes overcooked on the inside.

Perhaps best of all, roasting doesn't require a lot of fuss or attention, which makes it great for entertaining – it gives you time to mingle and socialize with your guests. And the clean-up afterward is almost nothing to speak of. We'll toast to that!

ROASTING TIP #1

Use the right temperature. The larger the piece of food, the slower it needs to cook so the outside won't be overcooked by the time the inside is done. Smaller portions need a hotter oven so they can brown on the outside before the inside is overdone. What's so great about browning? It adds flavor, plus it keeps the outside of a roast from looking unappealingly pale.

During the week, all I do is roast because it's so easy and locks in maximum flavor!

This tent might protect you from rain, but it won't keep anything warm!

ROASTING TIP #2

Give it a rest. Letting meat rest before carving helps it retain its juices – that way, they end up in your mouth instead of on your cutting board. The larger the roasted item, the longer it needs to rest. A steak or chicken breast needs 5 to 10 minutes. A small roast, such as a pork tenderloin or a whole chicken, needs 10 to 15 minutes. A medium-sized roast, such as a beef tenderloin, pork loin or rack of lamb, needs 15 to 20 minutes. And a large roast, such as a prime rib or whole turkey, should rest for 20 to 30 minutes.

ROASTING TIP #3

Check the internal temperature. The best way to test for doneness is to measure the roast's internal temperature (it should be a minimum of 145°F and no higher than 170°F, depending on how well done you like your meat). And for that, you need an internal thermometer. Be sure to measure at the centermost point of the thickest part of the roast, avoiding any bones or pockets of fat.

Easily Cut & Serve
An Oven-Roasted Whole Fish

ONE: With the fish on a platter or work surface, use a knife to cut about halfway deep into the fish along the spine. Note that the spine runs head to tail about halfway between the belly and the back.

TWO: Use your knife, a fork or a soup spoon to gently scrape along the spine towards the back, removing the flesh in chunks. Transfer the flesh to plates. Use the same method to scrape off the flesh between the spine and the belly.

THREE: Gently lift the tail, using your knife, fork or spoon to separate the flesh so that it stays on the platter. Continue down the spine, separating it from the flesh and lifting away the tail, spine and head.

FOUR: Gently scrape away any fin bones along the belly or back. Transfer the remaining flesh to plates. Remind your guests to watch for any remaining bones.

Your Best Tools FOR ROASTING

Does the term "roasting" send you into a panic, scouring the back of your cupboards for your large turkey roasting pan and rack? Well, you won't need those here. Our roasting recipes call for kitchen multitaskers you undoubtedly already have on hand... and may have already used today!

LARGE RIMMED BAKING SHEET

Unlike cookie sheets, which are rimless for easy transferring, your rimmed baking sheet is a multi-purpose workhorse in the kitchen. Also known as sheet pans, jelly roll pans (typically 10 x 15 inches) or half-sheet pans (typically 18 x 13 inches) in restaurant supply stores, baking sheets should be of a heavy weight to avoid warping.

WOODEN SPOON

Whether using it to stir your fare as it browns before going into the oven or scraping up those flavorful browned bits from the bottom of your baking pan or sheet, a straight-edged wooden spoon does the trick. Alternatively, use a silicone or other heat-proof spoon or spatula.

LARGE OVENPROOF SKILLET

Sear your protein on the stove top for a browned crust, then finish it off with a roast in the oven – all in one pan! Look for skillets made of cast iron, copper or aluminum and that are marked "ovenproof" or "safe for broiler" to accommodate higher temperatures.

INSTANT-READ THERMOMETER

Available in analog (using a dial) or digital displays, these thermometers quickly gauge the internal temperature of roasted proteins to indicate doneness. Simply insert into the thickest part of the food, avoiding bone or pockets of fat. TIP: Sanitize the thermometer's needle after each use to avoid cross-contamination.

149

Summer Squash Pasta p.204

Main Courses: Poultry

Curried Buttermilk Chicken &
Grilled Pineapple, p. 155

As the perfect source of lean protein, chicken and turkey are your go-to meats. Let us help make them more interesting and flavorful! Feast on succulent Maple-Simmered Chicken with Cranberries & Mashed Butternut Squash. Or if you're strapped for time, enjoy kid-friendly *Clean Eating* favorites like clean Chicken Fingers and easy-to-make Spicy Chicken Burgers. Don't forget the turkey! A comforting classic, Turkey Chili & Squash Lasagna is sure to have your family piping up for seconds!

Chicken Fingers
WITH RANCH-STYLE DIPPING SAUCE

Serves 4 to 6. **Hands-on time:** *15 minutes.* **Total time:** *15 minutes.*

Your kids can still enjoy their favorite fun finger food without the deep-fried fats that normally accompany this dish. Quick and easy to make, you can fit this meal in between homework and soccer practice.

INGREDIENTS:

- Olive oil cooking spray
- 6 oz baked multigrain tortilla chips
- ¼ cup raw pumpkin seeds (aka pepitas)
- 1 tsp ground coriander
- ¼ cup light olive oil mayonnaise
- ¼ cup skim milk
- 1 tsp hot sauce
- Sea salt and fresh ground black pepper, to taste
- 4 4-oz boneless, skinless chicken breasts, sliced into ½-inch-thick strips
- 10 oz mixed green and yellow wax beans, trimmed
- 1 orange or red bell pepper, cut into strips

DIPPING SAUCE

- ⅓ cup low-fat sour cream
- 3 Tbsp light olive oil mayonnaise
- 1 tsp white or red wine vinegar
- ½ tsp hot sauce
- ¼ tsp dried basil
- 1 green onion, thinly sliced

INSTRUCTIONS:

ONE: Preheat oven to 450°F. Line a large baking sheet with foil and mist with cooking spray.

TWO: In the bowl of a food processor, grind tortilla chips, pumpkin seeds and coriander into crumbs. (Mixture should yield 1¾ cups crumbs.) Transfer to a large bowl.

THREE: In a separate large bowl, whisk ¼ cup mayonnaise, milk, 1 tsp hot sauce, salt and black pepper. Add chicken and toss to coat. Remove chicken and shake strips to remove excess liquid; toss chicken in crumb mixture, pressing crumbs into each piece to coat. Arrange chicken on sheet and mist tops with cooking spray. Bake, turning once, until chicken is crisp and no longer pink inside, about 12 minutes.

FOUR: Meanwhile, fit a steamer basket over a pot of boiling water. Place beans in basket and cook until tender-crisp, about 4 minutes. Transfer to a colander and rinse under cold water to chill. Set aside.

FIVE: Prepare dipping sauce: In a medium bowl, combine sour cream, 3 Tbsp mayonnaise, vinegar, ½ tsp hot sauce and basil; stir in green onion. Serve chicken with beans, bell pepper and dipping sauce on the side.

Nutrients per serving (4 chicken strips, 3 oz vegetables, 2 Tbsp dipping sauce; based on 6 servings): *Calories: 354, Total Fat: 14 g, Sat. Fat: 3 g, Monounsaturated Fat: 3 g, Polyunsaturated Fat: 4 g, Carbs: 30 g, Fiber: 4 g, Sugars: 2 g, Protein: 25 g, Sodium: 356 mg, Cholesterol: 55 mg*

Jamaican
Jerk Chicken

Nutritional Bonus:
Chicken breast is an excellent source of vitamin K2. Similar to vitamin B, vitamin K is actually a group of vitamins – K1 and K2. A number of studies have revealed that K2, which is harder to source than K1, is the most powerful of the set, particularly when it comes to heart and bone health. Its ability to regulate calcium in the body may reduce buildup in your arteries while ensuring your bones have a sufficient supply to stay healthy and strong.

Jamaican Jerk Chicken
WITH SPICY TURNIP GREENS & BLACK-EYED PEAS

*Serves 4. **Hands-on time:** 25 minutes. **Total time:** 25 minutes.*

Jerk chicken is traditionally made with a good helping of Scotch bonnet chile peppers, but we've toned down the heat for those who are faint of tongue. If you prefer a spicier version, add more cayenne pepper or even a minced, seeded jalapeño to the spice blend.

INGREDIENTS:

- 1 tsp dried thyme
- ¼ tsp sea salt
- 1 tsp ground ginger
- ¼ tsp ground allspice
- ¼ tsp ground cayenne pepper, divided, plus additional for garnish
- 2 tsp extra-virgin olive oil
- 1 lb boneless, skinless chicken breast, trimmed of visible fat
- 5 cloves garlic, minced
- 1 Spanish onion, chopped
- ¾ lb turnip greens, coarsely chopped
- 1 15-oz can BPA-free can black eyed peas, drained, not rinsed
- ½ cup 2% plain Greek yogurt, optional

INSTRUCTIONS:

ONE: Prepare spice blend: In a small bowl, combine thyme, salt, ginger, allspice and ⅛ tsp cayenne.

TWO: In a large nonstick skillet, heat oil on medium for 1 minute. Rub chicken with spice blend and add to skillet with garlic; cook for 10 minutes per side, until cooked through. Using a slotted spatula, transfer chicken to a plate and cover to keep warm.

THREE: Add onion to skillet and cook for 5 minutes, stirring occasionally. Add remaining ⅛ tsp cayenne and greens and cook for 3 more minutes, constantly stirring greens to wilt evenly. Stir in peas and cook for 1 minute.

FOUR: Cut chicken into ½-inch wide x 3-inch long strips. Serve chicken with greens mixture, dividing evenly. Garnish greens with yogurt and additional cayenne, if desired.

Nutrients per serving (3 oz chicken and ¾ cup greens mixture): *Calories: 280, Total Fat: 7 g, Sat. Fat: 1.5 g, Monounsaturated Fat: 3 g, Polyunsaturated Fat: 1 g, Carbs: 25 g, Fiber: 7 g, Sugars: 4 g, Protein: 33 g, Sodium: 240 mg, Cholesterol: 65 mg*

Curried Buttermilk Chicken & Grilled Pineapple

*Serves 4. **Hands-on time:** 20 minutes. **Total time:** 35 minutes (plus marinating time).*

Savory, sweet and brimming with Indian flavors and aromas, this moist chicken can also be topped with fresh mango salsa or diced grilled peppers instead of coconut. And, if you (somehow!) have leftovers, try them in a curried chicken salad the next day.

INGREDIENTS:

- 4 6-oz boneless, skinless chicken breasts
- 1½ cups Curried Buttermilk Marinade (see recipe, p. 234)
- ½ cup unsweetened coconut flakes
- High-heat cooking oil (such as sunflower, safflower, peanut or grape seed oil), as needed
- 4 crosswise slices pineapple (aka rounds), about ½-inch thick, trimmed
- 1 tsp curry powder
- 4 sprigs fresh cilantro

INSTRUCTIONS:

ONE: Place chicken in a large zip-top bag. Add Curried Buttermilk Marinade and seal, squeezing out as much air as possible. Refrigerate for 2 to 6 hours, turning occasionally.

TWO: Meanwhile, in a small nonstick skillet, heat coconut on medium until lightly browned, stirring occasionally, about 3 minutes. Transfer to a plate to cool.

THREE: Heat grill on medium-high and lightly oil grate. Remove chicken from marinade, pat dry with paper towel and grill until cooked through, about 3 minutes per side. Meanwhile, sprinkle both sides of pineapple with curry and grill until lightly charred, about 2 minutes per side. Transfer chicken and pineapple to a platter and loosely cover with foil. Let rest for 5 minutes.

FOUR: To serve, arrange pineapple slices on a large serving platter or each of 4 plates and top with chicken, coconut and cilantro.

Nutrients per serving (1 chicken breast, 1 pineapple slice, 2 Tbsp coconut): *Calories: 298, Total Fat: 9 g, Sat. Fat: 6 g, Carbs: 11 g, Fiber: 2 g, Sugars: 7 g, Protein: 41 g, Sodium: 119 mg, Cholesterol: 98 mg*

NUTRITIONAL BONUS: Although selenium may contribute to your thyroid health, you only need a small amount of the trace mineral – no more than 400 mcg (micrograms) per day for adults. Dig into 1 serving of our tropical chicken dish and you'll meet almost 45% of your daily need.

Quesadilla Casserole

*Serves 6. **Hands-on time:** 5 minutes. **Total time:** 1 hour, 10 minutes.*

Get a load of this oversized version of your favorite Mexican snack! Chock full of hearty black beans and chunks of chicken, this casserole is a protein-packed paradise!

INGREDIENTS:

- 2 4-oz boneless, skinless chicken breasts
- 2 small whole-wheat tortillas, cut into ½-inch strips
- ½ Tbsp olive oil
- 2 cups frozen corn, thawed
- 1 15-oz BPA-free can black beans, drained and rinsed well
- ½ cup low-sodium, all-natural barbecue sauce (no more than 7 to 10 g carbs and 1 g fat per 2-Tbsp serving)
- ½ cup shredded low-fat cheddar cheese

INSTRUCTIONS:

ONE: Preheat oven to 425°F.

TWO: In a large pot, bring 2 qt water to a boil. Add chicken, reduce heat to medium-low, cover and cook for 15 to 20 minutes, until no longer pink. Transfer chicken to a plate to cool.

THREE: Meanwhile, place tortilla strips on a large baking sheet. Drizzle with oil, toss and spread in a single layer. Bake for 15 to 20 minutes, until crispy, tossing halfway through; set aside to cool. Reduce oven temperature to 350°F.

FOUR: Shred chicken with a fork. In a 10-inch square casserole dish, combine chicken, corn, beans and barbecue sauce. Spread mixture in an even layer. Transfer dish to oven and bake for 25 minutes. Remove from oven, top with tortilla strips and cheese and bake for 5 to 10 more minutes until brown and bubbly and cheese is melted. Serve immediately.

Nutrients per 1-cup serving: Calories: 254, Total Fat: 4 g, Sat. Fat: 1 g, Carbs: 36 g, Fiber: 5 g, Sugars: 6 g, Protein: 18 g, Sodium: 178 mg, Cholesterol: 24 mg

NUTRITIONAL BONUS: The dark-hued coating on black beans is a very rich source of 3 anthocyanin flavonoids: delphiniden, petunidin and malvidin. These 3 antioxidants boast many benefits, but a few of their properties are anti-inflammatory, free radical fighting and muscle repairing, respectively.

Chicken Enchiladas
WITH SALSA VERDE

*Serves 6. **Hands-on time:** 55 minutes. **Total time:** 1 hour, 20 minutes.*

You can make these enchiladas through Step Three up to one day in advance. Cover and refrigerate the cooked chiles and salsa separately.

INGREDIENTS:

- Olive oil cooking spray
- 2 poblano or pasilla chiles, halved lengthwise, cored and seeded
- 1 lb tomatillos (about 8 medium), husked, rinsed and quartered
- 1 cup thinly sliced white onion, divided
- ¾ cup coarsely chopped fresh cilantro, divided
- 3 cloves garlic
- ½ tsp fine sea salt, or more to taste
- 12 6-inch corn tortillas, divided
- 3 cups shredded cooked chicken breast (about 2 small skinless breasts), divided
- 3 cups romaine lettuce, finely shredded
- ½ cup tomato, chopped
- ½ cup crumbled queso fresco

INSTRUCTIONS:

ONE: Preheat broiler and arrange a rack about 6 inches from heat element. Line a large rimmed baking sheet with foil and mist with cooking spray. Arrange chiles on baking sheet cut side down and broil until they begin to soften and blacken, about 10 minutes (check occasionally to avoid burning). Set aside until cool enough to handle.

TWO: Meanwhile, in a medium saucepan on medium-high heat, combine tomatillos and enough water to cover. Bring to a boil, then reduce to a simmer and cook until tomatillos are tender, about 3 minutes. Drain, reserving cooking liquid.

THREE: Prepare salsa verde: In a blender, add ¼ cup reserved cooking liquid, ¼ cup onion, ½ cup cilantro, garlic and salt and process to coarsely chop. Add tomatillos, a few at a time, along with additional cooking water as needed to make a medium-bodied sauce. Season with additional salt, if desired. Transfer sauce to a shallow bowl.

FOUR: Preheat oven to 350°F. Mist a 9 x 13 x 2-inch baking pan with cooking spray. Peel or rub charred skin from chiles. Cut chiles crosswise into thin slices. Heat a small nonstick skillet on medium. Add 1 tortilla and cook until soft and pliable, 15 to 30 seconds per side. Immerse warmed tortilla in salsa verde to coat, then transfer to prepared baking pan. Arrange a scant ¼ cup chicken down center of tortilla. Top with a few chile slices and some onion. Roll up tortilla, enclosing filling, and place seam side down. Repeat with remaining tortillas, chicken, chiles and all but ¼ cup onion. Spoon remaining salsa verde over enchiladas.

FIVE: Bake enchiladas until heated through, about 20 minutes. Meanwhile, divide lettuce among 6 plates. Top with tomato, queso fresco, remaining ¼ cup onion and remaining ¼ cup cilantro, dividing evenly. Serve alongside warm enchiladas.

Nutrients per serving (2 enchiladas plus salad): Calories: 315, Total Fat: 7 g, Sat. Fat: 2 g, Carbs: 37 g, Fiber: 7 g, Sugars: 5 g, Protein: 29 g, Sodium: 251 mg, Cholesterol: 366 mg

Chicken Enchiladas

Nutritional Bonus:
Largely because of the poblanos, these enchiladas are a great source of vitamin C – a single serving provides 33% of your daily need. Serving the enchiladas with romaine instead of iceberg lettuce provides nearly twice the vitamin K and almost 5 times the vitamin A.

Kung Pao
Chicken

Kung Pao Chicken

Serves 4. **Hands-on time:** *40 minutes.* **Total time:** *50 minutes.*

Ideally, wear rubber gloves when handling chiles. Their heat can transfer to your fingers, which can make wiping your eyes or nose a painful experience. And note that you probably don't want to eat the chiles on their own – they infuse the dish with great flavor, but a bite of one will likely be too much of a good thing.

INGREDIENTS:

- 1 cup long-grain brown rice
- 3 Tbsp low-sodium soy sauce, divided
- 1 tsp aji-mirin (Japanese rice wine)
- 12 oz boneless, skinless chicken breasts, cut into ¾-inch dice
- ½ cup low-sodium chicken broth
- ¼ cup Chinese black vinegar or balsamic vinegar
- 4½ tsp arrowroot
- 1 tsp organic evaporated cane juice
- 1 tsp toasted sesame oil
- 1 Tbsp peanut, safflower or sunflower oil
- 6 to 10 small dried red chiles (preferably Szechuan chiles), halved crosswise and seeded
- 2 tsp whole Szechuan peppercorns
- 1 large red bell pepper, cut into ¾-inch dice
- 6 scallions, white and light green parts only, cut into ¾-inch pieces
- 6 cloves garlic, thinly sliced
- 1 1-inch piece fresh ginger, peeled and thinly sliced
- 2 Tbsp roasted unsalted peanuts

INSTRUCTIONS:

ONE: Prepare rice according to package directions.

TWO: Meanwhile, in a medium bowl, combine 1 Tbsp soy sauce and aji-mirin. Stir in chicken and set aside at room temperature.

THREE: In a small bowl, combine broth, vinegar, 2 Tbsp water, arrowroot, cane juice, sesame oil and remaining 2 Tbsp soy sauce. Set aside.

FOUR: When rice is about 10 minutes from being done, heat peanut oil in a large wok or skillet on high. Add chiles and peppercorns and cook, stirring almost constantly, until fragrant, about 1 minute. Add chicken mixture, spreading chicken in a single layer in wok, and cook undisturbed for 1 minute. Then stir chicken constantly for 1 minute.

FIVE: Add bell pepper, scallions, garlic and ginger and cook, stirring frequently, until bell pepper begins to soften, about 1 minute. Add broth-vinegar mixture and stir until sauce thickens, about 1 minute. Stir in peanuts. Serve chicken mixture over rice, dividing evenly.

Nutrients per serving (1 cup chicken mixture and ¾ cup rice): Calories: 410, Total Fat: 9 g, Sat. Fat: 1.5 g, Monounsaturated Fat: 4 g, Polyunsaturated Fat: 3 g, Carbs: 51 g, Fiber: 4 g, Sugars: 6 g, Protein: 27 g, Sodium: 372 mg, Cholesterol: 51 mg

Ginger Soy Chicken & Edamame Stir-Fry
WITH CASHEWS

Serves 6. **Hands-on time:** *15 minutes.* **Total time:** *24 minutes.*

Most stir-fry sauces are thickened with cornstarch, but we opted for a bit of all-natural almond butter to give this quick and colorful version its texture. If you'd like to bulk up the blend even further, try tossing in a handful of cubed firm tofu or cooked shrimp during its final few minutes on the stove top.

INGREDIENTS:

- ½ cup low-sodium chicken broth
- ¼ cup low-sodium soy sauce
- 3 Tbsp unsalted almond or cashew butter
- 1 Tbsp grated fresh ginger
- 2 tsp raw honey
- 1 tsp dry mustard
- 1 Tbsp safflower oil, divided
- 1 lb boneless, skinless chicken breast, cut into 1-inch pieces
- 3 cloves garlic, minced
- 1 medium red bell pepper, cut into 1-inch chunks (about 1 cup)
- ⅔ cup unsalted raw cashews
- 1 cup frozen shelled edamame, thawed
- 4 green onions, cut into 2-inch lengths
- 1½ cups cooked brown rice, optional

INSTRUCTIONS:

ONE: In a medium bowl, whisk broth with soy sauce, almond butter, ginger, honey and mustard. Set aside.

TWO: In a large nonstick wok or skillet on medium-high, heat ½ Tbsp oil. Add chicken and garlic and cook until chicken is browned and cooked through, about 3 minutes. Transfer to a small bowl; heat remaining ½ Tbsp oil in wok. Add pepper, cashews and edamame and cook for 3 minutes.

THREE: Return chicken to wok. Add onions and sauce. Bring to a boil on medium-high, then reduce heat to medium-low and cook until thickened, about 2 minutes. Serve stir-fry over rice, if desired.

Nutrients per 1¼-cup serving (not including rice): Calories: 263, Total Fat: 13 g, Sat. Fat: 1.5 g, Monounsaturated Fat: 7 g, Polyunsaturated Fat: 4 g, Carbs: 12 g, Fiber: 2 g, Sugars: 4 g, Protein: 24 g, Sodium: 409 mg, Cholesterol: 44 mg

Five-Spice Chicken
WITH FRESH PLUM SAUCE

*Serves 4. **Hands-on time:** 45 minutes. **Total time:** 1 hour.*

Available in many skin colors, plums offer a sweet-tart flavor at thier peak time of year. If you only ever think to eat the juicy stone fruit out of hand, consider this: Plums are equally as delicious when paired with savory recipes or an array of warm and sweet spices.

INGREDIENTS:

SAUCE

- 3 firm plums
- 1 tsp safflower oil
- 2 tsp chopped fresh ginger
- 2 cloves garlic, chopped
- 1 cup low-sodium chicken broth
- ¼ tsp Chinese five-spice powder
- 1 Tbsp raw honey

CHICKEN

- ¼ cup sliced unsalted almonds
- 2 tsp Chinese five-spice powder

- 4 6-oz boneless, skinless chicken breasts
- Sea salt and fresh ground black pepper, taste
- 2 tsp safflower oil

RABE

- 1 large bunch broccoli rabe, trimmed (about 1 lb)
- Zest 1 orange
- 2 Tbsp fresh orange juice
- 1½ tsp sesame oil
- 2 Tbsp sliced unsalted almonds, toasted
- Sea salt and fresh ground black pepper, to taste

INSTRUCTIONS:

ONE: Prepare sauce: Cut plums in half. Remove pits and cut each half into 4 slices. In a medium saucepan, heat oil on medium. Add plums and ginger. Cook, stirring frequently, until plums begin to brown slightly, 3 to 4 minutes. Add garlic and cook, stirring often, for 2 minutes. Add broth and five-spice powder, cover and simmer for 4 minutes. Uncover and continue to cook at a steady simmer until liquid reduces by about two thirds and plums are soft. Stir in honey and continue simmering until sauce thickens slightly, about 2 minutes. (Sauce can be made up to 1 day in advance and refrigerated. Reheat on stovetop on low.)

TWO: Prepare chicken: Preheat oven to 400°F. Place almonds in a heavy duty zip-top bag and crush with a rolling pin to make fine crumbs. Add five-spice powder and shake to combine. Season both sides of chicken with salt and pepper. With a spoon, sprinkle half of almond mixture over chicken and lightly press into meat to help almonds adhere. Flip chicken over and repeat with remaining almond mixture on opposite side.

THREE: Heat oil in a large oven-safe skillet on medium-high. Add chicken and cook, without moving, until golden brown on bottom, about 5 minutes. Flip over and repeat on opposite side. Transfer skillet to oven and roast until thickest part of chicken is no longer pink and temperature reaches 170°F on an instant-read thermometer, 10 to 15 minutes.

FOUR: Meanwhile, prepare rabe: Add about 2 inches water to a large saucepan and fit with a steaming rack. Cover and bring water to a boil. Add broccoli rabe, cover and reduce heat to medium. Steam until broccoli rabe is tender, 6 to 8 minutes. Transfer to a large bowl. Add orange zest and juice, oil and almonds. Season with salt and pepper; toss to combine. Place 1 chicken breast on each of 4 plates. Top each with about ⅓ cup plum sauce and serve broccoli rabe on the side, dividing evenly.

Nutrients per serving (1 chicken breast, ⅓ cup plum sauce, ⅔ cup rabe): *Calories: 402, Total Fat: 15 g, Sat. Fat: 2 g, Monounsaturated Fat: 8 g, Polyunsaturated Fat: 4 g, Carbs: 21 g, Fiber: 2 g, Sugars: 11 g, Protein: 48 g, Sodium: 223 mg, Cholesterol: 99 mg*

Chicken Marsala

*Serves 2. **Hands-on time:** 20 minutes. **Total time:** 1 hour.*

If you're tired of the same old baked chicken, this recipe will really make your poultry pop! Using apple juice instead of wine, plus the added zing of parsley, subtly sweetens this Franco-Italian meal.

INGREDIENTS:

- ¼ cup whole-wheat flour or brown-rice flour
- 1 tsp dried oregano
- ⅛ tsp ground black pepper
- 2 5-oz boneless, skinless chicken breasts, pounded ¼-inch thick
- 1 Tbsp olive oil
- 4 cups chopped shiitake or cremini mushrooms (5 oz)
- 2 cups 100% apple juice
- 2 Tbsp chopped fresh parsley

TIP: Opt for brown-rice flour and this chicken dinner becomes gluten free!

INSTRUCTIONS:

ONE: In a small bowl, combine flour, oregano and pepper. Spread on a plate; dredge chicken through mixture to coat. Set aside.

TWO: In a large skillet, heat oil on medium. Add mushrooms and sauté until soft, about 5 minutes. Remove from skillet and set aside on a plate.

THREE: Add chicken to skillet and brown on medium heat for about 5 minutes per side. (Add ¼ cup water if needed to prevent chicken from sticking to pan.) Remove chicken and transfer to a plate. Add ¼ cup apple juice and deglaze skillet by scraping any browned bits from bottom with a wooden spoon. Increase heat to medium-high; add parsley and remaining 1¾ cups apple juice and cook until juice is reduced by half, about 20 minutes. Return chicken and mushrooms to skillet and cook for 5 more minutes, until heated through.

Nutrients per serving (4½ oz chicken, ½ cup mushrooms, ½ cup sauce): *Calories: 370, Total Fat: 11 g, Sat. Fat: 2 g, Monounsaturated Fat: 7 g, Polyunsaturated Fat: 2 g, Carbs: 33 g, Fiber: 3 g, Sugars: 17 g, Protein: 35 g, Sodium: 95 mg, Cholesterol: 80 mg*

Chicken Cabbage Pad Thai

Serves 2. **Hands-on time:** *10 minutes*. **Total time:** *10 minutes*.

Pad Thai in 10 minutes! No more waiting for water to boil; use shredded cabbage instead! It's quick, easy and cuts out extra carbs found in traditional noodles.

INGREDIENTS:

- 1 tsp safflower oil
- 10 oz firm tofu, drained and crumbled
- 3 cups thinly sliced cabbage
- 1 medium carrot, peeled and shredded
- 4 scallions, cut into ¾-inch pieces
- 2 large egg whites
- 1 tsp low-sodium tamari
- 1 tsp Thai red curry paste
- 4 oz cooked boneless, skinless chicken breast, cut into 1-inch chunks

INSTRUCTIONS:

ONE: Heat a large nonstick or well-seasoned cast-iron skillet on high. Add oil and swirl to coat skillet. Add tofu, cabbage, carrot and scallions and stir to combine.

TWO: In a small bowl, whisk egg whites, tamari and curry paste.

THREE: Stir tofu mixture, scraping bottom of pan with a sturdy spoon, until tofu is firm and starts to turn golden in spots, about 5 minutes.

FOUR: Add chicken to skillet and toss. Pour egg mixture over top and stir, cooking until egg is set, about 2 minutes. Serve warm.

Nutrients per 2-cup serving: *Calories: 303, Total Fat: 11 g, Sat. Fat: 1.5 g, Monounsaturated Fat: 4 g, Polyunsaturated Fat: 5 g, Carbs: 15 g, Fiber: 5 g, Sugars: 3 g, Protein: 37 g, Sodium: 450 mg, Cholesterol: 48 mg*

NUTRITIONAL BONUS: Cabbage, the inexpensive and easy-to-grow staple, is an antioxidant superstar. The humble leaves carry a symphony of phytochemicals, including indoles that help the body detoxify and fight free radicals. Studies associate eating cabbage and other cruciferous veggies (such as kale, Brussels sprouts, broccoli and turnips) with a reduced risk of several types of cancer.

Eggplant
& Sausage
Linguine

162

Nutritional Bonus:
You can still have savory Italian
sausage without blowing your
calorie budget. Just make sure
it's the fresh, lean turkey variety, which is lower in fat and sodium than traditional links, and
keep portions small – we used 2
oz per person. In addition, this
hearty pasta's eggplant helps
provide a boost in potassium
(22% DV), an electrolyte that
helps regulate muscle and
heart function.

Eggplant & Sausage Linguine

Serves 4. ***Hands-on time:*** *45 minutes.* ***Total time:*** *55 minutes.*

Native to southern India, eggplant is frequently used in vegetarian soups and curries. The vegetable's English name came from the first cultivated plants that bore round, whitish fruit that resembled eggs. The large purple variety is known as Italian eggplant, while the smaller, slender ones are called Japanese eggplant.

INGREDIENTS:

- Olive oil cooking spray
- 1¼ lb eggplant, cut into ¾-inch cubes
- Fresh ground black pepper, to taste
- 8 oz whole-wheat linguine
- ½ onion, chopped
- 8 oz deli-fresh, all-natural turkey sausage, casing cut open and meat crumbled
- ½ tsp dried oregano
- ¼ tsp red pepper flakes
- 2 cloves garlic, chopped
- 1½ cups chopped tomatoes
- ¼ cup unsweetened golden raisins
- 1 Tbsp capers, rinsed and drained
- 2 Tbsp red wine vinegar
- ⅓ packed cup chopped parsley
- Sea salt, to taste, optional
- ½ cup low-fat ricotta cheese

INSTRUCTIONS:

ONE: Preheat oven to 400°F. Coat a rimmed baking sheet with cooking spray; add eggplant in a single layer. Coat eggplant with cooking spray and season with black pepper. Bake for 20 to 25 minutes, until tender and lightly browned, stirring once or twice. Remove from oven and set aside.

TWO: Meanwhile, cook linguine according to package directions. Drain and set aside.

THREE: Coat a large skillet with cooking spray and heat on medium-high. Add onion and sausage and cook, stirring frequently, until sausage is cooked through, about 8 minutes. Add oregano, red pepper flakes and garlic and cook for 1 more minute. Add tomatoes and bring to a simmer, then reduce heat to medium. Stir in eggplant, raisins and capers and simmer until thickened slightly, 5 to 7 minutes. Stir in vinegar and all but 1 Tbsp parsley. If desired, season with salt and black pepper.

FOUR: Return linguine to pot it was cooked in and place on low heat. Immediately add eggplant-sausage mixture and mix well. Divide among 4 bowls and top each with 2 Tbsp ricotta. Sprinkle evenly with remaining 1 Tbsp parsley and serve.

Nutrients per serving (1½ cups pasta and 2 Tbsp ricotta): *Calories: 385, Total Fat: 7 g, Sat. Fat: 2 g, Monounsaturated Fat: 1.5 g, Polyunsaturated Fat: 1.5 g, Carbs: 64 g, Fiber: 13 g, Sugars: 14 g, Protein: 23 g, Sodium: 486 mg, Cholesterol: 48 mg*

Creole Chicken & Okra
WITH PARSLEY RICE

Serves 4. ***Hands-on time:*** *8 minutes.* ***Total time:*** *20 minutes.*

Creole dishes are slow simmered, which, unfortunately, translates to a loss of vitamins, minerals and antioxidants throughout the long cooking process. In order to minimize nutrient depletion and help your vegetables retain their texture, we kept the stovetop time for our chicken and okra brief.

INGREDIENTS

- Olive oil cooking spray
- 2 6-oz boneless, skinless chicken breasts, rinsed and patted dry, cut into bite-size pieces
- 2 Tbsp olive oil, divided
- ½ cup diced onion
- ½ green bell pepper, chopped
- 2 cloves garlic, minced
- 5 oz grape tomatoes, halved (1 cup)
- ½ cup fresh chopped or frozen cut okra (thawed, if frozen)
- ½ tsp dried thyme
- 2 dried bay leaves
- 1 Tbsp Louisiana hot sauce
- ½ tsp sea salt
- ½ cup chopped fresh parsley, divided
- 2 cups cooked brown rice

INSTRUCTIONS:

ONE: Heat a large nonstick skillet on medium-high. Coat skillet with cooking spray, add chicken and cook for 2 minutes or until chicken is almost cooked through, stirring frequently. Remove chicken from skillet and set aside on a separate plate.

TWO: Return skillet to medium-high and heat 1 Tbsp oil. Add onion and pepper and cook for 4 minutes or until beginning to lightly brown, stirring frequently. Add garlic and cook for 15 seconds, stirring constantly. Add ½ cup water, tomatoes, okra, thyme and bay leaves. Reduce heat to medium-low, cover and simmer for 10 minutes or until okra is just tender. Remove from heat, stir in hot sauce, salt, remaining 1 Tbsp oil and ¼ cup parsley. Add chicken, stir to blend, cover and let stand for 5 minutes to absorb flavors and heat chicken thoroughly.

THREE: Toss rice with remaining ¼ cup parsley and serve chicken mixture over top.

Nutrients per serving (¾ cup chicken mixture and ½ cup rice): *Calories: 294, Total Fat: 9 g, Sat. Fat: 1.5 g, Monounsaturated Fat: 6 g, Polyunsaturated Fat: 1 g, Carbs: 28 g, Fiber: 4 g, Sugars: 2 g, Protein: 23 g, Sodium: 310 mg, Cholesterol: 49 mg*

Maple-Simmered Chicken
WITH CRANBERRIES & MASHED BUTTERNUT SQUASH

Serves 4. *Hands-on time:* 25 minutes. *Total time:* 35 minutes.

In this warm and decadent dish, sweet maple and buttery squash balance out tart cranberries. Simmering seasonal cranberries for 10 minutes before adding the chicken will release the pectin in the fruit, creating a naturally thickened, rich sauce.

INGREDIENTS:

- 1½ lb butternut squash, trimmed, peeled, seeded and cut into 1-inch cubes
- ¼ cup 2% plain Greek yogurt
- ¼ tsp sea salt
- ¼ cup pure maple syrup
- 8 oz fresh cranberries
- 1 tsp dried thyme, plus additional for garnish
- 1 lb boneless, skinless chicken breast, trimmed of visible fat

INSTRUCTIONS:

ONE: Fill a medium pot halfway with water and bring to a boil on high heat; reduce heat to medium. Add squash and simmer, partially covered, for 10 minutes. Drain well and return to pot. Add yogurt and salt and mash with a potato masher. Cover and set aside.

TWO: In a large nonstick skillet, add maple syrup, cranberries, thyme and ¼ cup water. Bring mixture to a boil on high heat; reduce to medium-low and gently simmer for 10 minutes. Using the back of a heatproof rubber spatula, mash cranberries until all are broken up.

THREE: Cut chicken into 4 equal pieces. Add chicken to cranberry mixture and cover skillet. Increase heat to medium and cook for 5 minutes. Flip chicken and cook for an additional 5 minutes. Cut into thickest piece of chicken to check for doneness; if still pink, flip chicken and cook for 2 more minutes or until chicken is opaque throughout. Divide chicken among serving plates and top each with 2 Tbsp cranberry mixture. Divide squash evenly between plates, and garnish with additional thyme.

Nutrients per serving (4 oz chicken, 2 Tbsp cranberry mixture, ½ cup squash): Calories: 290, Total Fat: 3 g, Sat. Fat: 1 g, Carbs: 41 g, Fiber: 6 g, Sugars: 21 g, Protein: 26 g, Sodium: 190 mg, Cholesterol: 65 mg

NUTRITIONAL BONUS: Brimming with antioxidants in their scarlet globules, cranberries are more than just a pretty garnish. Studies have linked the regular consumption of cranberries to higher levels of HDL and reduced levels of LDL (good and bad cholesterol, respectively). And they don't merely keep arterial plaque at bay: The berries also contain proanthocyanidins, plant polyphenols that may reduce plaque formation on your teeth!

Skillet Chicken
WITH TOMATOES, FENNEL & FRESH THYME

Serves 4. *Hands-on time:* 10 minutes. *Total time:* 25 minutes.

If your family's main complaint about boneless, skinless chicken breasts is that they're dry, then braising may be your answer! The slow-and-low technique keeps meat moist.

INGREDIENTS:

- 4 4-oz boneless, skinless chicken breasts
- Pinch sea salt
- ½ tsp fresh ground black pepper
- 1 Tbsp olive oil
- 1 yellow onion, diced
- 4 large cloves garlic, minced
- ¼ tsp crushed red pepper flakes, plus additional to taste
- 1 large fennel root, quartered, cored and thinly sliced crosswise
- 2 cups sliced cremini mushrooms
- 1¾ cups crushed tomatoes in purée (boxed or jarred)
- 2 tsp dried oregano
- 2 large sprigs fresh thyme
- ¼ cup chopped Kalamata olives, pitted, optional
- Fresh oregano leaves and minced flat-leaf parsley for garnish, optional

INSTRUCTIONS:

ONE: Pat chicken dry with paper towel and season with salt and black pepper. In a large braiser or heavy skillet, heat oil on medium-high. Add chicken and sear for 2 minutes per side, until lightly browned. Transfer to a plate and keep warm.

TWO: Reduce heat to medium, add onion and cook, stirring, until softened, about 3 minutes. Add garlic and red pepper flakes and cook for 1 minute, stirring. Stir in fennel, mushrooms, tomatoes, oregano and thyme. Return chicken to braiser, spooning vegetables and sauce over top. Cover and simmer for 12 to 15 minutes, until chicken's juices run clear and no pink remains. Remove and discard thyme.

THREE: Divide mixture evenly among serving plates. Top with olives, fresh oregano and parsley, if desired.

Nutrients per serving (1 chicken breast and 1¼ cups vegetable sauce): Calories: 260, Total Fat: 9 g, Sat. Fat: 1.5 g, Monounsaturated Fat: 5 g, Polyunsaturated Fat: 1 g, Carbs: 20 g, Fiber: 5 g, Sugars: 3 g, Protein: 27 g, Sodium: 380 mg, Cholesterol: 65 mg

Skillet
Chicken

Chicken
WITH SAUTÉED BLACKBERRY SAUCE & STEAMED POTATOES

*Serves 4. **Hands-on time:** 20 minutes. **Total time:** 35 minutes.*

This recipe uses a classic technique called deglazing, which is essentially the first step in making a sauce in the same pan following a sauté. In short, you add a little liquid, then use a gentle scrape of your spoon or spatula to release the skillet's browned bits into the liquid. Easy… and tasty!

INGREDIENTS:

- 1 lb small potatoes (white, red or a combination), scrubbed and halved
- 4 6-oz boneless, skinless chicken breasts
- ½ tsp each fine sea salt and fresh ground black pepper
- 2 Tbsp olive oil
- ⅓ cup chopped shallots
- 1 tsp chopped fresh rosemary
- 1 cup blackberries
- ½ cup 100% pomegranate or blueberry-pomegranate juice
- 2 scallions, white and light green parts only, thinly sliced

INSTRUCTIONS:

ONE: Fill a large pot with 1 inch of water and fit with a steamer basket. Place potatoes in steamer basket and bring water to a boil on high heat. Cover and cook until potatoes are tender, 10 to 15 minutes depending on size of potatoes.

TWO: Meanwhile, season chicken on both sides with salt and pepper. In a large skillet or sauté pan (not nonstick), heat oil on medium. Add chicken and cook for 6 minutes per side or until cooked through, cooking in batches if necessary. Transfer chicken to serving plates and let rest for 5 minutes.

THREE: Meanwhile, place same skillet on medium-high heat. Add shallots and rosemary and cook, stirring occasionally, until shallots are tender, about 1 minute. Stir in blackberries and pomegranate juice, deglazing pan by scraping up any browned bits from bottom of skillet with a heatproof spoon or spatula. Cook until liquid is reduced to a thin layer, 1 to 2 minutes. Remove from heat. Top chicken with berry mixture and arrange potatoes alongside, dividing evenly. Sprinkle potatoes with scallions and serve.

Nutrients per serving (1 chicken breast, 3 Tbsp berry sauce, 4 oz potatoes):
Calories: 388, Total Fat: 9 g, Sat. Fat: 1.5 g, Monounsaturated Fat: 6 g, Polyunsaturated Fat: 1 g, Carbs: 31 g, Fiber: 3 g, Sugars: 7 g, Protein: 43 g, Sodium: 363 mg, Cholesterol: 94 mg

How to Prep & Deglaze our Blackberry Sauce

ONE: In a large skillet or sauté pan (not nonstick), heat oil on medium. Add chicken and cook for 6 minutes per side or until cooked through. Transfer chicken to serving plates.

TWO: Place same skillet on medium-high heat. Add shallots and rosemary and cook, stirring occasionally, until shallots are tender, about 1 minute.

THREE: Stir in blackberries and pomegranate juice, deglazing pan by scraping up any browned bits from bottom of skillet with a heatproof spoon or spatula.

FOUR: Cook until liquid is reduced to a thin layer, 1 to 2 minutes.

Sweet Tomato Barbecue Chicken
WITH SLAW & GRILLED BREAD

*Serves 4. **Hands-on time:** 15 minutes. **Total time:** 45 minutes (includes chilling of slaw).*

Store-bought BBQ sauces are often bursting with sugars and empty calories. Your best bet is to make your own homemade blend (plus, tinker with our recipe and you can whip together your own signature secret sauce).

INGREDIENTS:

- Sprinkling fresh ground black pepper
- 4 4-oz boneless, skinless chicken breasts, pounded thin

SAUCE
- ¼ cup no-salt-added tomato paste
- 3 Tbsp balsamic vinegar
- 2 Tbsp pure maple syrup
- 2 tsp Worcestershire sauce
- 1 clove garlic, minced
- 1 tsp onion powder
- ½ tsp sea salt
- ⅛ to ¼ tsp red pepper flakes
- 2 tsp extra-virgin olive oil

SLAW
- 3 cups coleslaw with carrots
- ½ cup celery, thinly sliced

- 1 banana pepper, seeded and diced or ½ medium green bell pepper, seeded and diced
- 2 Tbsp apple cider vinegar
- 1 Tbsp safflower oil
- 1 stevia packet
- ⅛ tsp red pepper flakes
- ¼ tsp sea salt
- ¼ tsp fresh ground black pepper

BREAD
- 4 oz whole-grain or multigrain loaf bread, cut into 4 slices
- Olive oil cooking spray
- 2 cloves garlic, halved crosswise
- 2 tsp extra-virgin olive oil
- ½ tsp dried oregano

INSTRUCTIONS:

ONE: Prepare sauce: In a medium saucepan, whisk together ½ cup water, tomato paste, vinegar, maple syrup, Worcestershire, garlic, onion powder, salt and pepper flakes. Bring sauce to a boil on medium-high; continue boiling for 3 to 4 minutes or until mixture reduces to ½ cup. Remove from heat, stir in oil, divide sauce between 2 small bowls and let cool completely.

TWO: Meanwhile, prepare slaw: In a medium bowl, combine slaw ingredients, cover and refrigerate for at least 30 minutes.

THREE: Prepare bread: Preheat a grill or grill pan to medium-high. Lightly coat both sides of each bread slice with cooking spray and grill for 2 to 3 minutes per side or until golden. Remove bread from grill, gently rub top of each slice with garlic, brush or drizzle with oil and sprinkle with oregano, dividing evenly. Set aside.

FOUR: Sprinkle black pepper on both sides of chicken breasts. Place chicken on grill or grill pan and cook for 3 minutes on medium-high. Flip chicken over, brush 2 Tbsp sauce over top and cook for 3 minutes. Again, flip chicken over, brush with 2 Tbsp sauce and cook for 1 minute. Finally, flip chicken over and spoon remaining ¼ cup sauce over top. Cook for 1 more minute or until no longer pink in center. Serve with coleslaw and bread.

Nutrients per serving (3 oz chicken, ¾ cup coleslaw, 1 slice bread): Calories: 313, Total Fat: 11 g, Sat. Fat: 1.5 g, Monounsaturated Fat: 6 g, Polyunsaturated Fat: 2 g, Carbs: 24 g, Fiber: 5 g, Sugars: 7 g, Protein: 29 g, Sodium: 553 mg, Cholesterol: 58 mg

NOTE: **You may be tempted to flip the chicken only once or twice, but stick to the recipe: Not only does it keep the chicken from burning, but it also allows the sauce to adhere better and evenly.**

Nutritional Bonus:
If you're looking to maximize the health benefits of this meal, be sure to include the slaw. At only 22 calories per cup, the humble cabbage packs a nutrient-loaded punch that includes high levels of antioxidants, vitamin K and essential fatty acids. In a 2012 study in China, women whose consumption of cruciferous vegetables, including cabbage, was in the top 25th percentile were 62 percent less likely to die of breast cancer than those in the bottom 25 percent.

Mango
Mojito
Chicken

Southwest
Meatballs

Southwest Meatballs
WITH WARM CORN-BLACK BEAN SALSA

*Serves 4. **Hands-on time:** 15 minutes. **Total time:** 20 minutes.*

To ensure your meatballs boast their best flavor, create a caramelized crust by first searing them on all sides until they're golden brown. The colorful and hearty blend of black beans, corn, tomatoes, lime and cilantro enveloping the meatballs fills out this dish, plus it's a unique take on salsa: It's served warm!

INGREDIENTS:

- 1 lb ground turkey breast
- 2 large egg whites
- ¼ cup whole-wheat bread crumbs
- ¼ tsp sea salt
- ¼ tsp fresh ground black pepper
- 2 tsp olive oil
- 1 cup frozen yellow or white corn
- 1 15-oz BPA-free can low-sodium black beans, drained and rinsed well
- 2 cups diced vine-ripened tomatoes
- ½ cup low-sodium chicken broth
- 1 Tbsp fresh lime juice
- 1 tsp ground cumin
- ¼ cup chopped fresh cilantro

INSTRUCTIONS:

ONE: In a large bowl, combine turkey, egg whites, bread crumbs, salt and pepper and mix well. Shape into 16 meatballs, each about the size of a golf ball.

TWO: In a large skillet, heat oil on medium-high. Add meatballs and cook for 3 to 5 minutes, turning frequently, until browned on all sides. Add corn, beans, tomatoes, broth, lime juice and cumin and mix well. Reduce heat to medium, partially cover and cook for an additional 3 to 5 minutes, until meatballs are cooked through. Stir in cilantro and serve.

Nutrients per serving (4 meatballs and 1 cup corn-bean mixture): *Calories: 320, Total Fat: 4.5 g, Sat. Fat: 0 g, Carbs: 32 g, Fiber: 7 g, Sugars: 5 g, Protein: 37 g, Sodium: 340 mg, Cholesterol: 55 mg*

NUTRITIONAL BONUS: Protein is a clean eater's best friend, and with 37g per serving of this dish, we know you'll love the benefits. Consuming protein at each of your five or six meals throughout the day keeps you satisfied, keeps your blood sugar stable and keeps your metabolism burning at a steady rate throughout the day.

Mango Mojito Chicken

*Serves 4. **Hands-on time:** 15 minutes. **Total time:** 15 minutes.*

This spin-off of the classic rum-and-mint cocktail is sure to please your at-home brood and dinner guests alike. Instead of sweet rum, succulent mango creates a perfect balance of flavors when coupled with fresh mint and tangy lime. No highball glass required!

INGREDIENTS:

- 2 tsp olive oil
- 4 4-oz boneless, skinless chicken breasts
- ¼ tsp each sea salt and fresh ground black pepper
- 2 ripe mangos, pitted and diced
- 1 green bell pepper, chopped
- 1 cup low-sodium chicken broth
- ⅓ cup scallions, chopped
- 2 Tbsp fresh mint, chopped
- 1 Tbsp fresh lime juice
- 1 tsp finely grated lime zest
- 1 tsp finely grated garlic
- 2 cups cooked brown rice

INSTRUCTIONS:

ONE: In a large skillet, heat oil on medium-high. Season both sides of chicken with salt and black pepper. Add chicken to skillet and cook for 1 to 2 minutes per side, until golden brown.

TWO: Add mangos, bell pepper, broth, scallions, mint, lime juice, lime zest and garlic and bring to a simmer. Reduce heat to medium, partially cover and cook for 5 minutes, undisturbed, until chicken is cooked through. Add rice to skillet and stir to combine. Cook for 1 minute to heat through.

Nutrients per serving (1 chicken breast and 1 cup mango-rice mixture): *Calories: 340, Total Fat: 7 g, Sat. Fat: 1.5 g, Monounsaturated Fat: 3 g, Polyunsaturated Fat: 1 g, Carbs: 44 g, Fiber: 4 g, Sugars: 3 g, Protein: 27 g, Sodium: 200 mg, Cholesterol: 65 mg*

Grilled Chicken
WITH MANGO BARBECUE SAUCE

*Serves 6. **Hands-on time:** 1 hour. **Total time:** 1 hour, 15 minutes.*

Perfect for a sunny summer day, this zesty mango barbecue sauce really gives you an "on-the-island" taste. But you can enjoy this tropical barbecue dish in the comfort of your own backyard!

INGREDIENTS:

- 2 tsp olive oil
- 1 red onion, chopped
- ¾ tsp sea salt, divided
- 1 medium tomato, peeled, seeded and chopped
- 1 mango, peeled and cubed
- 2 Tbsp plus 1 tsp apple cider vinegar
- 1 Tbsp Sucanat
- 2 tsp Dijon mustard
- 6 4-oz boneless, skinless chicken breasts
- 1 lemon, halved
- Olive oil cooking spray
- ½ tsp fresh ground black pepper, divided

INSTRUCTIONS:

ONE: In a medium saucepan, heat oil on medium. Add onion and ¼ tsp salt and cook, stirring, until softened and lightly browned, 10 to 12 minutes. Stir in tomato, mango, vinegar, ¼ cup water, Sucanat and Dijon. Bring to a boil, then cover and reduce heat to low. Simmer, covered, for 15 minutes, stirring occasionally. Remove from heat and let cool slightly before processing in a blender or mini food processor until smooth. Pour ½ cup mango barbecue sauce into a bowl to brush on chicken while grilling. Reserve remaining sauce to serve at table. (Sauce can be made up to 1 day in advance and stored in a covered container in refrigerator.)

TWO: Preheat gas or charcoal grill to medium.

THREE: Rinse chicken breasts and pat dry with paper towels. Arrange in a single layer on a tray. Squeeze juice from half of lemon over chicken, then mist lightly with cooking spray. Sprinkle ¼ tsp salt and ¼ tsp pepper evenly over chicken. Flip chicken breasts over and repeat with remaining half of lemon, a mist of cooking spray and remaining ¼ tsp salt and ¼ tsp pepper.

FOUR: Grill chicken for about 15 minutes or until cooked through and no longer pink, flipping once. Brush with mango barbecue sauce during final 5 minutes of cooking. Let chicken rest for 10 minutes before serving. While chicken is resting, reheat remaining sauce. Serve chicken with sauce on the side.

Nutrients per serving (1 chicken breast with 2 Tbsp sauce): Calories: 186, Total Fat: 3 g, Sat. Fat: 1 g, Carbs: 12 g, Fiber: 1 g, Sugars: 8 g, Protein: 27 g, Sodium: 359 mg, Cholesterol: 66 mg

Spicy Chicken Burgers
WITH MANGO KETCHUP

*Serves 6. **Hands-on time:** 25 minutes. **Total time:** 45 minutes.*

Blending ketchup with mango creates a vibrant, sweet sauce you'll want to make again and again! Add a dash of cayenne to your custom condiment to mirror the heat in our alluringly crisp burgers.

INGREDIENTS:

- Olive oil cooking spray
- 6 4-oz boneless, skinless chicken breast cutlets
- 2 pinches sea salt, divided
- ¾ tsp fresh ground black pepper, divided
- ⅓ cup white whole-wheat flour
- 1 large egg
- 1 Tbsp 2% milk
- ¾ cup whole-wheat panko bread crumbs
- 1 tsp onion powder
- ¾ tsp ground cayenne pepper, plus additional to taste
- ½ tsp garlic powder
- ½ tsp dried thyme
- ½ tsp dried oregano
- ½ cup frozen mango chunks, thawed and drained
- ¼ cup organic ketchup
- 6 whole-grain sandwich buns, split
- 1 large red bell pepper, sliced into thin rings
- ½ cup jarred banana pepper rings (packed in water), drained
- 1½ cups baby arugula

INSTRUCTIONS:

ONE: Preheat oven to 375°F. Mist a large rimmed baking sheet with cooking spray. Season all sides of chicken with a pinch salt and ¼ tsp black pepper. In a shallow dish, add flour. In a separate shallow dish, lightly beat egg and milk. In a third shallow dish, combine panko, onion powder, cayenne, garlic powder, thyme, oregano and remaining pinch salt and ½ tsp black pepper.

TWO: Dredge chicken in flour, turning to coat and shaking off excess. Transfer to egg mixture, then press both sides into bread crumb mixture to coat thoroughly. Transfer to baking sheet and bake until cooked through, 18 to 22 minutes.

THREE: Meanwhile, prepare mango ketchup: In a food processor, process mango and ketchup, stopping to scrape down sides of bowl, until smooth. If desired, season with additional cayenne.

FOUR: Spread mango ketchup on bottom halves of buns. Sandwich chicken, bell pepper, banana pepper and arugula between buns.

Nutrients per serving (1 sandwich and 2 Tbsp mango ketchup): Calories: 340, Total Fat: 5 g, Sat. Fat: 1 g, Monounsaturated Fat: 1 g, Polyunsaturated Fat: 1 g, Carbs: 41 g, Fiber: 6 g, Sugars: 10 g, Protein: 34 g, Sodium: 490 mg, Cholesterol: 101 mg

Spicy
Chicken
Burgers

Yogurt & Herb Chicken
WITH CUCUMBER-LENTIL SALSA

*Serves 4. **Hands-on time:** 40 minutes. **Total time:** 40 minutes (plus marinating time).*

A creamy marinade of yogurt, fresh herbs and warm spices soaks into fast-cooking chicken cutlets, infusing them with flavor and moisture. French green (aka du Puy) lentils are ideal because they cook quickly and hold their shape, though brown lentils work well in a pinch.

INGREDIENTS:

- 4 cloves garlic, roughly chopped
- 1 1-inch piece fresh ginger, peeled and roughly chopped
- ½ white onion, roughly chopped
- 1⅓ cups roughly chopped mixed fresh herbs, divided, plus additional sprigs for garnish (BLEND TO TRY: Cilantro, dill, parsley, oregano, mint and/or basil)
- 2 tsp ground cumin, divided
- 2 tsp ground coriander, divided
- 1 tsp ground turmeric
- 1¼ cups low-fat plain yogurt, divided
- 4 5-oz boneless, skinless chicken breast cutlets, ¼-inch thick (TIP: Alternatively, pound regular chicken breasts ¼-inch thick)

- ¾ cup French green lentils (aka du Puy lentils), picked over and rinsed
- 1 Tbsp olive oil
- 2 carrots, peeled and finely chopped
- 1 red onion, finely chopped
- ¾ tsp sea salt, divided
- ¼ tsp fresh ground black pepper
- ½ field-grown cucumber, peeled, seeded and finely chopped
- 2 Roma tomatoes, finely chopped
- Juice 1 lemon
- Olive oil cooking spray
- Lime slices for garnish, optional

INSTRUCTIONS:

ONE: In a food processor, pulse garlic, ginger, white onion, half of fresh herbs and 1 tsp each cumin, coriander and turmeric until finely chopped. Add 1 cup yogurt and process until combined. Transfer mixture to a large heavy-duty zip-top bag. Add chicken to bag and massage bag to coat. Refrigerate, turning once or twice, for 4 to 24 hours.

TWO: In a medium saucepan, add lentils and enough water to cover by about 3 inches. Heat on high, cover and bring to a boil. Uncover, reduce heat to medium, and cook until tender but not mushy, 14 to 16 minutes. Drain and set aside.

THREE: Meanwhile, in a large skillet, heat oil on medium-low. Add carrots and red onion and sauté, stirring, until soft and light brown, 12 to 15 minutes. Stir in lentils, remaining 1 tsp each cumin and coriander, ¼ tsp salt and pepper. Sauté until heated through, about 4 minutes. Transfer to a large bowl and gently fold in cucumber, tomatoes, lemon juice and remaining half of fresh herbs.

FOUR: Arrange oven rack 8 to 10 inches from top heat source and preheat broiler to high. Line a large baking sheet or broiler pan with foil and mist with cooking spray. Remove chicken from marinade, scraping off excess, and transfer to sheet; discard marinade. Sprinkle chicken with remaining ½ tsp salt. Transfer to top rack and broil, turning once, until cooked through and edges are lightly browned, 10 to 14 minutes. Serve chicken with lentil mixture and top with remaining ¼ cup yogurt. If desired, garnish with lime.

Nutrients per serving (1 chicken breast, 1 cup lentil mixture, 1 Tbsp yogurt):
Calories: 407, Total Fat: 8 g, Sat. Fat: 2 g, Monounsaturated Fat: 3 g, Polyunsaturated Fat: 1 g, Carbs: 38 g, Fiber: 8.5 g, Sugars: 11 g, Protein: 46 g, Sodium: 542 mg, Cholesterol: 87 mg

175

Nutritional Bonus:
With all those fresh herbs, you can be sure this dish will be flavorful and full of nutrients – especially if you choose to include parsley. The activity of parsley's volatile oils qualifies it as chemoprotective and, in particular, a food that can help neutralize carcinogens. In animal studies, parsley's volatile oils have been shown to inhibit tumor formation, particularly in the lungs.

Chicken, Blackberry & Barley Toss
WITH YOGURT-THYME DRESSING

*Serves 4. **Hands-on time:** 20 minutes. **Total time:** 20 minutes.*

In this summertime dish, the sweet juiciness of the blackberries complements the rich herbed yogurt and hearty barley. And keep our Yogurt-Thyme Dressing in mind when preparing chicken or lamb – the topping works double duty as a marinade.

INGREDIENTS:
- 1 cup pearled barley
- ¼ cup 2% plain Greek yogurt
- ⅛ tsp sea salt
- 1 tsp raw honey
- 2 tsp dried thyme
- 1 Tbsp extra-virgin olive oil, divided
- 1 lb boneless, skinless chicken breast, cut into ¼-inch-thick strips
- 6 oz blackberries
- ¼ cup minced radish tops, rinsed well and patted dry, optional

OPTION: If you'd like to lighten up the taste of our grain salad even further, try 1 Tbsp dried mint in lieu of the thyme called for in this recipe. Look for the dried herb in the spice aisle of your local supermarket.

INSTRUCTIONS:

ONE: In a medium pot, bring 2 cups water to a boil. Add barley, cover and reduce heat to low. Simmer for 10 minutes, then check to see if barley has reached desired tenderness. If too chewy, cook for an additional 2 minutes and check again. Drain barley well and transfer to a large mixing bowl.

TWO: Meanwhile, prepare Yogurt-Thyme Dressing: In a small bowl, combine yogurt, salt, honey, thyme, 1 Tbsp water and 1½ tsp oil. Whisk with a fork and set aside.

THREE: In a large nonstick pan, heat remaining 1½ tsp oil on medium. Add chicken and cook for 5 to 6 minutes, occasionally flipping pieces over to ensure they cook evenly. When cooked through and lightly browned, use a slotted spoon to remove chicken and transfer it to bowl with barley.

FOUR: Add blackberries and Yogurt-Thyme Dressing to barley-chicken mixture and toss well. Garnish with radish tops, if desired.

Nutrients per 1½-cup serving: Calories: 373, Total Fat: 6 g, Sat. Fat: 1 g, Monounsaturated Fat: 3 g, Polyunsaturated Fat: 1 g, Carbs: 46 g, Fiber: 10 g, Sugars: 3 g, Protein: 32 g, Sodium: 112 mg, Cholesterol: 66 mg

Turkey & Butter Bean Cassoulet
Serves 4.

Feisty Chef Nadia G from the Cooking Channel's *Bitchin' Kitchen* offers *CE* readers this exclusive recipe for a saucy cassoulet.

INGREDIENTS:
- 2 Tbsp olive oil
- 4 6-oz skinless turkey legs
- Pinch paprika
- Fresh cracked black pepper, to taste
- ¼ tsp sea salt
- 5½ cups low-sodium chicken broth, divided
- 3½ cups crushed tomatoes, divided (TRY: San Marzano variety)
- 2 Tbsp pure maple syrup
- 2 large yellow onions, chopped
- 2 cloves garlic, minced
- 1 sprig fresh thyme
- ¼ cup flat-leaf parsley, chopped
- 1 bay leaf
- ½ cup cooked butter beans

INSTRUCTIONS:

ONE: Preheat oven to 325°F.

TWO: In a large nonstick pan, heat oil on medium-high. Add turkey legs and sprinkle with paprika, pepper and salt. Sear for 2 to 3 minutes per side, until golden.

THREE: In a 4-qt roasting pan, combine 4 cups broth, 2 cups tomatoes, maple syrup, onions, garlic, thyme, parsley, bay leaf and beans. Add turkey legs, cover with foil and cook in oven on middle rack for 2 hours. Every 30 minutes, add ½ cup broth and ½ cup tomatoes to pan. Remove roasting pan from oven and serve.

Nutrients per serving (6 oz turkey and 1 cup bean-sauce mixture): Calories: 452, Total Fat: 13 g, Sat. Fat: 3 g, Monounsaturated Fat: 7 g, Polyunsaturated Fat: 2 g, Carbs: 40 g, Fiber: 6 g, Sugars: 19 g, Protein: 77 g, Sodium: 516 mg, Cholesterol: 142 mg

NUTRITIONAL BONUS: How does turkey keep you slim? Let us count the ways. Turkey's protein content helps regulate hunger by stabilizing blood sugar levels, and its tryptophan content helps keep stress levels down, which means fewer fat-storing stress hormones are released into your system. Turkey is also an excellent source of protein, which keeps you full and increases your metabolic rate.

Turkey &
Butter Bean
Cassoulet

Spicy
Sausage Hash
Brown Pie

Spicy Sausage Hash Brown Pie

*Serves 8. **Hands-on time:** 30 minutes. **Total time:** 45 minutes.*

Enjoy clean hash browns and spicy sausages all in one meal. Opt for natural sausages from your local deli for the freshest flavor with less sodium than their prepackaged counterparts.

INGREDIENTS:

- ¼ lb deli-fresh, natural, spicy chicken sausage, casings removed
- ¼ lb deli-fresh, natural, hot chorizo, casings removed
- 1 Tbsp olive oil
- 1 Yukon gold potato, scrubbed well and shredded
- 1 cup diced yellow onion
- 1 cup diced sweet bell pepper (red, yellow and/or orange)
- 1 jalapeño pepper, diced
  (TIP: For less heat, remove ribs and seeds.)
- 1 clove garlic, minced
- 8 egg whites
- ¼ cup skim milk
- 1 tsp fresh ground black pepper
- 1 tsp garlic powder
- 1 Tbsp Dijon mustard
- ½ cup shredded low-fat cheddar cheese

INSTRUCTIONS:

ONE: Preheat oven to 350°F.

TWO: Heat a large cast-iron or ovenproof skillet on medium-high. Add sausage and chorizo and cook for 7 to 8 minutes, until browned, breaking up with a wooden spoon. Transfer sausage mixture to a plate lined with paper towel to absorb excess fat.

THREE: Drain and wipe out skillet; heat oil on medium-high. Add potato, onion, bell pepper, jalapeño and garlic. Sauté, stirring occasionally, until soft, about 10 minutes.

FOUR: Meanwhile, in a medium bowl, whisk egg whites, milk, black pepper, garlic powder and Dijon until smooth. Set aside.

FIVE: Add sausage mixture to skillet, stirring until thoroughly combined. Pour egg mixture evenly over top and sprinkle with cheese. Transfer skillet to oven and bake until eggs are cooked through and cheese is bubbly, 10 to 15 minutes.

Nutrients per serving (⅛ of pie): Calories: 174, Total Fat: 9 g, Sat. Fat: 3 g, Monounsaturated Fat: 4 g, Polyunsaturated Fat: 1 g, Carbs: 10 g, Fiber: 1 g, Sugars: 3 g, Protein: 13 g, Sodium: 406 mg, Cholesterol: 26 mg

Turkey Chili & Squash Lasagna

*Serves 10. **Hands-on time:** 25 minutes. **Total time:** 1 hour, 45 minutes.*

Ground turkey is a great clean alternative to ground beef. Plus, the tryptophan in turkey helps to decrease stress and causes feelings of calm, making this a feel-good comfort meal.

INGREDIENTS:

- 2 tsp extra-virgin olive oil
- 1 large yellow onion, finely chopped
- 1 green bell pepper, diced
- 1 lb ground turkey breast
- 3 cloves garlic, minced
- 2 tsp chile powder
- ¼ tsp hot chile pepper flakes
- ¼ tsp ground cumin
- Pinch each sea salt and fresh ground black pepper
- 4 cups peeled and cubed butternut squash (1 small squash)
- 2 cups strained tomatoes
- 1 cup low-sodium chicken broth
- 1 cup BPA-free canned unsalted black beans, drained and rinsed
- ⅓ cup chopped fresh cilantro
- 1 egg white
- 1½ cups pressed skim cottage cheese
- 6 fresh whole-wheat lasagna sheets, divided
- 1 cup part-skim mozzarella cheese
- 2 Tbsp grated low-fat Parmesan cheese

INSTRUCTIONS:

ONE: Preheat oven to 375°F.

TWO: In a large nonstick skillet, heat oil on medium. Add onion, green pepper, turkey, garlic, chile powder, pepper flakes, cumin, salt and black pepper. Cook, breaking up turkey with a wooden spoon, until browned, about 6 minutes. Stir in squash, tomatoes, broth and beans and bring mixture to a boil. Reduce heat to medium-low, cover and simmer until thickened, about 20 minutes. Stir in cilantro.

THREE: In a small bowl, combine egg white and cottage cheese. Set aside.

FOUR: In a 13 x 9-inch baking dish, add enough turkey mixture to just coat bottom of dish, avoiding squash pieces (to prevent creating a lumpy base). Arrange 2 lasagna sheets over top of turkey mixture, overlapping to fit. Layer a third of cottage cheese mixture, then a third of turkey mixture over top. Repeat with remaining 4 lasagna sheets, cottage cheese mixture and turkey mixture. Top with mozzarella and Parmesan. Cover with foil and bake until bubbly, about 40 minutes. Uncover and continue baking until browned, about 10 minutes.

Nutrients per 1-cup serving: Calories: 306, Total Fat: 6 g, Sat. Fat: 2 g, Carbs: 16 g, Fiber: 7 g, Sugars: 5 g, Protein: 26.5 g, Sodium: 185 mg, Cholesterol: 85 mg

Salts & Oils

Adding bold flavors to healthy oils and salts means using less and tasting more!

Salt and fat. Two of the baddest guys in town, right?

Well, that's only partly true. In moderation, healthy fats and salt are important components of a balanced diet. Fats are essential in the body for vitamin absorption, blood clotting and brain development. Salt, on the other hand, is indispensible in maintaining the pH balance of the blood.

Many people who are eating clean mistakenly eschew all fats and salt, when they should really be just consuming a little less of them. Fats and salt are amazing flavor enhancers, which means you need very little of them to add a lot of taste to your dishes. A drizzle of oil or a shake of salt is more than enough to liven up any dish.

So to help you get the most mileage out of your oils and salt, we've created four infused oil and four flavored salt recipes – each bursting with rich, aromatic flavor. Remember that when it comes to oil and salt, moderation is key. But each of these recipes will help you make the most out of the oils and salts that you use on a daily basis. They're easy and straightforward, but they'll add intense and indulgent flavor to every meal you make!

FLAVORED OILS

1. Grape Seed Masala
2. Roasted Garlic
3. Citrus Splash
4. Basil Zinger

4 Flavored Oils

Roasted Garlic

How to use it: Drizzle over popcorn, pastas and salads.

How to make it: Preheat oven to 350°F. In an ovenproof casserole dish, add 3 cups extra-virgin olive oil. Peel and separate cloves of 1 whole head garlic and add to oil. Roast in oven until garlic is golden, 30 to 35 minutes. Remove from oven and let cool slightly. With a slotted spoon, remove garlic from oil and discard. (Alternatively, if refrigerated and used within the same day, you can spread those cloves on toast for quick and tasty garlic bread.) With a funnel, pour oil into a resealable bottle and refrigerate for 3 to 4 days.

Nutritional bonus: We've all heard about garlic's superpowers when it comes to boosting heart health, but garlic is now being studied for its potential to curb weight gain and obesity!

Grape Seed Masala

How to use it: Mix with plain yogurt or over fish, chicken or rice.

How to make it: Heat a deep skillet on low. Add 2 Tbsp mustard seeds and cook, stirring continuously, until seeds begin to pop. Add 2 Tbsp curry powder and toast, stirring continuously, for 1 minute. Add 2 cups grape seed oil, stirring and pressing out any lumps with the back of a spoon. Add 5 strips lime peel (each about the size of a martini garnish) and cook until just hot. Remove from heat and set aside for about 2 hours. With a cheesecloth-lined funnel, strain oil into a resealable bottle. Store in the fridge for up to 1 week.

Nutritional bonus: Omega-3 fatty acids in mustard seeds? It's true, they're considered a very good source of the essential nutrient, which may help boost cognitive performance.

Citrus Splash

How to use it: Add to marinades or drizzle over white fish, grilled shellfish and chicken.

How to make it: In a medium pot, add 3 cups extra-virgin olive oil, 4 strips lemon peel (each about the size of a martini garnish), 2 sprigs fresh lime leaves and 1 bunch lemongrass, tough tops and bottoms removed and stalks cut into 3 pieces each. Heat on low just until hot, about 5 minutes. Set aside for about 4 hours. With a slotted spoon, remove and discard peel, leaves and lemongrass. With a funnel, pour oil into a resealable bottle and refrigerate for up to 1 week.

Nutritional bonus: Extra-virgin olive oil (EVOO) contains polyphenols, nutrients that have anti-inflammatory properties. EVOO contains more polyphenols than regular olive oil, so opt for it whenever possible!

Basil Zinger

How to use it: As a finishing touch to grilled portobellos, salads or pastas.

How to make it: In a medium pot, add 3 cups extra-virgin olive oil and 2 sprigs rinsed and dried fresh basil (leaves and stems). Heat on low just until hot, about 5 minutes. With a slotted spoon, remove basil from oil. With a funnel, carefully pour oil into a resealable bottle and refrigerate for up to 1 week.

Nutritional Bonus: Basil contains flavonoids, powerful plant-based compounds that function as antioxidants in the body and protect your cells from damage.

SO, WHAT'S A SMOKE POINT?

It's the temperature at which oil starts to break down and release harmful chemicals. For high-heat cooking, choose oils with higher smoke points such as grape seed or safflower oil.

---

4 Flavored Rock & Sea Salts

Tokyo Salt Blend

How to use it: To liven up white fish, oysters, rice or noodles.

How to make it: Heat a large skillet on medium. Add ¼ cup white sesame seeds and toast, swirling skillet constantly, until golden. Transfer to a food processor with ¼ cup green tea leaves, 2 sheets thinly sliced nori (sushi seaweed) and 1 cup coarse-grain sea salt. Process until finely ground. Transfer to a tightly sealed jar and store in the fridge for up to 6 months.

Nutritional bonus: Considered a sea vegetable, nori is an excellent source of iodine – a key factor in thyroid health.

Chocolate Pink Himalayan Salt

How to use it: Sprinkle on anything with chocolate, such as low-fat brownies or truffles.

How to make it: In a large bowl, combine ¼ cup medium-coarse Himalayan salt, ¼ cup finely grated dark chocolate (70% cocoa or greater) and 1 Tbsp unsweetened cocoa powder. Mix well, transfer to a tightly sealed jar and store in a cool, dark place for up to 6 months. (**TIP:** Can't find Himalayan salt? No worries, coarse sea salt will do!)

Nutritional bonus: Ever wonder why eating chocolate makes you feel so good? Cocoa contains serotonin, a neurotransmitter that plays a valuable role in your mood, sleep and anxiety levels.

Porcini Sea Salt

How to use it: Best with lean beef or game. Can be used to make a wet rub for steak by adding a few drops of oil, roasted garlic and coarse ground black pepper.

How to make it: In a food processor, whirl ½ cup dried porcini mushrooms and ¼ cup French fleur de sel or sel gris until finely ground. (If fleur de sel or sel gris is unavailable, substitute coarse sea salt.) Transfer to a tightly sealed jar and store in the fridge for up to 6 months.

Nutritional bonus: With their strong earthy notes, porcini mushrooms are a great way to add flavor and fiber to your meals without adding excess calories – a ½-oz serving of dried porcini mushrooms is only about 50 calories!

Indian Black Salt

How to use it: Add depth of flavor to roasted cauliflower, grilled fish, chicken or pork.

How to make it: In a large bowl, whisk ¼ cup Indian black salt with ¼ cup garam masala and ½ cup fine sea salt. Transfer to a tightly sealed jar and store in a cool, dark place for up to 1 year.

Nutritional bonus: A blend of dried South-Asian spices, garam masala not only comes packed with exotic flavors, but also provides a punch of immune-boosting antioxidants!

Main Courses: Seafood

Light and Easy Prawn Pasta, p. 195

The clean cooking secrets of the sea have been brought straight to your kitchen! Full of nutritious omega-3 fats, our watery delicacies are infused with the *Clean Eating* flavors you love. If you have a hankering for fish and chips, try our perfectly spiced Cajun Catfish with Plantain Fritters. Or cook up a Light & Easy Prawn Pasta for a fast meal. Have fun expanding your seafood horizons – not your waistline.

Cajun Catfish
WITH PLANTAIN FRITTERS

*Serves 4. **Hands-on time:** 45 minutes. **Total time:** 45 minutes.*

Cajun dishes aren't for the faint of heart, but tonight's dinner is a not-too-spicy compromise sure to suit everyone's tastes. Feel free to double up on the spice mix so you have some left over – Cajun flavors are a perfect match for shrimp and chicken.

INGREDIENTS:

- 2 green plantains, cut into 3-inch-long segments
- 1 bunch collard greens, chopped
- ¾ tsp sea salt, divided
- 2 egg whites
- 2 tsp extra-virgin olive oil, divided
- 1½ tsp sweet paprika
- ¾ tsp dried thyme
- ¾ tsp dried oregano
- ½ tsp fresh cracked black pepper
- ⅛ tsp ground cayenne pepper
- ¾ lb boneless, skin-on catfish fillets (4 fillets total), rinsed and patted dry
- 3 cloves garlic, minced

NOTE: Plantains change from green to yellow as they ripen and sweeten. If you can only find yellow plantains at the market, feel free to use them as well. Your end result will be a bit sweeter.

INSTRUCTIONS:

ONE: Bring a large stockpot of water to boil on high heat. Add plantains and cook, uncovered, for 15 minutes. Drain and transfer to a large bowl of cold water.

TWO: Rinse stockpot and add greens and ¼ cup water. Cook, covered, on medium heat for 8 minutes or until greens are wilted. Drain and set aside.

THREE: When plantains are cool enough to handle, drain and peel, using a sharp knife to cut away any brown spots. Return to bowl. Add ½ tsp salt and egg whites. Using a potato masher, mash until smooth. Divide plantain mixture into 8 equal portions and form into flat patties, about 3 inches wide each.

FOUR: In a large nonstick skillet, heat ¾ tsp olive oil on medium for 1 minute. Add 4 patties and cook for 5 minutes, flipping once at the start to evenly coat patties in oil. Flip again and cook for an additional 5 minutes. Reduce heat if patties start to brown too quickly. Remove from heat and stack on a warm plate, covering with foil to keep warm. Add ¾ tsp olive oil to skillet and repeat steps with remaining patties.

FIVE: Prepare spice mixture: In a small bowl, combine paprika, thyme, oregano, black pepper, cayenne and remaining salt. Spread mixture on a large plate, then dredge catfish fillets in mixture, pressing into both sides. Place garlic on a separate large plate and dredge fillets in garlic, pressing into both sides.

SIX: Wipe out skillet. Add remaining olive oil and heat on medium for 1 minute. Add fillets, skin side up, cover and cook for 3 minutes, then gently flip and cook for an additional 2 minutes. Fish is done if fillets flake easily at center. Serve with plantain fritters and greens.

Nutrients per serving (3 oz catfish, 2 fritters, ½ cup greens): *Calories: 250, Total Fat: 5 g, Sat. Fat: 1 g, Monounsaturated Fat: 3 g, Polyunsaturated Fat: 1 g, Omega-3s: 490 mg, Omega-6s: 500 mg, Carbs: 34 g, Fiber: 5 g, Sugars: 14 g, Protein: 19 g, Sodium: 460 mg, Cholesterol: 50 mg*

186

TRY IT:
On the side, serve brown jasmine rice or soba noodles – either will nicely complement the Ginger Teriyaki Shrimp's Asian flavors and contrast with its delicacy.

Ginger Teriyaki Shrimp & Scallion Skewers

Ginger Teriyaki Shrimp & Scallion Skewers
WITH SESAME CUCUMBER SALAD

Serves 6. **Hands-on time:** *35 minutes.* **Total time:** *1 hour, 20 minutes (includes marinating time).*

Pair thin and tender shrimp with this relatively acidic marinade and the result is a brief 30 to 60 minutes of marinating time.

INGREDIENTS:

- 48 large raw shrimp, peeled and deveined (about 2¼ lb), tail on or off
- 1½ cups Ginger Teriyaki Marinade (see recipe, p. 234)
- 3 Tbsp rice vinegar
- 2 tsp toasted sesame oil
- 2 large cucumbers, peeled, halved lengthwise, seeded and sliced
- ¼ cup thinly sliced red onion
- 16 scallions, white and light green parts only, cut into 1½-inch pieces
- ½ avocado, pitted, peeled and diced
- High-heat cooking oil (such as sunflower, safflower, peanut or grape seed oil), as needed
- 1½ tsp sesame seeds, toasted

INSTRUCTIONS:

ONE: Place shrimp in a large zip-top bag. Add Ginger Teriyaki Marinade and seal, squeezing out as much air as possible. Refrigerate for 30 to 60 minutes, turning occasionally.

TWO: Meanwhile, in a medium bowl, whisk together vinegar and sesame oil. Add cucumbers and onion. Set aside in refrigerator (while shrimp marinates), stirring occasionally, 30 to 60 minutes.

THREE: Remove shrimp from marinade and pat dry with paper towel. Thread 4 shrimp and a few scallion pieces onto each skewer. Remove cucumber mixture from refrigerator and stir in avocado.

FOUR: Heat grill to high and lightly oil grate with cooking oil. Grill skewers for 1½ to 2 minutes per side or until shrimp is barely opaque. Remove from grill and arrange on plates.

FIVE: Drain excess liquid from cucumber salad. Transfer to a serving bowl, sprinkle with sesame seeds and serve alongside shrimp.

Nutrients per serving (2 shrimp skewers and ½ cup salad): Calories: 186, Total Fat: 7 g, Sat. Fat: 1 g, Monounsaturated Fat: 3 g, Polyunsaturated Fat: 2 g, Omega-3s: 300 mg, Omega-6s: 380 mg, Carbs: 15 g, Fiber: 3 g, Sugars: 9 g, Protein: 14 g, Sodium: 309 mg, Cholesterol: 85 mg

Pan-Roasted Mahi Mahi
WITH FRUIT SALSA & GRILLED SQUASH

Serves 4.

Chef Dominic Tedesco shared this fresh and hearty fish dish with *CE*. His advice: If you can't find mahi mahi, simply substitute with cod or wild salmon.

INGREDIENTS:

- 2 zucchini, sliced on a ½-inch-thick diagonal
- 2 yellow squash, sliced on a ½-inch-thick diagonal
- 2 Tbsp olive oil, divided
- 4 4-oz boneless fresh mahi mahi fillets, skin on
- ¼ tsp each sea salt and fresh ground black pepper
- 3 Tbsp low-sodium broth (chicken, vegetable or fish)

FRUIT SALSA

- 1 ripe avocado, pitted, peeled and diced
- 1 sweet red grapefruit, peeled, segmented and chopped
- 1 medium orange, peeled, segmented and chopped
- 1 small red bell pepper, finely chopped
- 1 clove garlic, minced
- ½ cup finely chopped red onion
- ¼ cup chopped fresh cilantro
- 2 Tbsp fresh lime juice
- Sea salt and fresh ground black pepper, to taste

INSTRUCTIONS:

ONE: Preheat the oven to 350°F.

TWO: In a large bowl, combine all salsa ingredients; set aside.

THREE: Heat a grill pan or barbecue to medium-high. In a separate large bowl, toss zucchini and squash with 1 Tbsp oil. Add zucchini and squash to grill pan and cook, turning once, until golden brown and tender. Transfer to a plate; set aside.

FOUR: Sprinkle mahi mahi with salt and black pepper. In an ovenproof skillet, heat remaining 1 Tbsp oil on medium-high. Add mahi mahi, flesh side down, and cook until golden brown, 2 to 3 minutes. Carefully flip mahi mahi and cook, skin side down, for 1 minute. Pour broth over top, transfer to oven and bake for about 5 minutes, or until mahi mahi is just cooked through.

FIVE: To serve, remove skin from mahi mahi, if desired. Top with fruit salsa and serve with grilled zucchini-squash mixture.

CHEF'S TIP: If the fish is hard to flip, it's not ready to be turned yet! When the flesh releases naturally, it's ready to be flipped over. (NOTE: This rule does not apply if using a nonstick pan.)

Nutrients per serving (1 fillet, ½ cup zucchini-squash mixture, ¾ cup salsa): Calories: 300, Total Fat: 14 g, Sat. Fat: 2 g, Monounsaturated Fat: 9 g, Polyunsaturated Fat: 2 g, Carbs: 23 g, Fiber: 7 g, Sugar: 13 g, Protein: 25 g, Sodium: 270 mg, Cholesterol: 85 mg

For a photo of this recipe, see page 182.

Collard-Wrapped Cod
WITH ROOT VEGETABLE SALAD

Serves 4. Hands-on time: 45 minutes. Total time: 45 minutes.

Wrapping cod in collard greens gives both the fish and the greens an extra boost: The cod lends the collards a buttery flavor, while the collards prevent the cod from touching the hot pan directly, meaning it steams instead of sautéing. The result is a more tender dish.

INGREDIENTS:

- ½ lb turnips, peeled and cut into ½-inch cubes
- ½ lb black radishes, peeled and cut into ½-inch cubes
- ½ lb beets, peeled and cut into ½-inch cubes
- 2 medium carrots, peeled and grated
- ½ tsp dried dill
- ¼ tsp sea salt
- 1 Tbsp apple cider vinegar
- 1 Tbsp extra-virgin olive oil, divided
- 8 large leaves collard greens, rinsed well in cold water, tough bottom stems removed
- 1 lb boneless, skinless cod fillet, rinsed and patted dry

INSTRUCTIONS:

ONE: Fill 2 medium pots halfway with water and bring each to boil on high heat. In 1 pot, add turnips and radishes; in the other, add beets. (**NOTE:** Turnips, radishes and beets can be cooked in same pot, but beets will stain the other vegetables.) Reduce heat of both burners to medium and simmer, partially covered, for 10 minutes, then drain.

TWO: In a large bowl, combine carrots, dill, salt, vinegar and 1 tsp oil. Add turnip, radish and beets; toss to combine. Cover and set aside.

THREE: Fill a large stockpot halfway with water and bring to boil on high heat. Add collard greens and boil for 1 minute, using a wooden spoon to immerse greens in water if they pop up. Drain immediately, return to pot and cover with cold water to prevent greens from over-cooking.

FOUR: Using a sharp knife, cut cod into 8 equal portions. Place collard greens on a cutting board, rib side down. Place 1 piece cod lengthwise on top of each leaf; fold up 1 long side, then both short sides. Roll the leaf over to completely wrap cod.

FIVE: In a large nonstick skillet, heat 1 tsp oil for 1 minute on medium. Add 4 cod-collard wraps, seam side down; cover and cook, undisturbed, for 7 minutes. (**NOTE:** Wraps will make a loud snapping noise as cod steams.) Remove skillet from heat and let sit, covered, for 1 minute. Remove lid and transfer wraps to a large plate. Add remaining oil to skillet and repeat process with remaining cod-collard wraps. Add 2 wraps and 1 cup carrot-beet mixture to each of 4 plates.

NOTE: Be sure to let the cooked packages sit off of the heat, covered, for 1 minute before peeking inside – the crackle-and-pop action will die down and you won't risk getting burned by the steam.

Nutrients per serving (2 cod-collard wraps and 1 cup carrot-beet mixture): Calories: 210, Total Fat: 5 g, Sat. Fat: 0.5 g, Monounsaturated Fat: 3 g, Polyunsaturated Fat: 1 g, Omega-3s: 350 mg, Omega-6s: 460 mg, Carbs: 19 g, Fiber: 7 g, Sugars: 9 g, Protein: 25 g, Sodium: 320 mg, Cholesterol: 50 mg

Cracker Catfish Sticks
WITH CAJUN RED PEPPER SAUCE & WILTED SWISS CHARD

Serves 4 to 6. Hands-on time: 15 minutes. Total time: 15 minutes.

This update on the classic kid favorite is bursting with Cajun flavor and zest. Cooking up these catfish sticks with healthy olive oil means you cut down on calories and fat, and boost the yum factor.

INGREDIENTS:

- Olive oil cooking spray
- ¼ cup buttermilk or skim milk
- ¼ cup Dijon mustard
- 1 cup whole-wheat or whole-grain cracker crumbs (about 28 crackers)
- ½ tsp dried thyme
- 2 tsp paprika, divided
- ½ tsp ground cayenne pepper, divided
- 1 lb boneless, skinless catfish fillets, cut crosswise into 1-inch strips
- 1 cup jarred water-packed roasted red peppers, drained and rinsed
- 2 cloves garlic, minced, divided
- 1 Tbsp fresh lemon juice
- 3 Tbsp extra-virgin olive oil, divided
- ¼ tsp red pepper flakes
- 1 bunch Swiss chard (about 1 lb), coarsely chopped

INSTRUCTIONS:

ONE: Preheat oven to 450°F. Line a large baking sheet with foil and mist with cooking spray.

TWO: In a small bowl, whisk buttermilk and Dijon. In a separate small bowl, combine cracker crumbs, thyme, 1 tsp paprika and ¼ tsp cayenne. Dip each catfish strip into buttermilk mixture, turning to coat; shake strips to allow excess liquid to drip off. Immediately transfer each strip to crumb mixture, turning and pressing to coat. Transfer catfish to baking sheet and mist tops with cooking spray. Place in oven and bake until crispy and golden brown, about 10 minutes.

THREE: Meanwhile, prepare Cajun Red Pepper Sauce: In the bowl of a food processor, process red peppers, 1 clove garlic, lemon juice and remaining 1 tsp paprika and ¼ tsp cayenne until smooth, about 30 seconds. While processing, slowly pour in all but 2 tsp oil until combined. Set aside.

FOUR: In a large nonstick skillet, heat remaining 2 tsp oil on medium-high. Add remaining 1 clove garlic and pepper flakes and cook, stirring, until fragrant, about 10 seconds. Add chard, cover and cook, stirring occasionally, until wilted and tender, about 5 minutes. Serve catfish with dipping sauce and chard, dividing evenly.

Nutrients per serving (3 oz catfish, ½ cup chard, ¼ cup dipping sauce; based on 6 servings): Calories: 252, Total Fat: 13 g, Sat. Fat: 2 g, Monounsaturated Fat: 7 g, Polyunsaturated Fat: 2 g, Omega-3s: 450 mg, Omega-6s: 1,840 mg, Carbs: 19 g, Fiber: 5 g, Sugars: 4 g, Protein: 16 g, Sodium: 460 mg, Cholesterol: 44 mg

Cracker
Catfish
Sticks

Crab Pot Pie in a Bread Bowl

Crab Pot Pie in a Bread Bowl

*Serves 5. **Hands-on time:** 20 minutes. **Total time:** 35 minutes.*

What makes this super-easy recipe even better? The fact that you can eat the bowl virtually eliminates cleanup! Enjoy this rich take on chicken pot pie to save time and effort in the kitchen.

INGREDIENTS:

- 3 Tbsp olive oil, divided
- 1 Yukon gold potato, scrubbed well and diced
- 1 cup diced yellow onion
- 1 cup peeled and diced carrots
- 1 leek, diced
- 2 Tbsp whole-wheat flour
- 1 cup clam juice
- ½ cup skim milk
- 1 cup frozen peas
- 1 cup frozen corn
- 1 cup fresh lump crabmeat
- 5 whole-wheat bread bowls

INSTRUCTIONS:

ONE: Preheat oven to 350°F.

TWO: In a large skillet, heat 1 Tbsp oil on medium-high. Add potato, onion, carrots and leek. Cook for 10 minutes, stirring frequently, until onion is translucent and carrots soften.

THREE: Meanwhile, in a medium skillet, heat remaining 2 Tbsp oil on medium-high. Sprinkle in flour and whisk to combine until smooth. Slowly whisk in clam juice and milk until combined and sauce begins to thicken, about 5 minutes.

FOUR: Add clam juice mixture to skillet with potato-leek mixture and stir to combine; reduce heat to medium. Stir in peas, corn and crab and cook until heated through, about 3 minutes.

FIVE: Set bread bowls on a baking sheet and remove tops. Ladle mixture into bread bowls, dividing evenly. Loosely cover each bowl with bread top, leaving space for steam to escape. Transfer to oven and bake for 15 minutes. Serve immediately.

Nutrients per bowl: Calories: 572, Total Fat: 11 g, Sat. Fat: 1 g, Monounsaturated Fat: 6.5 g, Polyunsaturated Fat: 1 g, Carbs: 90 g, Fiber: 12 g, Sugars: 7.5 g, Protein: 26 g, Sodium: 620 mg, Cholesterol: 38 mg

TIP: Save 310 calories, 61 g of carbs and 291 mg of sodium by eating just the filling and passing on the bowl!

Crab Cakes
WITH HONEYDEW-STRAWBERRY SALSA

*Serves 5. **Hands-on time:** 1 hour. **Total time:** 1 hour, 10 minutes.*

These crab cakes pair well with quinoa or black beans to make a main course. For a decadent (yet still healthy!) brunch, skip the salsa and top each crab cake with a poached egg and a drizzle of your favorite hot sauce or homemade pesto.

INGREDIENTS:

- 1 lb crabmeat, drained and picked over for shells
- 1 Tbsp Dijon mustard
- 4 Tbsp whole-wheat panko bread crumbs
- 2 Tbsp chopped fresh parsley
- 4 scallions (white and some green parts), thinly sliced
- Zest ½ lemon
- 1½ tsp salt-free chile or Cajun seasoning blend
- 1 tsp smoked paprika
- ⅛ tsp sea salt
- 1 large egg
- 1 large egg white
- ¼ cup white whole-wheat flour
- Fresh ground black pepper, to taste
- 2 Tbsp safflower oil, divided
- Lemon wedges for serving, optional

SALSA

- 1 cup diced honeydew melon
- 1 cup diced strawberries
- ½ small red onion, chopped (about ½ cup)
- 1 jalapeño pepper, seeded and chopped (about ¼ cup)
- 3 Tbsp chopped fresh parsley
- 1½ Tbsp fresh lemon juice
- Pinch sea salt

NOTE: We recommend the affordable "Special" grade of pre-packed crabmeat for convenience. "Lump" crabmeat is also a great choice.

INSTRUCTIONS:

ONE: Prepare crab cakes: In a large bowl, combine crabmeat, Dijon, panko, parsley, scallions, lemon zest, chile seasoning, paprika, salt, egg and egg white. Gently fold mixture with a rubber spatula to blend.

TWO: To form patties, firmly pack crab mixture into a ¼-cup measuring cup. Invert crab into your palm and press into the shape of a disk, about 1 inch thick. Transfer to a plate and repeat with remaining crab mixture, making about 10 patties. Cover patties with plastic wrap and chill for at least 30 minutes or up to 24 hours to firm up crab cakes.

THREE: Meanwhile prepare salsa: In a medium bowl, combine all salsa ingredients. Stir gently to combine. May be made up to 4 hours ahead. Cover and chill; bring to room temperature before serving.

FOUR: Line a plate or baking sheet with parchment paper. Put flour in a wide bowl or pie plate and season with black pepper. Gently dredge each crab cake in flour and transfer to parchment. Add 1 Tbsp oil to a large, heavy skillet and heat on medium. Add half of crab cakes and cook until golden brown, 4 to 5 minutes per side. Transfer to plate or sheet, cover with foil to keep warm and repeat with remaining oil and crab cakes. Serve immediately with salsa and lemon wedges, if desired.

Nutrients per crab cake: Calories: 254, Total Fat: 9 g, Sat. Fat: 1 g, Carbs: 21 g, Fiber: 3 g, Sugars: 5 g, Protein: 24 g, Sodium: 445 mg, Cholesterol: 133 mg

MAKE IT FASTER: To make this dish even more quickly, pick up fresh all-natural mango or peach salsa in your market's produce section.

Smoky Barbecued Halibut
WITH SCALLIONS

*Serves 4. **Hands-on time:** 10 minutes. **Total time:** 20 minutes.*

Turn up the heat with this smoky grilled halibut. Smothered in a chipotle barbecue sauce and grilled to perfection, this fish will pair well with brown rice or a salad of crisp greens.

INGREDIENTS:

- 1¼ lb boneless, skinless halibut fillet, about 1 inch thick
- 2 Tbsp tomato paste
- 1 Tbsp raw honey
- 1 Tbsp balsamic vinegar
- 2 cloves garlic, minced
- ½ tsp minced chipotle chile pepper in adobo sauce
- 3 tsp extra-virgin olive oil, divided
- 2 bunches scallions, tops and bottoms trimmed
- ⅛ tsp each sea salt and fresh ground black pepper
- High-heat cooking oil (such as sunflower, safflower, peanut or grape seed oil), as needed

INSTRUCTIONS:

ONE: Place halibut in a 7 x 9-inch baking dish and set aside.

TWO: Prepare barbecue sauce: In a small bowl, combine tomato paste, honey, vinegar, garlic, chile pepper in adobo sauce and 1 tsp olive oil; stir well to combine. Spread sauce over entire halibut.

THREE: In a separate baking dish, add scallions. Drizzle with remaining 2 tsp olive oil, sprinkle with salt and pepper and toss to coat.

FOUR: Preheat a grill to medium and lightly oil grate with cooking oil. Place halibut on 1 side of grill rack and scallions on the opposite side. Close grill hood and cook scallions for 2 minutes per side, until soft and lightly charred. Grill halibut until it flakes when tested with a fork and is opaque in center, about 10 minutes. (**NOTE:** Alternatively, to cook under a broiler, simply coat a broiler pan with olive oil cooking spray and broil on medium.) Remove from grill and place on a platter. Arrange scallions around halibut and serve.

Nutrients per serving (5 oz halibut and 3 scallions): Calories: 220, Total Fat: 7 g, Sat. Fat: 1 g, Monounsaturated Fat: 4 g, Polyunsaturated Fat: 1 g, Carbs: 6 g, Fiber: 1 g, Sugars: 4 g, Protein: 30 g, Sodium: 150 mg, Cholesterol: 45 mg

Thin-Crust Shrimp Pizza
WITH FRESH CORN

*Serves 4. **Hands-on time:** 30 minutes. **Total time:** 45 minutes.*

All you need for a pizzeria-style thin crust is a very hot oven and a pizza stone! We preheat the stone for 30 minutes so your pizza starts to crisp as soon as it hits the oven. A fresh corn and tender shrimp topping provides the perfect textural contrast to your delicate crust.

INGREDIENTS:

- 1 Tbsp olive oil, divided
- 1 large red onion, sliced into half-moons
- ¼ tsp sea salt, divided
- ⅛ tsp fresh ground black pepper, plus additional to taste
- 1 large red bell pepper, thinly sliced
- Olive oil cooking spray
- 8 oz raw medium shrimp, peeled and deveined
- ½ tsp chile powder
- 1 to 2 Tbsp whole-wheat flour, for dusting
- 1 lb fresh or frozen whole-grain pizza dough, room temperature
- 2 oz grated low-fat pepper jack cheese (about ¾ cup)
- 1¼ cups fresh corn kernels (from 1 to 2 ears)
- ¼ cup chopped fresh cilantro, optional
- Lime wedges for garnish, optional

INSTRUCTIONS:

ONE: Arrange a large pizza stone in center of oven and preheat oven to 550°F. Let heat for 30 minutes before baking.

TIP: If you don't have a pizza stone, use a large heavy-duty baking sheet and heat in center of oven for 10 minutes before baking; if rimmed, turn sheet upside down.

TWO: In a large nonstick skillet, heat ½ Tbsp oil on medium-low. Add onion, ⅛ tsp salt and black pepper, to taste, and sauté, stirring occasionally, until onion is very tender and light brown, 15 to 18 minutes.

THREE: Meanwhile, in a medium skillet, heat remaining oil on medium-high. Add bell pepper and black pepper, to taste, and sauté, stirring frequently, until bell pepper is tender, about 8 minutes. Transfer to a small bowl; reduce heat on skillet to medium and mist with cooking spray. Season shrimp with remaining salt, black pepper and chile powder. Add to skillet and cook, turning, until just cooked through, about 4 minutes. Remove from heat and set aside.

FOUR: Arrange a large piece of parchment paper over a large cutting board and dust lightly with flour. With floured hands or a floured rolling pin, shape dough into a 12-inch circle. Top with cheese, onion, bell pepper, corn and shrimp. Carefully transfer pizza on parchment paper to pizza stone or baking sheet. Bake until edges are puffed and crust is lightly browned, 9 to 11 minutes. Remove from oven and let rest for 5 minutes. If desired, top with cilantro and serve with lime.

Nutrients per serving (¼ of pizza): Calories: 482, Total Fat: 13 g, Sat. Fat: 3 g, Monounsaturated Fat: 3 g, Polyunsaturated Fat: 1 g, Carbs: 66 g, Fiber: 9 g, Sugars: 5 g, Protein: 26 g, Sodium: 303 mg, Cholesterol: 101 mg

Thin-Crust
Shrimp
Pizza

Creamy
Dijon
Halibut

Creamy Dijon Halibut
WITH SPINACH-LEMON BULGUR

Serves 4. **Hands-on time:** *15 minutes.* **Total time:** *1 hour, 30 minutes.*

We've kept the hands-on time minimal for this recipe thanks to the addition of a slow cooker. The halibut requires only minutes of prep work, and takes absolutely no effort to cook!

INGREDIENTS:

- Olive oil cooking spray
- 1 yellow onion, thinly sliced
- 2 tsp chopped fresh thyme
- 1 tsp chopped fresh rosemary
- ½ tsp garlic powder
- ½ tsp coarsely ground black pepper
- ½ tsp sea salt, divided
- 4 4-oz boneless, skinless halibut fillets, rinsed and patted dry (or other lean, thick white fish fillets)
- ½ cup low-fat sour cream
- 1 Tbsp extra-virgin olive oil
- 2 tsp coarse-grain Dijon mustard
- ½ tsp Worcestershire sauce
- 2 cups cooked bulgur
- 2 packed cups baby spinach, coarsely chopped
- 1 clove garlic, minced
- 1 tsp lemon zest
- 2 tomatoes, sliced or cut into wedges
- 1 lemon, quartered, optional

INSTRUCTIONS:

ONE: Coat a 3- to 3½-qt slow cooker with cooking spray; arrange onion along bottom. In a small bowl, combine thyme, rosemary, garlic powder, pepper and ¼ tsp salt. Sprinkle mixture on both sides of halibut fillets, dividing evenly. Place halibut over top of onions, cover and cook until opaque in center, 1 hour and 15 minutes on high or 2½ hours on low.

TWO: Meanwhile, in a small bowl, whisk sour cream, oil, Dijon and Worcestershire sauce; cover and refrigerate.

THREE: In a medium bowl, toss bulgur, spinach, garlic, lemon zest and remaining ¼ tsp salt until combined; divide among serving plates. With a slotted spoon, remove halibut fillets from slow cooker, discarding onions. Place halibut alongside bulgur mixture and top with sour cream mixture, dividing evenly. Serve with tomatoes and lemon wedges, if desired.

Nutrients per serving (3 oz halibut, ½ cup bulgur mixture, 2 Tbsp sour cream mixture): *Calories: 363, Total Fat: 10 g, Sat. Fat: 4 g, Monounsaturated Fat: 3 g, Polyunsaturated Fat: 2 g, Carbs: 41 g, Fiber: 8 g, Sugars: 5 g, Protein: 29 g, Sodium: 510 mg, Cholesterol: 70 mg*

Light & Easy Prawn Pasta

Serves 8.

Actress Debi Mazar and her husband Gabriele Corcos kindly shared this simple, protein-packed pasta dish with *CE*. Its quick cooking time makes it a busy mom's secret weapon!

INGREDIENTS:

- 1½ lb medium to large raw prawns or shrimp, peeled and deveined, preferably tail on
- Juice ½ lemon
- 3 cloves garlic, minced
- ⅛ tsp chile pepper flakes
- 3 Tbsp olive oil, plus additional to serve
- ½ cup Italian parsley, finely chopped
- ½ cup dry white wine
- 14 oz ripe cherry tomatoes, chopped
- ⅛ tsp sea salt
- 1 lb whole-wheat spaghettini, fettuccine or linguine
- ¼ cup chopped fresh basil, optional

INSTRUCTIONS:

ONE: Rinse prawns in a large bowl filled with water and lemon juice. Set aside.

TWO: In a large nonstick pan, sauté garlic and pepper flakes in oil on medium-high for 2 to 3 minutes. Add parsley and prawns and cook until prawns turn vivid pink. Add wine, stirring until reduced by half. Add tomatoes and cook for 5 more minutes. Remove prawns from sauce and set aside in a shallow dish.

THREE: Meanwile, fill a large pot with water, add salt and bring to a boil. Add pasta and cook according to package directions. Drain and transfer pasta to pan with sauce and sauté on medium-high heat for 1 minute.

FOUR: Transfer pasta to a serving platter and arrange prawns over top. Serve with a drizzle of oil and basil, if desired.

Nutrients per 1½-cup serving: *Calories: 382, Total Fat: 10 g, Sat. Fat: 1 g, Monounsaturated Fat: 4 g, Polyunsaturated Fat: 0.5 g, Carbs: 44 g, Fiber: 9 g, Sugars: 4 g, Protein: 26 g, Sodium: 50 mg, Cholesterol: 0 mg*

Seared Scallops
OVER PEA PESTO LINGUINE

*Serves 4. **Hands-on time:** 30 minutes. **Total time:** 30 minutes.*

This scallop dinner shines with a little extra lemon juice squeezed over the finished dish.

INGREDIENTS:

- 8 oz whole-wheat linguine or spaghetti pasta
- 2 cups fresh asparagus spears, cut into 2-inch pieces
- 12 sea scallops (about 1 lb)
- Sea salt and fresh gound black pepper, to taste (or four peppercorn blend)
- 1 Tbsp olive oil

PEA PESTO

- ½ cup low-sodium chicken broth, divided
- 3 Tbsp minced garlic (4 to 6 cloves)
- 1 cup frozen peas, thawed
- 1 oz shredded Parmesan cheese (¼ cup)
- 1 oz chopped unsalted walnuts (¼ cup)
- Juice ½ lemon
- Sea salt and fresh gound black pepper, to taste

INSTRUCTIONS:

ONE: In a large pot, cook pasta according to package directions. Add asparagus to pot during the last 2 to 3 minutes of cooking. Before draining pasta, reserve ¼ cup pasta cooking water in a small dish. Drain pasta and asparagus and return to pot.

TWO: See the step-by-step guide "How to Prep and Sear Scallops" and follow steps 1 through 6.

THREE: Prepare Pea Pesto: Reduce heat to medium. Deglaze scallop pan by pouring ¼ cup broth into pan and scraping up browned bits from bottom of pan with a wooden spoon. Add garlic and sauté until fragrant, 1 to 2 minutes. Add remaining ¼ cup broth and peas and sauté until broth and peas are just heated, about 2 minutes.

FOUR: Transfer pea mixture, including liquid, to a mini food processor or blender. Add Parmesan, walnuts, lemon juice, salt and pepper; process until combined, scraping down sides of processor as needed. Add pesto to pot with drained pasta and asparagus; toss until evenly coated. Add 2 Tbsp reserved pasta-cooking water (and additional as needed to thin sauce) and stir until desired coating and texture is achieved. Divide pasta mixture among 4 plates. Top each serving with 3 seared scallops. If desired, garnish with additional chopped walnuts and Parmesan.

Nutrients per serving (1½ cups pasta and 3 scallops): Calories: 395, Total Fat: 11 g, Sat. Fat: 2 g, Monounsaturated Fat: 3 g, Polyunsaturated Fat: 4 g, Omega-3s: 790 mg, Omega-6s: 3,330 mg, Carbs: 54 g, Fiber: 11 g, Sugars: 4 g, Protein: 23 g, Sodium: 311 mg, Cholesterol: 21 mg

How to Prep and Sear Scallops

ONE: Some scallops may come with a small band of muscle still attached. If you find one, simply peel it off, as this part becomes rubbery when cooked. Pat scallops dry with paper towels.

TWO: Sprinkle salt and pepper on both sides. Heat a stainless steel sauté pan on high for 1 minute (a nonstick pan will work, but stainless is preferred for searing and caramelizing). Add oil and swirl to coat bottom; heat for 30 seconds.

THREE: Place scallops around the outside of pan and cook 1 side for 1 to 2 minutes, or until visibly browned around bottom edge.

FOUR: Use a thin metal spatula to scrape under each scallop and release from pan. Turn scallops over and cook other side for 1 to 2 minutes.

FIVE: Scallops are done when they feel slightly firm but still tender when pressed gently. It's easy to overcook scallops, so you generally shouldn't exceed a cooking time of 5 to 6 minutes total.

SIX: Remove scallops to a plate and serve immediately or keep warm by covering with foil or another plate while finishing recipe.

Nutritional Bonus:
Scallops pack an especially heart-healthy dose of B12, a vitamin that converts harmful body chemicals into harmless substances. In addition, scallops are a rich source of omega-3 fatty acids, magnesium and potassium – all nutrients the body requires in order to maintain a healthy heart, good circulation and normal blood pressure.

Seared
Scallops

Quick-
Braised
Salmon &
Broccoli

Quick-Braised Salmon & Broccoli
WITH TANGY LEMON-HERB SAUCE

*Serves 4. **Hands-on time:** 10 minutes. **Total time:** 24 minutes.*

This super-fast fish dish is ideal for entertaining: The colorful combination and silky sauce will wow guests yet won't relegate you to the kitchen, thanks to minimal hands-on time.

INGREDIENTS:

- 2 8-oz thick-cut boneless, skinless wild salmon fillets
- ¼ tsp fresh ground black pepper, plus additional to taste
- 1 Tbsp olive oil
- 1 cup low-sodium fish or vegetable broth, divided
- 1 medium leek, thinly sliced crosswise, white and pale green parts only
- 1 medium head broccoli, cut into thin spears
- Juice 1 lemon, divided
- 6 oz nonfat plain Greek yogurt
- 2 Tbsp finely minced fresh tarragon
- 2 Tbsp finely minced fresh mint leaves
- Sea salt, to taste

INSTRUCTIONS:

ONE: Preheat oven to 350°F.

TWO: Pat salmon dry with paper towel and season with pepper. In a large braiser or ovenproof sauté pan, heat oil on medium-high. Add salmon and sear for 3 minutes per side, until lightly golden. Transfer salmon to a plate and keep warm.

THREE: Reduce heat to medium and add ¼ cup broth to pan. Add leek and cook for 2 minutes, stirring, until liquid evaporates and leeks soften. Add remaining ¾ cup broth and broccoli; mix well.

FOUR: Return salmon to center of braiser, nestling between leeks and broccoli. Drizzle half of lemon juice over salmon; cover and transfer pan to oven. Cook for 12 to 14 minutes, until salmon and broccoli are tender. Remove from oven and, using a slotted spoon, transfer salmon and vegetables to a platter; cover with foil to keep warm. Reserve ½ cup pan juices.

FIVE: Prepare Lemon-Herb Sauce: In a small bowl, combine yogurt, tarragon, mint, remaining lemon juice and reserved ½ cup pan juices; mix well. (Add additional lemon juice or pan juices as needed to reach desired consistency.) Season with salt and additional pepper.

SIX: To serve, halve salmon fillets and plate each with Lemon-Herb Sauce and leek-broccoli mixture.

Nutrients per serving (4 oz salmon, 1½ cups vegetables, ¼ cup sauce): *Calories: 300, Total Fat: 12 g, Sat. Fat: 2.5 g, Monounsaturated Fat: 5 g, Polyunsaturated Fat: 3 g, Omega-3s: 2,050 mg, Omega-6s: 820 mg, Carbs: 17 g, Fiber: 5 g, Sugars: 4 g, Protein: 32 g, Sodium: 190 mg, Cholesterol: 60 mg*

Lobster Mac & Cheese

*Serves 6. **Hands-on time:** 20 minutes. **Total time:** 35 minutes.*

Adding lobster to the classic mac and cheese dish makes it that much more savory, but our clean touches mean this is an indulgence you won't be regretting!

INGREDIENTS:

- Olive oil cooking spray
- 3 cups brown-rice elbow macaroni
- 1 tsp olive oil
- 1½ lb steamed lobster, meat removed (about 1 cup) and shell reserved
- 1½ cups low-sodium chicken broth
- 1 Tbsp natural olive oil buttery spread or organic unsalted butter
- 2 small shallots, minced
- 1 Tbsp brown-rice flour
- ½ tsp paprika
- ¼ tsp each sea salt and fresh ground black pepper
- 1 cup 1% milk
- 1 cup shredded low-fat sharp cheddar cheese, divided
- 1 large vine-ripened tomato, seeded and diced
- ¼ cup whole-wheat panko bread crumbs

INSTRUCTIONS:

ONE: Preheat oven to 375°F. Place 6 1-cup ramekins on a large baking sheet and mist each with cooking spray; set aside.

TWO: Bring a large pot of water to boil on high heat. Add macaroni and cook until al dente, 8 to 10 minutes. Drain, return macaroni to pot and cover to keep warm.

THREE: In a large saucepan, heat oil on medium-high. Add lobster shell and sauté, stirring occasionally, for 3 minutes. Add broth and bring to a boil; reduce heat to medium and simmer for 5 minutes. Set a fine mesh sieve over a large bowl; carefully strain and reserve broth, discarding shell.

FOUR: Rinse saucepan and place on medium heat; melt buttery spread. Add shallots and sauté, stirring occasionally, for 2 minutes, until softened and pale in color. Add flour, paprika, salt and pepper, stirring to coat, and sauté for 1 minute. Add reserved broth and whisk constantly until thickened, about 3 minutes.

FIVE: Add milk and cook, stirring, until heated through, 1 to 2 minutes. Remove from heat and add lobster meat and ¾ cup cheese; stir until cheese is melted. Add lobster-cheese mixture to macaroni and stir to combine. Add tomato and stir. Spoon 1 cup macaroni-cheese mixture into each ramekin and top with panko and remaining ¼ cup cheese, dividing evenly. Transfer sheet with ramekins to oven and bake until cheese is melted and panko is golden, 7 to 9 minutes.

Nutrients per ramekin: *Calories: 444, Total Fat: 8 g, Sat. Fat: 2 g, Monounsaturated Fat: 2 g, Polyunsaturated Fat: 1 g, Carbs: 55 g, Fiber: 2 g, Sugars: 3 g, Protein: 37 g, Sodium: 456 mg, Cholesterol: 86 mg*

Scallops

WITH MINT VINAIGRETTE & PEA PURÉE

Serves 4. *Hands-on time: 30 minutes.* *Total time: 30 minutes.*

Looking for a quick dinner that delivers all the taste your family wants? This scallop dish will please you with its quick preparation, and please your family with its fresh and light taste.

INGREDIENTS:

- 6 tsp olive oil, divided
- 2 leeks, trimmed, rinsed and thinly sliced
- ¼ tsp sea salt, divided
- 1 tsp fresh thyme leaves
- 2 cups frozen green peas
- ¾ cup low-fat milk, plus additional if needed
- 1 lb sea scallops
- 1 tsp fresh lemon juice
- 2 tsp white wine vinegar
- 1 tsp minced fresh mint
- ½ tsp raw honey

INSTRUCTIONS:

ONE: Heat a skillet on medium-low. Add 1 tsp oil and swirl to coat skillet. Add leeks and ⅛ tsp salt and cook, stirring occasionally, until leeks are softened and just starting to brown. Add thyme, peas and milk. Increase heat to medium and cook, stirring, until peas are heated through, about 5 minutes. Remove mixture from heat.

TWO: Scrape pea-milk mixture into a blender and purée until smooth, adding a bit more milk to thin, if necessary.

THREE: Heat a large clean skillet on medium-high. Add 1 tsp oil and swirl to coat pan. Add scallops, leaving a bit of space between each to prevent steaming. Sear scallops for about 3 minutes per side, until golden brown and barely firm to the touch. Transfer scallops to a plate.

FOUR: In a small bowl, whisk together remaining 4 tsp oil, lemon juice, vinegar, 1 tsp water, mint, honey and remaining ⅛ tsp salt.

FIVE: To serve, spoon ½ cup pea purée onto each of 4 plates and top with 4 scallops. Spoon 2 tsp vinaigrette over top of scallops and serve.

Nutrients per serving (4 scallops, ½ cup pea purée, 2 tsp vinaigrette): Calories: 259, Total Fat: 9 g, Sat. Fat: 1 g, Monounsaturated Fat: 5.5 g, Polyunsaturated Fat: 1 g, Omega-3s: 376 mg, Omega-6s: 802 mg, Carbs: 22 g, Fiber: 4 g, Sugars: 8.5 g, Protein: 24 g, Sodium: 449 mg, Cholesterol: 40 g

NUTRITIONAL BONUS: Green peas offer loads of protein, fiber, vitamin K and C, manganese, and B-vitamins thiamin, folate and B6. Folate promotes healthy red blood cell formation while vitamin B6 helps keep your blood glucose levels within a normal range.

Broiled Figs & Scallops

WITH SHREDDED BEETS, WALNUTS & MINT

Serves 4. *Hands-on time: 30 minutes.* *Total time: 30 minutes.*

Black Mission figs are so named because the Spanish clergy, who established religious settlements called "missions," planted fig trees along the California coast. Most of the figs sold in the US are still grown in California. Other common types, such as Brown Turkey figs and Calimyrnas, may be used interchangeably in this recipe.

INGREDIENTS:

- 3 medium beets, trimmed, peeled and quartered
- 1 Tbsp walnut oil or extra-virgin olive oil
- 1 Tbsp red or white wine vinegar
- 1 tsp raw honey
- ½ tsp sea salt, divided
- Fresh ground black pepper, to taste
- Olive oil cooking spray
- 1 lb sea scallops
- 10 fresh Black Mission figs, trimmed and halved
- 1 oz unsalted walnuts, chopped and toasted
- 2 Tbsp chopped mint leaves

INSTRUCTIONS:

ONE: In a food processor, shred beets, then transfer to a large bowl. In a small bowl, whisk oil, vinegar and honey. Pour mixture over beets, season with ¼ tsp salt and pepper and mix well.

TWO: Preheat broiler. Coat a rimmed baking sheet with cooking spray. Season scallops on both sides with remaining ¼ tsp salt and pepper, then place on baking sheet in a single layer. Arrange figs, cut side up, around scallops and season lightly with pepper. Mist scallops and figs with cooking spray. Broil 6 to 8 inches from heat until tops of scallops appear opaque and figs are juicy and tender, 4 to 5 minutes. Transfer figs to a plate and set aside. Flip scallops and return to broiler, cooking until firm to the touch and opaque in the center, 2 to 3 minutes.

THREE: Divide beet mixture among 4 plates. Arrange figs and scallops over top, dividing evenly, and sprinkle with walnuts and mint. Enjoy!

TIP: If you don't have a food processor, shred the beets on the large holes of a box grater.

Nutrients per serving (⅔ cup beets, 3 to 4 scallops, 1 Tbsp walnuts, 5 fig halves): Calories: 310, Total Fat: 9 g, Sat. Fat: 1 g, Monounsaturated Fat: 2 g, Polyunsaturated Fat: 6 g, Omega-3s: 870 mg, Omega-6s: 2,760 mg, Carbs: 34 g, Fiber: 5 g, Sugars: 15 g, Protein: 22 g, Sodium: 471 mg, Cholesterol: 37 mg

Broiled Figs & Scallops

MAIN COURSES: SEAFOOD

Nutritional Bonus:
The small amount of walnuts here contributes 640 mg of omega-3 fatty acids per serving. Along with its connection to a reduced risk of cardiovascular disease, this healthy fat may help relieve joint pain in people with rheumatoid arthritis and inflammatory bowel disease, according to an analysis of 17 clinical studies.

Poblano
Rice with
Shrimp

THE BEST OF CLEAN EATING 3

Poblano Rice

WITH SHRIMP

Serves 4.

This recipe comes from New York-based chef Allison Fishman, who shared it exclusively with *CE*. Like it hot? Leave the seeds in the jalapeños and poblanos to kick up the spice factor.

INGREDIENTS:

- 1 large poblano pepper, halved lengthwise, seeded and stem discarded
- 1 jalapeño pepper, halved lengthwise, seeded and stem discarded
- 2 scallions, trimmed
- ¼ cup roasted sunflower seeds
- 1 cup fresh cilantro leaves, gently packed, plus additional for garnish
- Juice 1 lime (about 2 Tbsp)
- 2 Tbsp olive oil
- 1 cup long-grain brown rice
- ½ tsp kosher salt
- 1 lb frozen jumbo shrimp (16 to 20 count), deveined, tail on
- 1 small red onion, finely chopped, optional, for garnish
- Lime wedges, optional

INSTRUCTIONS:

ONE: Set broiler. Place both peppers, skin side up, on a broiler pan with scallions. Broil until blistered, about 5 minutes. Remove poblano to a bowl and cover with plastic wrap. Allow poblano to steam for 10 minutes; remove skin.

TWO: In the bowl of a food processor, combine peppers and scallions; pulse until puréed. Add sunflower seeds; pulse to make a paste. Add cilantro, lime juice and oil, pulsing until cilantro is incorporated. Scrape bowl as needed. Remove pesto and reserve.

THREE: Bring 1¼ cups water to boil. Add rice and salt; reduce heat to low, cover and simmer for 15 minutes. Remove rice from heat and allow to steam for 5 additional minutes, then use a fork to fluff. Add pesto to rice, a little at a time, and continue to toss gently with a fork until combined.

FOUR: Meanwhile, bring a large pot of water to boil. Add shrimp, return to a boil, and cook until pink and lightly curled; about 3 minutes. Remove from heat with a slotted spoon. When cool enough to handle, remove shells from shrimp.

FIVE: Spoon rice onto large serving platter and place shrimp on top; garnish with cilantro. Serve with onion and lime wedges, if desired.

Nutrients per 1-cup serving: Calories: 336, Total Fat: 13 g, Sat. Fat: 2 g, Monounsaturated Fat: 7 g, Polyunsaturated Fat: 4 g, Carbs: 42 g, Fiber: 4 g, Sugars: 1 g, Protein: 13 g, Sodium: 300 mg, Cholesterol: 53 mg

Hoisin-Chile Shrimp

WITH GREEN BEANS & WALNUTS

*Serves 4. **Hands-on time:** 20 minutes. **Total time:** 30 minutes.*

Savory tamari and the sweetness of hoisin make this chile-laced stir-fry an exciting dish. Whip it up when you're looking for an exotic answer to, "What's for dinner?"

INGREDIENTS:

- 1 Tbsp orange zest
- ¼ cup 100% orange juice
- 2 Tbsp hoisin sauce
- 1 Tbsp low-sodium tamari
- ½ tsp chile-garlic paste (TIP: Look for it in the Asian section of most grocery stores or in Asian markets.)
- 2 tsp toasted sesame oil
- 1½ lb fresh green beans, trimmed and halved crosswise
- 1 lb medium shrimp, peeled and deveined
- 4 scallions, ends trimmed and thinly sliced
- ¼ cup unsalted walnut pieces, toasted and coarsely chopped

INSTRUCTIONS:

ONE: In a small bowl, whisk orange zest, orange juice, hoisin sauce, tamari and chile-garlic paste; set aside.

TWO: In a wok or large nonstick skillet, heat oil on high. Add beans and stir-fry, stirring frequently, for 4 minutes. Add 3 Tbsp water and cook for 4 more minutes. Add shrimp, scallions and hoisin-chile mixture and stir-fry until shrimp are juicy and just cooked through, about 2 minutes. Top each serving with walnuts, dividing evenly.

Nutrients per 2-cup serving: Calories: 280, Total Fat: 10 g, Sat. Fat: 1 g, Monounsaturated Fat: 2 g, Polyunsaturated Fat: 5.5 g, Omega-3s: 1,300 mg, Omega-6s: 3,040 mg, Carbs: 21 g, Fiber: 7 g, Sugars: 6 g, Protein: 28 g, Sodium: 480 mg, Cholesterol: 170 mg

Nutritional Bonus:

Like all nuts, walnuts pack a punch when it comes to their fat content. But they also abound with antioxidants (more polyphenols than any other common nut, as a matter of fact!), protein and heart-healthy alpha-linolenic acid (ALA), a plant-based omega-3 essential fatty acid.

Summer Squash Pasta
WITH SCALLOPS & GOAT CHEESE

Serves 4. **Hands-on time:** *45 minutes.* **Total time:** *1 hour.*

With a mild flavor, summer squash is best roasted or grilled to bring out its natural sweetness. The most common variety, apart from zucchini, is the crookneck yellow squash with a long neck and round end.

INGREDIENTS:

- Olive oil cooking spray
- 5 yellow summer squash, cut into 1-inch chunks
- ½ tsp dried herbs (any combination of thyme, rosemary, oregano and marjoram)
- Fresh ground black pepper, to taste
- ¼ tsp sea salt, divided, plus additional to taste
- 1 Tbsp olive oil, divided
- 1 red onion, halved lengthwise and thinly sliced
- 2 cloves garlic, minced
- 1 tsp fresh rosemary leaves, chopped
- 8 oz whole-wheat penne pasta
- 3 oz goat cheese, crumbled, divided
- ½ cup fresh herbs (any combination of mint, basil, parsley, dill and thyme), chopped
- 1 lb sea scallops (about 8 large)

INSTRUCTIONS:

ONE: Preheat oven to 425°F. Coat a rimmed baking sheet with cooking spray. Add squash, dried herbs, pepper and ⅛ tsp salt. Coat with cooking spray and toss to combine, then spread out in a single layer. Roast for 20 to 22 minutes, stirring once or twice, until tender and richly browned. Set aside. (Squash may be roasted up to 1 day ahead and refrigerated; bring to room temperature before using.)

TWO: In a large nonstick skillet on medium-low, heat ½ Tbsp oil. Add onion and season to taste with salt and pepper. Cook for 20 minutes, stirring occasionally, or until very soft and golden brown. (Reduce heat if onion browns too quickly.) Add garlic and rosemary and cook for 2 minutes more. Transfer onion mixture to a bowl and set skillet aside.

THREE: Meanwhile, bring a large pot of water to a boil. Add penne and cook according to package directions. Right before pasta is done, reserve ½ cup pasta cooking water. Drain pasta and return to pot.

FOUR: Return pot to stove on low heat and add squash, onion mixture, 2 oz goat cheese, fresh herbs and ¼ cup reserved pasta cooking water. Mix well, adding pasta cooking water as desired. Divide penne mixture among 4 bowls.

FIVE: Wipe out skillet, add remaining oil and heat on medium-high. Season scallops with pepper and remaining salt. Add scallops to skillet and cook, without moving, for 4 to 6 minutes or until deeply browned on bottom side. Flip and repeat on opposite side until centers are no longer translucent, about 4 more minutes. Arrange 2 scallops over each bowl of pasta. Sprinkle with remaining goat cheese, dividing evenly, and serve.

Nutrients per serving (1½ cups pasta and 2 scallops): *Calories: 454, Total Fat: 11 g, Sat. Fat: 4 g, Monounsaturated Fat: 4 g, Polyunsaturated Fat: 1 g, Omega-3s: 390 mg, Omega-6s: 510 mg, Carbs: 57 g, Fiber: 8 g, Sugars: 8 g, Protein: 34 g, Sodium: 410mg, Cholesterol: 56 mg*

Coriander & Fennel Seed Trout
WITH TOMATO-FENNEL RELISH

Serves 4. **Hands-on time:** *20 minutes.* **Total time:** *30 minutes.*

Want to serve dinner in a snap? Trout to the rescue! A quick rub and brief cook is all it needs before gracing your table. And by adding our Tomato-Fennel Relish, you'll provide a bright counterpoint to the earthier flavors of the fish. This dish is so elegant that diners will assume you slaved for hours!

INGREDIENTS:

- 1½ cups coarsely chopped cherry tomatoes
- ¼ cup finely diced fennel bulb
- 2 Tbsp chopped feathery fennel fronds, plus additional for garnish
- 2 tsp white balsamic or white wine vinegar
- 2 tsp olive oil
- Sea salt and fresh ground black pepper, to taste
- High-heat cooking oil (such as sunflower, safflower, peanut or grape seed oil), as needed
- 2 boneless whole trout (10 to 12 oz each), head and tail removed, skin left on, each cut lengthwise along spine into 2 fillets (4 fillets total)
- 4 tsp Coriander & Fennel Seed Rub (see recipe, p. 234)

INSTRUCTIONS:

ONE: Prepare relish: In a medium bowl, combine tomatoes, fennel bulb and fronds, vinegar and olive oil. Season with salt and pepper. Set aside.

TWO: Heat grill to high and lightly oil grate with cooking oil. Sprinkle both sides of trout with Coriander & Fennel Seed Rub and grill for 2 minutes per side or until barely opaque.

THREE: Serve trout with relish over top, garnished with additional fennel fronds.

Nutrients per serving (1 trout fillet and ⅓ cup relish): *Calories: 191, Total Fat: 6 g, Sat. Fat: 1 g, Monounsaturated Fat: 2 g, Polyunsaturated Fat: 2 g, Omega-3s: 1,000 mg, Omega-6s: 580 mg, Carbs: 4 g, Fiber: 2 g, Sugars: 1 g, Protein: 30 g, Sodium: 311 mg, Cholesterol: 84 mg*

Nutritional Bonus:
Fill your plate with squash this summer and you'll have plenty of calories left over for a treat. With just 20 calories per cup of sliced squash and 35% of your daily vitamin C needs, this veggie is an excellent source of immunity-boosting nutrition.

Coriander
& Fennel
Seed Trout

Stove-Top Seafood & Veggie Bake

Stove-Top Seafood & Veggie Bake

Serves 8. **Hands-on time:** *12 minutes.* **Total time:** *42 minutes.*

Mop up the leftover broth from this delicious seafood and vegetable bake with a piece of crusty whole-grain bread.

INGREDIENTS:

- 1 1½-lb whole shell-on lobster, steamed
- 1 lb shell-on shrimp (16 to 20 count), deveined
- 1½ Tbsp olive oil, divided
- 1½ cups low-sodium chicken broth
- 1 medium yellow onion, minced
- 1 medium carrot, finely diced (about ½ cup)
- 3 cloves garlic, minced
- 1 bulb fennel, chopped into 1-inch chunks, fronds reserved for garnish
- ½ tsp sea salt
- 1 tsp fresh ground black pepper
- ¼ tsp ground cayenne pepper, optional
- 16 mini red potatoes, scrubbed and halved
- 2 lb littleneck clams, scrubbed
- 4 small ears corn, husks and silk removed, cut into 1-inch chunks
- 2 lb mussels, debearded and scrubbed
- 2 cups grape tomatoes, halved
- 8 sea scallops
- ½ cup chopped fresh Italian parsley

TIP: Save time and effort by asking your fishmonger or supermarket fish vendor to steam the lobster for you.

INSTRUCTIONS:

ONE: Using a small hammer and a heavy cutting board, smash shell of lobster and remove tail and claw meat. Cut into 1-inch chunks, reserving shell. Remove shells from shrimp, leaving tail on and reserving shells.

TWO: Prepare seafood stock: In a medium saucepan, heat ½ Tbsp oil on medium. Add shrimp and lobster shells and sauté until shrimp shells have turned completely pink. Add broth and bring to a boil. Reduce heat and simmer for 5 to 7 minutes, until broth becomes light brown in color. Strain and discard shells, reserving seafood stock.

THREE: In a very large stockpot on medium heat, sauté onion and carrot in remaining oil until onion is translucent and carrot has softened slightly, 2 to 3 minutes. Add garlic and fennel and sauté until fennel has softened slightly, 2 to 3 minutes. Season with salt, pepper and cayenne, if desired. Add potatoes and reserved stock, scraping up any bits from bottom of pot with a wooden spoon. Bring to a boil. Add clams and corn, stirring to combine. Cover with a tight-fitting lid. When clams begin to open, add mussels and tomatoes, stirring to combine; again cover with lid. When mussels begin to open, add shrimp and scallops, stirring to combine; again cover. When shrimp begin to turn pink, add lobster meat. Cover and heat through, about 3 minutes more. Discard unopened clams or mussels.

FOUR: To serve, divide seafood-vegetable mixture equally among 8 shallow bowls. Pour hot stock from bottom of pot over each serving, and garnish with parsley and reserved fennel fronds, dividing evenly.

Nutrients per 12-oz serving: *Calories: 440, Total Fat: 8 g, Sat. Fat: 1 g, Monounsaturated Fat: 3 g, Polyunsaturated Fat: 2 g, Omega-3s: 1,150 mg, Omega-6s: 580 mg, Carbs: 33 g, Fiber: 4 g, Sugars: 5 g, Protein: 56 g, Sodium: 586 mg, Cholesterol: 190 mg*

Thai Peanut Noodles
WITH SHRIMP

Serves 6 to 8. **Hands-on time:** *15 minutes.* **Total time:** *25 minutes.*

This fresh-tasting chilled salad is perfect for summertime picnics or any-time-of-year potlucks. Your family and friends will love the multiple layers of flavor (it includes all four traditional Thai cuisine taste components – hot, sour, salty and sweet). And you'll appreciate how quickly you'll be able to get back to your lazy days of summer (25 minutes from start to table!).

INGREDIENTS:

- ⅓ cup light coconut milk
- ⅓ cup no-salt-added tomato juice
- ¼ cup unsalted, natural peanut butter (crunchy or smooth)
- 2 Tbsp Thai fish sauce
- 3 Tbsp fresh lime juice
- 1 Tbsp raw honey
- ¼ tsp crushed red pepper flakes
- 1 lb medium raw shrimp, peeled and deveined, tails on or off
- 8 oz brown rice noodles
- 2 cups thinly sliced Napa cabbage (about ½ small head)
- 1 green onion, thinly sliced
- 3 Tbsp each chopped fresh mint and cilantro
- 3 Tbsp unsalted peanuts, crushed

INSTRUCTIONS:

ONE: In a large bowl, whisk coconut milk with tomato juice, peanut butter, fish sauce, lime juice, honey and pepper flakes.

TWO: Bring a large pot of water to a boil on high heat. Add shrimp and cook until opaque, about 3 minutes. Using a slotted spoon, transfer shrimp to bowl with coconut milk mixture.

THREE: In same pot, cook noodles according to package directions or until tender, about 6 minutes. Drain and rinse well. Add noodles to bowl with shrimp. Add cabbage, onion, mint and cilantro; toss to coat. Top with peanuts.

Nutrients per 1¼-cup serving (using 8 servings): *Calories: 224, Total Fat: 7 g, Sat. Fat: 2 g, Monounsaturated Fat: 3 g, Polyunsaturated Fat: 1 g, Omega-3s: 290 mg, Omega-6s: 610 mg, Carbs: 24 g, Fiber: 4 g, Sugars: 1 g, Protein: 18 g, Sodium: 548 mg, Cholesterol: 86 mg*

Nutritional Bonus:
Be careful not to judge a recipe by its coconut cover! While the fat content here may seem high, the saturated fat found in coconut milk is actually easily metabolized by the body. In fact, lauric acid – a saturated fat found in coconut milk – has both antiviral and antifungal properties.

Know Your
Shellfish

In addition to highlighting a few nutritional standouts from the most popular types of shellfish, we provide some tips to boost your know-how both at the fish counter and in the kitchen:

SHRIMP

The most sustainable options include wild-caught pink shrimp (think bay or cocktail) or spot prawns and US-farmed Pacific and west coast white shrimp. Avoid imported black tiger shrimp, tiger prawns and white shrimp (farmed white shrimp from Thailand, however, is a good alternative).

NUTRITION SNAPSHOT*: 90 calories; 1 g fat; 17 g of protein help fill you up and prevent fatigue.

BUYING AND COOKING: For a few more dollars, get fresh or frozen shrimp that have been peeled and deveined to save valuable prep time. Use in stir-frys, salads, soups or on the grill. Or, buy shell-on, deveined shrimp, peel them and freeze the shells to make fish stock for your next bisque or pasta sauce base (or our Stove-Top Seafood & Veggie Bake on p. 207!).

OYSTERS

NUTRITION SNAPSHOT*: 57 calories; 2 g fat; 68% of your daily need for vitamin D, which aids in the absorption of nutrients such as calcium and phosphorus, and may help reduce your risk of osteoporosis. Also provides more than 250% of your daily value of zinc, a mineral that helps maintain immune system function.

BUYING AND COOKING: Choose fresh, pre-shucked oysters for use in soups or casseroles. If you prefer to get them on the half-shell, many fish markets will shuck your order for you. You can also place the shelled variety on a grill; when they pop open, they're ready to eat (a drop of hot sauce and a squirt of lemon juice go a long way).

CRAB

Dungeness, Blue, US King, Snow, Jonah, Stone and Kona are good eco-friendly alternatives; avoid imported King crab.

NUTRITION SNAPSHOT*: 73 calories; 1 g fat; 127% of your day's worth of vitamin B12, which is necessary for the formation of red blood cells, proper maintenance of the nervous system, and like all B vitamins, it aids metabolism.

BUYING AND COOKING: Choose live, fresh crab or whole, cooked crab. Boil live crab for 15 to 20 minutes or until bright orange; reheat cooked variety in boiling water for 3 to 4 minutes. Crack shell and pick out the meat. After opening up the body, make sure to remove the spongy gills and small paddles at the front of the crab – these are not consumable. Add the meat to salads and pastas or wrap in rice paper to make spring rolls.

LOBSTER

NUTRITION SNAPSHOT*: 135 calories; 1 g fat; 50% of your recommended daily value of selenium. Deficiency of this trace mineral and antioxidant may contribute to heart disease and a weakened immune system.

BUYING AND COOKING: Purchase lobster tails and simmer until shell is red, 8 minutes for a ½-lb tail (some supermarkets and fishmongers will steam them while you wait). Use to make decadent ravioli, pasta primavera or Mac 'n' Cheese (p. 199); mix with olive oil-based mayonnaise and chopped celery for lobster rolls.

CLAMS

NUTRITION SNAPSHOT*: 63 calories; 1 g fat; 66% of your daily iron requirement to help your body produce energy.

BUYING AND COOKING: Buy fresh clams (littlenecks and steamers are the most common) with tightly closed shells. Scrub with a stiff brush and soak in cold water for 20 minutes; lift shells out of water with your hands, letting sand and grit sink to the bottom. Repeat until soaking water is clear. Steam as you would mussels.

SCALLOPS

Bay and sea varieties are available. Bay scallops are much smaller (approximately ½ inch in diameter), sweeter and more delicate. They are quicker-cooking and are often prepared using gentler methods. Large sea scallops (aka giant scallops; about 1½ inches in diameter) can withstand higher heats, making them well suited for pan-searing.

NUTRITION SNAPSHOT*: 75 calories; 1 g fat; 27% of your recommended daily intake of selenium promotes optimal thyroid gland function.

BUYING AND COOKING: Almost always sold out-of-shell, either fresh or frozen, so no extra prep is required. Add to chowder or sear until golden brown in olive oil.

MUSSELS

NUTRITION SNAPSHOT*: 73 calories; 2 g fat; 170% of your day's recommended dose of vitamin B12, vital in the growth of healthy skin cells.

BUYING AND COOKING: Buy fresh mussels with tightly closed shells. Scrub under running water with a stiff brush to remove any debris and pull off tendrils, or "beards," still clinging to shells. Steam over simmering water in a large covered pot, or cook in a seasoned broth to impart greater flavor; discard any that do not open fully.

* Per 3-oz serving

Main Courses:
Meatless Meals

Raspberry & Brie Flatbreads, p. 215

Clean Eating has created savory meatless masterpieces for you, whether you're vegan or just trying to incorporate more meatless meals into your diet. Our plant-based meals don't skimp on the protein and are made with the freshest ingredients, without the fake veggie meats. Top our flavorful Broccoli Rabe Linguine with feta instead of fatty ground beef. Revel in our Grilled Watermelon Skewers and White Bean Salad, and share them at any outdoor feast or backyard BBQ. Your meatless clean options are endless!

Farro-Corn Cakes
WITH HEIRLOOM TOMATO RELISH

*Serves 4. **Hands-on time:** 45 minutes. **Total time:** 1 hour, 20 minutes.*

You'll purposefully overcook the farro a bit in this crab cake-like dish to help make it sticky enough to shape into a disk. For fresh corn kernels, simply slice them right off the cob.

INGREDIENTS:

- ⅔ cup farro
- 1½ cups fresh corn kernels
- 2 small heirloom tomatoes, cut into ¼-inch dice
- 1½ tsp white balsamic or white wine vinegar
- 1 Tbsp chopped shallots, divided
- 2 Tbsp chopped fresh flat-leaf parsley, divided
- 1 Tbsp chopped fresh tarragon, divided
- ⅔ cup whole-wheat bread crumbs
- 3 large egg whites, lightly beaten
- ½ tsp fine sea salt
- ½ tsp fresh ground black pepper
- 2 Tbsp olive oil
- 3 cups shredded red or green leaf lettuce

INSTRUCTIONS:

ONE: Bring a large saucepan of water to a boil. Add farro and cook until very tender, 50 to 60 minutes. Add corn and cook for an additional 3 minutes or until tender. Drain and transfer to a large bowl. Set aside to cool to room temperature.

TWO: Meanwhile, prepare relish: In a medium bowl, combine tomatoes, vinegar, shallots, 1 Tbsp parsley and 1½ tsp tarragon; set aside.

THREE: In a separate medium bowl, combine bread crumbs, egg whites, salt, pepper and remaining 1 Tbsp parsley and 1½ tsp tarragon. Stir bread crumb mixture into farro mixture. With dampened hands, shape mixture into 8 cakes, each about 3 inches in diameter and ¾-inch thick.

FOUR: In a large skillet or sauté pan (not nonstick), heat oil on medium. Carefully add cakes and cook until golden brown, about 2 minutes per side. Arrange lettuce on 4 plates and top each with 2 farro-corn cakes. Top with relish, dividing evenly, and serve.

Nutrients per serving (2 corn cakes, ¾ cup lettuce, ⅓ cup relish): *Calories: 248, Total Fat: 9 g, Sat. Fat: 1 g, Monounsaturated Fat: 5 g, Polyunsaturated Fat: 1 g, Carbs: 33 g, Fiber: 4 g, Sugars: 4 g, Protein: 9 g, Sodium: 506 mg, Cholesterol: 0 mg*

Farro-Corn
Cakes

Spice-Rubbed Tofu Steaks

Spice-Rubbed Tofu Steaks
WITH GRILLED PEPPER SAUCE

Serves 4. ***Hands-on time:*** *30 minutes.* ***Total time:*** *1 hour.*

Here's a great dish for Meatless Mondays or any time you'd like to go vegetarian. Thanks to their time on the grill, the tofu "steaks" become pleasantly toothsome, and the rub lends delicious dimension to the otherwise plainly flavored protein.

TIP: If you have leftover Grilled Pepper Sauce, save it to top a piece of grilled chicken or fish, or use it as a perfect pizza sauce replacer.

INGREDIENTS:

- 1½ pkg extra-firm tofu (14 to 16 oz each pkg), drained
- ½ onion (halved through root end)
- High-heat cooking oil (such as sunflower, safflower, peanut or grape seed oil), as needed
- 2 Tbsp plus 2 tsp Smoky-Sweet Spice Rub, divided (see recipe, p. 234)
- 1 red bell pepper, cut into eighths
- 1 yellow bell pepper, cut into eighths
- 2 plum tomatoes, halved lengthwise and seeded
- 1 Tbsp no-salt-added tomato paste
- 1 tsp red wine vinegar

INSTRUCTIONS:

ONE: Cut tofu lengthwise into 6 slices total (whole pkg into 4 slices; ½ pkg into 2 slices) and pat dry with paper towel. Cut each slice in half diagonally, making 12 triangles. Arrange a few layers of paper towel in a baking dish, place tofu on top, then cover with a few more layers of paper towel. Place another baking dish on top and weigh down with a few heavy cans. Set aside at room temperature for 30 minutes or covered in refrigerator for up to 1 day.

TWO: Meanwhile, cut onion into 6 wedges, keeping root intact; set aside.

THREE: Heat grill to medium-high and lightly oil grate. Remove cans, additional baking dish and paper towels from tofu, rearrange tofu in dish and sprinkle with 2 Tbsp Smoky-Sweet Spice Rub, rubbing it into both sides. Grill until lightly browned, 3 to 4 minutes per side; remove from grill. Add onion and peppers to grill until softened and lightly charred, 4 to 5 minutes per side; remove from grill. Grill tomatoes, skin side down, until softened and lightly charred, about 2 minutes; remove from grill. Transfer tofu, half of peppers and 4 onion wedges to a platter and cover to keep warm.

FOUR: Prepare Grilled Pepper Sauce: In a food processor, purée remaining peppers, 2 onion wedges and 2 tsp Smoky-Sweet Spice Rub with tomatoes, tomato paste and vinegar. Serve tofu and vegetables with sauce on the side.

Nutrients per serving (3 tofu pieces, 2 pepper pieces, 1 onion wedge, 5 Tbsp sauce): *Calories: 191, Total Fat: 8 g, Sat. Fat: 0.25 g, Carbs: 17 g, Fiber: 5 g, Sugars: 8 g, Protein: 15 g, Sodium: 230 mg, Cholesterol: 0 mg*

Raspberry & Brie Flatbreads

Serves 4. ***Hands-on time:*** *40 minutes.* ***Total time:*** *48 minutes.*

Each of the tiny globules that make up a single raspberry contains its own seed. This means the raspberry is an "aggregate," made up of many tiny, individual fruits. In the United States, these ruby-red (you may also spot white raspberries) fruits are grown mostly in California, Washington and Oregon.

INGREDIENTS:

- Olive oil cooking spray
- 2 onions, halved lengthwise and thinly sliced
- 1½ tsp rosemary leaves, chopped
- Fresh ground black pepper, to taste
- 14 oz store-bought whole-wheat pizza dough
- Whole-wheat flour, as needed for rolling dough
- 3½ oz brie, thinly sliced
- 1½ cups raspberries
- 2 Tbsp basil leaves, chopped

INSTRUCTIONS:

ONE: If using a pizza stone, place stone on a rack in center of oven and preheat oven to 550°F. If using a rimmed baking sheet, preheat oven to 550°F for 15 minutes, then place baking sheet upside down on center rack in oven and heat for an additional 15 minutes.

TWO: Heat a large skillet on medium-low. Coat with cooking spray and add onions. Cook, stirring occasionally, for 15 to 20 minutes or until soft and golden brown, reducing heat if onions start browning too quickly. Stir in rosemary and pepper. Transfer mixture to a blender. Add 3 Tbsp water and purée to form a chunky paste. Set aside.

THREE: Divide dough into 4 equal portions. Place each portion on a piece of parchment paper approximately the size of your pizza stone or baking sheet and lightly sprinkle with flour. Roll each dough portion into a 7-inch-long by ¼-inch-thick oval. Spread onion purée evenly on each oval, leaving a 1-inch border. Divide brie and raspberries evenly on each.

FOUR: If using pizza stone, carefully remove stone from oven and use a pizza peel or baking sheet to transfer flatbreads and parchment paper onto stone. If using rimmed baking sheet, carefully remove sheet from oven and slide flatbreads and parchment paper onto upside-down sheet and return to oven. Bake until edges are puffed and browned, 5 to 8 minutes. Sprinkle with basil and serve.

OPTIONS: If you can't find fresh whole-wheat pizza dough, make this recipe with 6-inch prepared whole-wheat flat bread or pita bread. Just add toppings and bake on a rimmed baking sheet in a 400°F oven until cheese melts and bread is crisp, 6 to 10 minutes, depending on thickness of bread.

NOTE: Turning your baking sheet upside down in this recipe makes it easier to slide the parchment paper on and off.

Nutrients per flatbread: *Calories: 360, Total Fat: 10 g, Sat. Fat: 4 g, Carbs: 54 g, Fiber: 10 g, Sugars: 6 g, Protein: 13 g, Sodium: 452 mg, Cholesterol: 25 mg*

For a photo of this recipe, see page 210.

Butternut Squash Risotto
WITH CHESTNUTS & TALEGGIO

Serves 4. *Hands-on time:* 30 minutes. *Total time:* 1 hour, 30 minutes.

If you're looking to boost your dinner with a beverage, a happy wine pairing for this Italian rice dish is a Merlot. Its soft, round, black cherry fruit flavors complement the pungent Italian mountain cheese, sweet chestnuts and squash.

INGREDIENTS:

- 5 cups low-sodium chicken or vegetable broth
- 3 cups peeled and diced butternut squash
- 2 tsp extra-virgin olive oil
- ½ cup chopped red onion
- 3 cloves garlic, minced
- 1 Tbsp chopped fresh rosemary
- 1 cup brown arborio rice or short-grain brown rice
- ½ cup dry white wine
- 1 cup jarred, cooked chestnuts, quartered
- 3 oz taleggio cheese, shredded (about ¾ cup), divided
- Sea salt and fresh ground black pepper, to taste

INSTRUCTIONS:

ONE: In a medium saucepan, bring broth to a boil on high heat. Reduce heat to lowest setting.

TWO: Set a steamer basket in a pot and add enough water to reach bottom portion of basket. Bring water to a boil, add squash, cover and reduce heat to medium. Steam until squash is tender when pierced with a sharp knife, about 6 minutes. Turn off heat.

THREE: In a large saucepan, heat oil on medium. Add onion, garlic and rosemary and sauté, stirring occasionally, for 3 minutes, until onion is translucent. Add rice and stir for 30 seconds to coat with oil. Add wine and cook, stirring constantly, until liquid is almost fully absorbed, about 2 minutes. Reduce heat to low, stir in ½ cup broth and cook, stirring occasionally, until broth is almost absorbed. Stir in another ½ cup broth and cook, stirring occasionally, until almost absorbed. Repeat steps until all broth is added, about 45 minutes total. Stir in squash, chestnuts and all but 4 Tbsp taleggio cheese. Serve, garnishing each bowl with remaining taleggio cheese, dividing evenly.

Nutrients per 1¼-cup serving: *Calories: 480, Total Fat: 12 g, Sat. Fat: 5 g, Monounsaturated Fat: 5 g, Polyunsaturated Fat: 1 g, Carbs: 73 g, Fiber: 5 g, Sugars: 4 g, Protein: 18 g, Sodium: 310 mg, Cholesterol: 25 mg*

NUTRITIONAL BONUS: Brown arborio rice, though less creamy than its white counterpart, has more fiber and nutrients (including immunity-boosting vitamin B6) because its chewy bran coating has been left intact.

Spring Vegetable Ravioli
WITH MINT RICOTTA

Serves 4. *Hands-on time:* 45 minutes. *Total time:* 45 minutes.

Juicy, garden-fresh grape tomatoes burst into a fresh, sweet sauce in this veggie-loaded cheese ravioli, which we've accented with a dollop of minty ricotta.

INGREDIENTS:

- ½ Tbsp olive oil
- 2 yellow summer squash or zucchini, halved lengthwise and sliced ¼-inch thick
- ½ tsp dried thyme, divided
- ⅔ cup low-fat ricotta cheese
- 2 Tbsp chopped fresh mint or basil
- Olive oil cooking spray
- 1 lb thin asparagus, trimmed and cut into 2-inch pieces
- 1½ cups grape tomatoes
- 3 cloves garlic, chopped
- 1 cup frozen artichoke hearts, thawed and quartered
- Sea salt and fresh ground black pepper, to taste
- 1 9-oz pkg fresh spelt or whole-wheat cheese ravioli

INSTRUCTIONS:

ONE: In a large skillet, heat oil on medium-high. Add squash and ¼ tsp thyme and sauté, stirring occasionally, until tender and lightly browned, about 10 minutes.

TWO: Meanwhile, in a small bowl, combine ricotta and mint. Refrigerate until needed.

THREE: Transfer squash mixture to a medium bowl. Reduce heat on skillet to medium and mist with cooking spray. Add asparagus and sauté, stirring occasionally, until tender-crisp, 6 to 8 minutes. Add to bowl with squash.

FOUR: Increase heat to medium-high and add tomatoes. Sauté, stirring frequently, for 2 minutes. Add garlic and sauté, stirring frequently, for 1 minute. Add ¼ cup water and remaining ¼ tsp thyme and bring to a simmer. Cook, stirring occasionally, until water evaporates and tomatoes just begin to burst, 3 to 4 minutes. Stir in artichokes and squash-asparagus mixture and cook until heated through, about 2 minutes. Season with salt and pepper and remove from heat.

FIVE: Cook ravioli according to package directions. Drain and divide among serving bowls. Top each with squash-tomato mixture and ricotta mixture.

Nutrients per serving (11 ravioli, 1 cup vegetables and 2½ Tbsp ricotta mixture): *Calories: 325, Total Fat: 11 g, Sat. Fat: 5 g, Monounsaturated Fat: 1 g, Polyunsaturated Fat: 0 g, Carbs: 41 g, Fiber: 10 g, Sugars: 10 g, Protein: 18 g, Sodium: 528 mg, Cholesterol: 53 mg*

Spring
Vegetable
Ravioli

Gardener's Shepherd's Pie

Nutritional Bonus:
Your body absorbs more iron from plant-based foods when combined with vitamin C, and this pie boasts a healthy dose of both. Each 2-cup serving fulfills 58% of your daily need for the immunity-boosting vitamin and 36% of your requirement for the mineral vital in the transportation of oxygen to cells.

Gardener's Shepherd's Pie

Serves 4. Hands-on time: *30 minutes.* **Total time:** *1 hour, 15 minutes.*

Vegetarians and meat-eaters alike will be drawn to the comforts of this hearty stew, thick with creamy beans and the bright colors of garden fare. We've even topped the oven-baked classic with a layer of creamy mashed potatoes, just like signature shepherd's pie!

INGREDIENTS:

- 1½ lb Russet potatoes (about 4 small), peeled and cut into large pieces
- 2 tsp olive oil
- 1 large leek, white and light green parts thinly sliced, rinsed well
- 2 medium carrots, peeled and sliced into ¼-inch rounds (about 1 cup)
- 2 medium turnips, diced small (about 1½ cups)
- ½ cup fresh or frozen peas
- ¼ lb fresh green beans, trimmed and cut into ½-inch pieces
- 5 small cloves garlic, smashed with flat side of a knife
- 2 cups low-sodium vegetable broth, divided
- 3 large Swiss chard leaves, torn into medium pieces
- 2 sprigs thyme, leaves chopped
- 2 cups cooked cannellini beans
- ½ tsp sea salt
- ½ tsp fresh ground black pepper
- ⅓ cup low-fat milk
- 2 Tbsp low-fat sour cream
- 1 Tbsp chopped fresh chives

INSTRUCTIONS:

ONE: Preheat oven to 400°F. Place potatoes in a large pot filled with enough cold water to just cover them. Bring water to a boil, cover and reduce heat to low. Simmer until fork tender, about 15 minutes. Drain potatoes very well and set aside. Reserve pot.

TWO: Meanwhile, add oil to a large Dutch oven or wide saucepot on medium-high. Add leek and sauté for 5 minutes, stirring often, until it begins to soften. Add carrots, turnips, peas, green beans and garlic and sauté for 10 more minutes, stirring occasionally, until vegetables begin to soften and brown bits form on the bottom of the pan. Pour in ½ cup broth, scraping brown bits from bottom as broth evaporates.

THREE: Add chard and thyme and sauté until chard wilts, about 2 minutes. Add cannellini beans, remaining broth, salt and pepper and simmer for 10 minutes, until liquid reduces slightly and vegetables are fork tender.

FOUR: While vegetables cook, warm milk in pot reserved from potatoes. Add potatoes and mash with a potato masher until mostly smooth (potatoes will be thick with some chunks). Stir in sour cream and chives.

FIVE: Transfer stewed vegetables to a 10-inch pie dish. Spread potatoes over top of vegetables, to edges of dish. Put pie dish on a baking sheet and transfer to oven. Bake until vegetable liquid bubbles and potato topping begins to brown, about 20 minutes.

SIX: Remove from oven and let rest for about 10 minutes before serving.

Nutrients per 2-cup serving: *Calories: 366, Total Fat: 5 g, Sat. Fat: 1 g, Carbs: 68 g, Fiber: 12 g, Sugars: 9 g, Protein: 14 g, Sodium: 366 mg, Cholesterol: 4 mg*

Pasta Lentil Bolognese

Serves 4. Hands-on time: *20 minutes.* **Total time:** *1 hour, 10 minutes.*

Bolognese sauce is a rich ragoût that simmers for hours, coaxing flavor from aromatic vegetables and texture from at least one form of meat. Our plant-based version honors its roots with steady preparation (thankfully quicker than several hours!) that persuades sweet notes from caramelized vegetables and soft yet sturdy chew from meaty lentils. A splash of milk toward the end of an hour-long stovetop stay rounds out the zip of the tomato-based sauce.

INGREDIENTS:

- 2 tsp olive oil
- 1 medium onion, diced small (1 cup)
- 1 medium carrot, peeled and diced small (1 cup)
- 2 small celery stalks, diced small (½ cup)
- 1 small fennel bulb, diced small (1½ cups)
- 4 cloves garlic, minced
- 2 Tbsp white wine vinegar
- 2 cups low-sodium vegetable broth
- 1 cup green lentils
- 2½ cups jarred or tetra-packed no-salt-added chopped or crushed tomatoes with juices (about 28 oz)
- 2 tsp dried oregano
- 2 tsp dried parsley
- 1 tsp dried basil
- 8 oz wide whole-wheat pasta noodles such as linguine, fettucine, tagliatelle or rigatoni
- ½ cup low-fat milk
- ¼ tsp sea salt
- ½ tsp fresh ground black pepper

INSTRUCTIONS:

ONE: In a large Dutch oven or saucepot, heat oil on medium-high. Add onion, carrot, celery, fennel and garlic. Cook, stirring often, until released water evaporates and brown bits begin to form on bottom of pot, about 15 minutes. Add vinegar and scrape any brown bits from bottom of pot as liquid evaporates. Stir in broth, 1 cup water, lentils, tomatoes, oregano, parsley and basil. Reduce heat to medium and simmer, partially covered, for 45 minutes, stirring occasionally.

TWO: Meanwhile, bring a large pot of water to a boil and prepare pasta according to package directions. Drain pasta and set aside.

THREE: Add milk to bolognese and continue to simmer for an additional 10 minutes. Season with salt and pepper. Divide pasta among 4 bowls and top each with about 1½ cups bolognese.

Nutrients per serving (4 oz pasta and 1½ cups bolognese): *Calories: 337, Total Fat: 4 g, Sat. Fat: 1 g, Carbs: 68 g, Fiber: 15 g, Sugars: 8 g, Protein: 13 g, Sodium: 484 mg, Cholesterol: 1 mg*

Pineapple Curry Tofu

*Serves 6. **Makes** 7 cups.*

Have some leftover tofu to use up? Try this delectable, heart-healthy recipe from Chef Mayra Trabulse. It combines tropical flavors with the delightful crunch of veggies to satisfy even the biggest tofu skeptic.

INGREDIENTS:

- ¼ cup all-purpose whole-wheat flour
- 2 tsp curry powder, divided
- Sea salt and fresh ground black pepper, to taste
- 1 pkg extra-firm tofu (350 g), drained and cut into 1-inch cubes
- 1 Tbsp coconut oil, divided
- 1 green bell pepper, chopped
- 1 onion, chopped
- 2 cloves garlic, minced
- 8 oz fresh pineapple, cut into ½-inch pieces (about quarter of pineapple)
- 14 oz diced tomatoes, boxed or jarred
- 3 Tbsp unsweetened currants or raisins
- 2 tsp Asian hot sauce (such as Sriracha)
- 1¾ cups light coconut milk
- 1 tsp tapioca flour
- ⅓ cup chopped fresh cilantro, divided
- 2 Tbsp fresh lime juice
- ⅓ cup coarsely chopped raw unsalted cashews, optional

INSTRUCTIONS:

ONE: In a medium bowl, combine whole-wheat flour, 1 tsp curry powder, salt and black pepper. Add tofu, tossing to coat.

TWO: In a large nonstick skillet, heat ½ Tbsp oil on medium-high. Add tofu and cook, stirring occasionally, until lightly crisp on all sides, about 5 minutes. Transfer tofu to a plate; return skillet to stove top and reduce heat to medium. Add remaining ½ Tbsp oil. Add green pepper, onion and garlic and cook until tender, stirring occasionally, about 3 minutes.

THREE: Stir in pineapple, tomatoes and their juices, currants, remaining curry powder and hot sauce. Bring to a boil; return tofu to skillet and reduce to a simmer. Cover and cook for 10 minutes.

FOUR: In a separate medium bowl, whisk coconut milk and tapioca flour; stir into skillet. Cook, stirring, until thickened and bubbly, about 1 minute. Reduce heat to low and simmer for 2 more minutes. Stir in lime juice and half of cilantro. Sprinkle with remaining cilantro and cashews, if desired.

TRY IT: Serve over cooked brown rice, sweet potatoes, rice noodles or simply as is in a bowl.

Nutrients per 1-cup serving: Calories: 200, Total Fat: 9 g, Sat. Fat: 5.5 g, Carbs: 23 g, Fiber: 5 g, Sugars: 13 g, Protein: 8 g, Sodium: 77 mg, Cholesterol: 0 mg

Spaghetti
WITH KALE, FETA & POACHED EGG

*Serves 4. **Hands-on time:** 15 minutes. **Total time:** 45 minutes.*

Is spaghetti the only thing on your kids' minds? Shake up the usual fare with the addition of fresh kale, tangy feta and protein-packed eggs. Even your kids will slow down to enjoy each bite!

INGREDIENTS:

- 1 lb curly kale, rinsed
- 2 tsp olive oil
- 1 medium red onion, chopped
- ½ tsp red pepper flakes
- Pinch sea salt, plus additional to taste
- 2 cups low-sodium chicken or vegetable broth
- 4 cloves garlic, minced
- 4 large eggs
- ½ lb whole-wheat spaghetti (8 oz)
- 4 oz crumbled feta cheese (about 1½ cups)
- Fresh ground black pepper, to taste

INSTRUCTIONS:

ONE: Fill a large pot with water and bring to a boil on high heat.

TWO: Remove leaves from kale stems. Thinly slice stems and set aside; coarsely chop leaves. Add kale leaves to pot and cook for 2 minutes. Using tongs or a slotted spoon, remove kale leaves from pot; transfer to a mesh sieve. Keep pot with water simmering on low.

THREE: In a large nonstick skillet, heat oil on medium-high. Add kale stems, onion, red pepper flakes and salt. Cook, stirring frequently, until onion is golden, about 8 minutes. Add kale leaves and broth, stir and cook for 5 more minutes. Stir in garlic and reduce heat to low.

FOUR: In a large saucepan, bring 2 inches of water to a boil on high heat. Crack each egg separately into a small bowl or cup. Slowly pour each egg into water and reduce heat to low; cook for 4 minutes.

FIVE: Meanwhile, bring pot of water back to a boil and add spaghetti. Cook according to package directions. Drain and add spaghetti to kale mixture; toss to mix. Divide mixture evenly among serving bowls and top each with 1 poached egg and feta. Season with salt and pepper.

Nutrients per serving (2 cups spaghetti-kale mixture, 1 egg, 1 oz feta): Calories: 440, Total Fat: 13 g, Sat. Fat: 5 g, Monounsaturated Fat: 4 g, Polyunsaturated Fat: 2 g, Carbs: 60 g, Fiber: 10 g, Sugars: 4 g, Protein: 27 g, Sodium: 610 mg, Cholesterol: 220 mg

Pizza Margherita

*Serves 4. **Makes** 1 12- to 14-inch pizza, 12 oz dough and 3 cups sauce. **Hands-on time:** 30 minutes. **Total time:** 3 hours, 30 minutes (includes rising and chilling time).*

This pizza is classic in its simplicity, with bright tomato sauce, creamy cheese and sweet basil all in delicious harmony. Use the best ingredients you can find so the natural flavors really shine.

TIP: To save time, you can also opt for 12 oz frozen pizza dough, thawed.

INGREDIENTS:

- White whole-wheat flour, as needed for dusting
- 6 oz part-skim low-moisture mozzarella cheese, shredded (about 1½ cups)
- 16 fresh basil leaves, torn into pieces

DOUGH

- ¼ tsp active dry yeast
- 1⅔ cups white whole-wheat flour
- ¼ tsp fine sea salt
- Olive oil cooking spray

NAPOLETANA-STYLE SAUCE

- 1 24- to 26-oz jar or box unsalted strained tomatoes
- 3 cloves garlic, minced
- 1 tsp red wine vinegar, plus additional to taste
- 1½ tsp chopped fresh oregano leaves
- ¼ tsp fine sea salt
- ⅛ tsp fresh ground black pepper

INSTRUCTIONS:

ONE: Prepare dough: In the bowl of an electric mixer fitted with a dough hook attachment, add 3 Tbsp warm water (120°F). Sprinkle yeast over top and set aside for 15 minutes.

NOTE: If water is too hot, it will kill the yeast; too cool, and yeast will fail to activate.

TWO: Add ½ cup cool water, 1⅔ cups flour and salt to yeast mixture. Mix with dough hook on medium-low setting for 4 minutes; let rest for 5 minutes. Mix on medium-low for an additional 3 minutes, until smooth and slightly sticky.

THREE: Generously coat a large bowl with cooking spray; transfer dough to bowl, rolling to coat in oil. Cover bowl with plastic wrap and let sit at room temperature for 90 minutes, then refrigerate for 1 hour. Dough will increase in size – almost double. Return dough to room temperature before using.

NOTE: For a sweeter and chewier dough, let sit at room temperature for 30 minutes, then refrigerate overnight.

FOUR: Prepare sauce: In a large bowl, combine tomatoes, garlic, vinegar, oregano, salt and pepper. Add more vinegar, if desired. Set aside.

FIVE: Preheat oven to 500°F. (If using a pizza stone, transfer stone to oven and preheat as well.) On a lightly floured surface, roll or stretch dough out to a 12- to 14-inch round. Transfer to a pizza pan or pizza paddle dusted with flour. Top dough evenly with ¾ cup tomato sauce and cheese. Transfer to oven and bake until golden and crisp, 10 to 12 minutes. (If using a pizza stone and paddle, transfer to oven by sliding dough off of paddle and onto hot stone in oven.) Sprinkle with basil, cut into 8 slices and serve.

Nutrients per 2 slices: Calories: 360, Total Fat: 8 g, Sat. Fat: 4.5 g, Monounsaturated Fat: 2 g, Polyunsaturated Fat: 0 g, Carbs: 50 g, Fiber: 11 g, Sugars: 8 g, Protein: 19 g, Sodium: 520 mg, Cholesterol: 25 mg

Nutritional Bonus:
Another reason to enjoy pizza: It's a great source of calcium. A single serving of this recipe provides more than one-third of your daily recommended intake. In addition to helping reduce the risk of osteoporosis, calcium may also lower blood pressure.

Grilled Watermelon Skewers

WITH FETA & WHITE BEAN SALAD

*Serves 4. **Hands-on time:** 35 minutes. **Total time:** 35 minutes.*

Watermelons were first cultivated in Egypt 5,000 years ago and are now popular all over the globe. In fact, they are the most consumed melon in the US, perhaps because their 92% water content makes them exceptionally refreshing.

INGREDIENTS:

- 1½ cups cooked cannellini beans, rinsed (or BPA-free canned beans, drained and rinsed well)
- 2 packed cups arugula leaves
- 1 large shallot, thinly sliced
- 3 Tbsp chopped sun-dried tomatoes (not packed in oil)
- ½ Tbsp extra-virgin olive oil
- 2 oz feta cheese, crumbled
- Sea salt and fresh ground black pepper, to taste
- 1 seedless watermelon, rind removed and cut into 2-inch square chunks
- ½ cup balsamic vinegar

INSTRUCTIONS:

ONE: In a large bowl, combine beans, arugula, shallot, tomatoes and oil. Add cheese and mix gently. Season with salt and pepper. Divide among 4 plates.

TWO: Preheat a grill to medium (or set a broiler to high). Thread 5 chunks watermelon onto each of 4 metal skewers. Place skewers directly on grill grates and cook, turning 2 or 3 times, until light grill marks appear, 6 to 10 minutes total. (If broiling, place skewers on a broiler pan and cook 8 to 10 inches from heat, turning 2 or 3 times, until light browning is visible, 10 to 14 minutes total.) Rest 1 skewer over top of each salad.

THREE: In a small covered saucepan on medium-high heat, bring vinegar to a simmer. Uncover and reduce heat to medium-low to maintain a steady simmer. Cook, swirling pan occasionally, until vinegar coats bottom of pan when tilted, 6 to 8 minutes. Vinegar should be slightly thickened. Remove from heat and immediately drizzle vinegar over salads and watermelon, dividing evenly. Serve immediately.

Nutrients per serving (½ cup salad and 1 skewer watermelon): Calories: 219, Total Fat: 5 g, Sat. Fat: 2 g, Carbs: 36 g, Fiber: 5 g, Sugars: 18 g, Protein: 10 g, Sodium: 320 mg, Cholesterol: 4 mg

NUTRITIONAL BONUS: Watermelon, already everyone's favorite summer refresher, is also an antioxidant powerhouse. Like tomatoes, it contains lycopene, which is constantly being studied for its anticarcinogenic effects. Plus, you can thank the melon's red flesh for its rich stores of beta-carotene, a carotenoid that may help reduce the risk of heart attack, stroke, osteoarthritis and rheumatoid arthritis.

Roasted Squash & Apple Ravioli

*Serves 6 to 8. **Makes** 34 wonton ravioli. **Hands-on time:** 36 minutes. **Total time:** 1 hour, 15 minutes.*

Who doesn't love classic ravioli? To pump up the seasonal goodness, we've added the fresh tastes of squash and apple. Bet you can't resist this dish any time of year!

INGREDIENTS:

- 1 small butternut squash (about 1½ lb), halved and seeded
- 1 apple (such as Granny Smith or Spy), halved and cored
- 2 cloves garlic
- ⅛ tsp ground nutmeg
- Sea salt and fresh ground black pepper, to taste
- 1 cup part-skim smooth ricotta cheese
- 5 oz unripened soft goat cheese
- 68 whole-wheat wonton wrappers
- 2 tsp extra-virgin olive oil
- 1 large leek, trimmed and thinly sliced
- 1 cup low-sodium chicken broth
- ⅓ cup roasted unsalted pumpkin seeds for garnish, optional

INSTRUCTIONS:

ONE: Preheat oven to 425°F. In a roasting pan, place squash and apple, cut side down. Add garlic and roast until tender, about 40 minutes. Remove from oven and set aside until cool enough to handle. Scoop out flesh from squash and apple and transfer to a large bowl; discard peels. Add garlic and mash with a fork. Stir in nutmeg, salt and pepper. Stir in ricotta and goat cheese; set aside.

TWO: Bring a large pot of water to a boil while you make ravioli. Line a baking sheet with parchment paper. Arrange a small bowl of water near your work surface. Place 2 wonton wrappers in front of you; keep remaining wrappers covered with a kitchen towel to prevent them from drying out. Spoon 1 heaping Tbsp squash-ricotta mixture into center of 1 wrapper. Dip your finger into water and moisten edges of wrapper. Place second wrapper over top and press edges together firmly to seal. Transfer to baking sheet. Repeat with remaining mixture and wrappers.

THREE: Add ravioli to pot with boiling water and cook for 2 to 3 minutes (cooking in batches, if necessary). With a slotted spoon, transfer ravioli to serving plates, dividing evenly, and cover to keep warm.

FOUR: In a large skillet, heat oil on medium. Add leeks and cook until softened, about 4 minutes. Stir in broth and ¾ cup water and cook for 2 minutes. Ladle broth mixture over top of ravioli, dividing evenly. Garnish each serving with pumpkin seeds, if desired.

Nutrients per serving (4 to 6 ravioli and ⅓ to ¼ cup broth mixture): Calories: 330, Total Fat: 9 g, Sat. Fat: 4 g, Monounsaturated Fat: 3 g, Polyunsaturated Fat: 1 g, Carbs: 52 g, Fiber: 8 g, Sugars: 5 g, Protein: 16 g, Sodium: 245 mg, Cholesterol: 18 mg

Nutritional Bonus:
Butternut squash belongs to
the pumpkin family and is the
greatest source of vitamin A
in the brood. A natural antioxidant, the fat-soluble vitamin
aids in maintaining good vision
and the integrity of your skin
and mucus membranes.

**Roasted
Squash &
Apple
Ravioli**

Broccoli
Rabe
Linguine

THE BEST OF CLEAN EATING 3

Broccoli Rabe Linguine
WITH FETA

Serves 4. ***Hands-on time:*** *25 minutes.* ***Total time:*** *30 minutes.*

Closely related to turnip, lush broccoli rabe (also known as rapini) provides a sophisticated and slightly bitter punch of flavor to this classic and incredibly simple pasta.

INGREDIENTS:

- 1 bunch broccoli rabe, trimmed and cut into 3-inch pieces
- 8 oz whole-grain linguine pasta
- 1½ tsp olive oil
- 3 cloves garlic, chopped
- ¼ tsp red pepper flakes, or to taste
- Sea salt and fresh ground black pepper, to taste
- 1 15-oz BPA-free can cannellini beans, drained and rinsed
- 12 Kalamata olives, pitted and chopped
- ¼ cup sun-dried tomatoes (dry-packed), chopped
- 2½ oz feta cheese, crumbled

INSTRUCTIONS:

ONE: Bring a large saucepan of water to a boil. Add broccoli and return to a boil. Cook until just tender, 3 to 4 minutes. Remove from heat. With tongs or a slotted spoon, transfer broccoli to a colander to drain; do not discard cooking water.

TWO: Return saucepan to a boil. Add pasta and cook until al dente. Drain.

THREE: Meanwhile, in a large skillet, heat oil on low. Add garlic and pepper flakes and sauté, stirring constantly, for 1 minute. Stir in broccoli, salt and black pepper and increase heat to medium. Stir in beans, olives and tomatoes and remove from heat.

FOUR: Return pasta to saucepan and stir in broccoli mixture. To serve, garnish with cheese.

Nutrients per 2-cup serving: *Calories: 394, Total Fat: 9 g, Sat. Fat: 2.5 g, Monounsaturated Fat: 3.5 g, Polyunsaturated Fat: 1 g, Carbs: 66 g, Fiber: 11 g, Sugars: 4 g, Protein: 19 g, Sodium: 569 mg, Cholesterol: 6 mg*

Nutritional Bonus:
Broccoli rabe (aka rapini) is a member of the mustard family, which also includes cabbage, broccoli and cauliflower. Like its cruciferous relatives, broccoli rabe is high in cancer-fighting phytochemicals, as well as folate and free-radical-fighting vitamins A and C.

Cheesy Butternut Bake
WITH ALMONDS & RAISINS

Serves 4. ***Hands-on time:*** *20 minutes.* ***Total time:*** *45 minutes.*

Our blend of sweet and savory winter produce is baked to perfection with a cheesy topping to make this casserole hearty enough for a budget-friendly main.

INGREDIENTS:

- Olive oil cooking spray
- 1½ lb butternut squash, peeled, seeded and chopped into ½-inch cubes
- 1 head cauliflower, stalks removed and discarded
- ½ lb carrots, peeled and cut into ¼-inch rounds
- 1 lb green cabbage, trimmed and thinly sliced
- 1 egg
- ¼ cup 2% milk
- ½ cup low-sodium chicken broth
- ½ tsp fresh ground black pepper
- 1 tsp dried sage
- ¼ tsp sea salt
- 4 oz shredded part-skim mozzarella cheese
- 1 large red pear
- 1 oz sliced raw unsalted almonds
- 2 oz unsweetened raisins

INSTRUCTIONS:

ONE: Preheat oven to 350°F. Coat a 9 x 13-inch baking dish with cooking spray.

TWO: Fill a large pot halfway with water and bring to a boil. Add squash, reduce heat to medium-high and simmer for 5 minutes. Add cauliflower and simmer for 5 more minutes. Drain and transfer mixture to a large bowl. Add carrots and cabbage and toss gently.

THREE: In a small bowl, beat egg lightly with a fork. In a medium pot, add milk and broth and place on medium-low heat for 3 minutes until simmering. Remove from heat and whisk in egg, pepper, sage and salt. Place on low heat and gradually whisk in cheese, stirring constantly until mostly melted; do not let mixture come to a simmer, so reduce heat if necessary. Remove from heat and set aside.

FOUR: Thinly slice pear. Spoon squash-cabbage mixture into baking dish and top evenly with pears, gently pressing pear into vegetables so slices lie flat. Spoon cheese mixture over top and sprinkle with almonds and raisins. Transfer to oven and bake for 25 minutes or until pears are lightly browned. Serve immediately.

Nutrients per 2½-cup serving: *Calories: 395, Total Fat: 11 g, Sat. Fat: 4 g, Monounsaturated Fat: 4 g, Polyunsaturated Fat: 1 g, Omega-3s: 100 mg, Omega-6s: 1,240 mg, Carbs: 63 g, Fiber: 14 g, Sugars: 21 g, Protein: 19 g, Sodium: 450 mg, Cholesterol: 73 mg*

NUTRITIONAL BONUS: Cauliflower contains glucosinolates and isothiocyanates, phytochemical compounds that are often under study for their aggressive cancer-fighting and detoxifying properties. Cauliflower also contains impressive amounts of vitamin C – in fact, one serving of this dish provides 311% of your daily requirement of the antioxidant-rich, immune-boosting vitamin.

Classic Tacos

Serves 4. ***Hands-on time:*** *15 minutes.* ***Total time:*** *45 minutes.*

Tex-Mex tacos have won the hearts of many with their saucy, chile-spiked ground beef tucked into corn tortillas and a selection of fixin's that can outshine any sundae bar. Our vegetarian twin – dripping with homemade, savory mushroom-cauliflower sauce that mimics a traditional beef filling – will wow meat lovers.

INGREDIENTS:

- 2 tsp olive oil
- 1 small onion, diced small (1½ cups)
- 2 large cloves garlic, minced
- 1 lb cremini mushrooms, stems trimmed, roughly chopped into small pieces
- 1 cup cauliflower florets, roughly chopped into small pieces
- 3 Tbsp tomato paste
- 2 tsp chile powder
- 1 tsp ground cumin
- ½ tsp sea salt
- ½ tsp fresh ground black pepper
- 1 cup frozen corn kernels
- 12 small corn tortillas
- 5 large romaine lettuce leaves, sliced into ¼-inch strips
- ½ avocado, pitted, peeled and cubed
- ½ cup grated low-fat cheddar cheese
- ¼ cup low-fat sour cream

INSTRUCTIONS:

ONE: In a large, high-sided skillet, heat oil on medium-high. Add onion and sauté for 5 minutes, until it begins to soften. Stir in garlic and sauté for 30 more seconds.

TWO: Add mushrooms and cauliflower and stir constantly for 2 minutes, until vegetables start to release water and shrink. Continue to cook, stirring occasionally until mushrooms are about half their original size and cauliflower is fork tender, about 15 minutes.

THREE: In a small mixing bowl, whisk together tomato paste, ¼ cup water, chile powder, cumin, salt and pepper. Add to mushroom mixture along with corn. Stir to combine, then cover. Reduce heat to medium-low and simmer for 15 minutes.

FOUR: Warm tortillas over the flame of a gas stove or in a warm oven. To assemble tacos, fill each tortilla with ¼ cup mushroom filling. Top with lettuce, avocado, cheese and sour cream, dividing evenly.

Nutrients per 3 tacos: *Calories: 379, Total Fat: 12 g, Sat. Fat: 3 g, Monounsaturated Fat: 5 g, Polyunsaturated Fat: 2 g, Carbs: 58 g, Fiber: 10 g, Sugars: 8 g, Protein: 15 g, Sodium: 394 mg, Cholesterol: 11 mg*

Huevos Rancheros
WITH PIQUANT SALSA

Serves 4. ***Hands-on time:*** *40 minutes.* ***Total time:*** *40 minutes.*

A quick jalapeño-peppered salsa spikes the heat and tickles your palate in our take on this quintessential Mexican dish. Chile-simmered black beans add satisfying fill-you-up fiber.

INGREDIENTS:

- 1 15-oz BPA-free can black beans, 2 Tbsp juices reserved, drained and rinsed
- ½ tsp ground cumin
- ½ tsp chile powder
- Olive oil cooking spray
- 4 large eggs
- Sea salt and fresh ground black pepper, to taste
- 8 6-inch corn tortillas
- 2 Tbsp chopped fresh cilantro
- Lime slices for garnish, optional

SALSA

- 1 tsp safflower oil
- ½ large yellow onion, chopped
- ¼ tsp plus 1 pinch sea salt, divided
- 2 cloves garlic, chopped
- 15 oz boxed or jarred unsalted diced tomatoes, 2 Tbsp juices reserved
- 1 tsp ground cumin
- 1 tsp chile powder
- 1 to 2 jalapeño chile peppers, halved lengthwise and sliced (TIP: For less heat, remove seeds)

INSTRUCTIONS:

ONE: Prepare salsa: In a medium saucepan, heat safflower oil on medium-low. Add onion and 1 pinch salt. Sauté, stirring occasionally, until light brown, about 10 minutes. Add garlic and sauté, stirring frequently, for 1 minute. Add tomatoes and juices, 1 tsp cumin, 1 tsp chile powder and remaining ¼ tsp salt. Cook, stirring occasionally, for 2 minutes. Stir in jalapeño and remove from heat.

MAKE AHEAD: Salsa can be made up to 1 day ahead; cover and refrigerate. Reheat before serving.

TWO: In a small saucepan, heat beans and juices, 2 Tbsp water, ½ tsp cumin and ½ tsp chile powder on medium. Cook, stirring occasionally, until beginning to simmer, 1 to 2 minutes. With a potato masher or fork, mash beans into a chunky consistency and cook until steaming hot, 1 to 2 minutes. Cover and remove from heat.

MAKE-AHEAD: Prepare this step up to 1 day ahead; cover and refrigerate. Reheat before serving.

THREE: Mist a large nonstick skillet with cooking spray and heat on medium-low. Working in batches, carefully break eggs into skillet, keeping yolks intact. Season with salt and pepper and cook until whites are set and yolks reach desired doneness, 3 to 4 minutes.

FOUR: To serve, top tortillas with bean mixture, eggs, salsa and cilantro, dividing evenly. If desired, serve with lime.

Nutrients per serving (2 tortillas, ⅓ cup bean mixture, 1 egg, ¼ cup salsa): *Calories: 319, Total Fat: 8 g, Sat. Fat: 2 g, Monounsaturated Fat: 3 g, Polyunsaturated Fat: 2 g, Carbs: 46 g, Fiber: 9.5 g, Sugars: 4 g, Protein: 16 g, Sodium: 319 mg, Cholesterol: 211 mg*

Huevos
Rancheros

Exotic Mixed Mushroom Pasta

Nutritional Bonus:
Mushrooms are bursting with riboflavin, or vitamin B2, an essential compound required in the metabolism of carbohydrates, amino acids and lipids.

Exotic Mixed Mushroom Pasta
WITH LIMA BEANS

Serves 8. *Hands-on time:* 13 minutes. *Total time:* 50 minutes.

Traditional mushroom pasta is a perennial favorite, but smothered with cream sauce and loaded with fat, it is no friend to your waistline. Do your body some good and try this *CE*-approved version instead.

INGREDIENTS:

- 1 1-oz pkg dried porcini mushrooms or other dried mushrooms
- 2 cups low-sodium chicken or vegetable broth
- 1 Tbsp extra-virgin olive oil
- 1 yellow onion, finely chopped
- 1 leek, white and light green parts only, finely chopped
- 8 oz cremini mushrooms, sliced
- 4 oz shiitake mushrooms, sliced
- 4 oz oyster mushrooms, sliced
- 3 cloves garlic, minced
- ½ tsp sea salt, plus additional to taste
- ½ tsp fresh ground black pepper, plus additional to taste
- 12 oz whole-grain linguine, broken into small pieces
- 1½ cups frozen lima beans, thawed
- 3 Tbsp finely chopped fresh tarragon
- 3 Tbsp finely chopped chives

INSTRUCTIONS:

ONE: Fill a small bowl with 1 cup hot water. Add porcini mushrooms and soak for 20 minutes or until softened. Drain over a large bowl, reserving liquid. Thinly slice mushrooms; set aside.

TWO: In a small saucepan, heat broth on medium-low. Cover to keep warm.

THREE: In a large saucepan, heat oil on medium. Add onion and leek and cook, stirring until softened, about 5 minutes. Stir in remaining mushrooms, garlic, salt and pepper. Cook until mushrooms release juices, about 4 minutes, adding porcini mushrooms near end of cooking time.

FOUR: Meanwhile, cook linguine for half the amount of time indicated on package directions; drain.

FIVE: Add linguine and lima beans to leek-mushroom mixture, stirring. Stir in reserved porcini mushroom liquid until absorbed, about 5 minutes. Gradually add broth in ½-cup increments, stirring until liquid is absorbed after each addition, about 4 minutes total. Stir in tarragon and cook for 1 more minute. Sprinkle with chives before serving.

TIP: Dried porcini mushrooms may require rinsing under cold water after the soaking and draining process to remove any grit.

Nutrients per 1¾-cup serving: *Calories: 307, Total Fat: 5 g, Sat. Fat: 1 g, Carbs: 53 g, Fiber: 11 g, Sugars: 5 g, Protein: 14 g, Sodium: 265 mg, Cholesterol: 0 mg*

Summertime Zucchini & Eggplant Lasagna

Serves 4. *Hands-on time:* 15 minutes. *Total time:* 1 hour.

Using cottage cheese instead of ricotta in this lasagna translates to half the fat with the same amount of protein in every bite. And, if you'd like to enjoy this dish again with a slightly different twist, swap out the cottage cheese for another low-fat naturally creamy cheese, such as soft goat cheese or Neufchâtel.

INGREDIENTS:

- 1 1-lb eggplant, cut into ½-inch-thick rounds
- 1 zucchini, cut into ½-inch-thick rounds
- 1 yellow squash, cut into ½-inch-thick rounds
- 1 tsp extra-virgin olive oil
- ½ large yellow onion, chopped
- 4 cloves garlic, chopped
- 1½ cups 2% small-curd cottage cheese
- 2 tsp dried oregano
- Olive oil cooking spray
- 6 oz shredded part-skim mozzarella
- Fresh basil for garnish, optional

INSTRUCTIONS:

ONE: Preheat oven to 375°F. Line 2 baking sheets with parchment paper and spread eggplant, zucchini and squash out in a single layer on sheets, leaving a slight space between each round. Bake for 30 minutes; remove from oven and set aside.

TWO: In a large nonstick skillet, heat oil on medium for 1 minute. Add onion and cook, stirring often, for 5 minutes or until translucent. Add garlic and cook for an additional 2 minutes. Remove from heat and stir in cottage cheese and oregano.

THREE: Lightly coat an 11 x 7-inch baking dish with cooking spray. Line bottom of dish with zucchini and squash, using all rounds and overlapping them so dish is completely covered. Top with cottage cheese mixture. Arrange eggplant over cottage cheese in overlapping rows, then top with mozzarella. Bake at 375°F for 30 minutes or until cheese is golden and bubbling. Serve immediately, garnishing with basil, if desired.

Nutrients per 8-oz serving: *Calories: 250, Total Fat: 10 g, Sat. Fat: 6 g, Monounsaturated Fat: 3 g, Polyunsaturated Fat: 1 g, Carbs: 19 g, Fiber: 6 g, Sugars: 9 g, Protein: 23 g, Sodium: 600 mg, Cholesterol: 40 mg*

Veggie Satay

WITH CUCUMBER QUINOA SALAD & SPICY PEANUT SAUCE

Serves 4. Hands-on time: *45 minutes.* **Total time:** *1 hour, 15 minutes.*

Satay traditionally consists of marinated and skewered strips of meat grilled over a charcoal fire pit. Here, vegetables and tofu soak in a spicy coconut marinade before a quick grill (no fire pit required!).

INGREDIENTS:

- ½ cup nonfat plain Greek yogurt, divided
- ½ cup light coconut milk
- 1 Tbsp minced ginger root
- 1 large clove garlic, minced and pressed into a paste with flat side of a knife
- 2 tsp curry powder
- ⅛ tsp cayenne pepper
- ¼ tsp sea salt
- ¼ tsp fresh ground black pepper
- 3 large scallions, white parts minced and green parts thinly sliced, divided
- 2 medium zucchini, quartered and sliced into 1-inch chunks
- 1 12-oz block firm tofu, pressed and cut into 1-inch cubes (about 2 cups)
- 1 bunch asparagus, trimmed and sliced into 2-inch pieces
- 1 Tbsp natural unsalted peanut butter

QUINOA SALAD

- 1 cup quinoa
- ¼ tsp sea salt
- ¼ tsp fresh ground black pepper
- 1 large cucumber, halved, seeds scraped out and diced small (about 2 cups)
- ¼ lb sugar snap peas, sliced diagonally into ¼-inch pieces (about 1 cup)

INSTRUCTIONS:

ONE: In a large mixing bowl, combine ¼ cup yogurt with coconut milk, ginger, garlic, curry powder, cayenne, salt, black pepper and scallions (white parts). Add zucchini and tofu and toss gently to coat. Marinate for 30 minutes at room temperature (refrigerate if marinating longer).

TWO: Meanwhile, prepare quinoa salad: In a medium saucepan on medium-high, bring 1⅔ cups water to a boil. Stir in quinoa, cover, reduce heat to low and cook for 15 minutes. Remove from heat and keep quinoa covered for 10 more minutes.

THREE: Transfer cooked quinoa to a large, wide serving bowl and let cool to room temperature. Stir in salt, black pepper, sliced scallions (green parts), cucumber and sugar snap peas. Set aside at room temperature until ready to serve (refrigerate if making ahead of time).

FOUR: Heat a large grill pan on high until very hot. Grill asparagus for 3 to 5 minutes, until just tender. Transfer to a bowl and keep covered. Grill zucchini until just tender, about 2 minutes per side. Add to bowl with asparagus. Grill tofu cubes on 2 sides until grill marks are visible, about 2 minutes per side. Add to bowl with vegetables. Reserve marinade.

FIVE: Whisk remaining ¼ cup yogurt and peanut butter into leftover marinade. Place grilled vegetables over top of quinoa salad, drizzle with marinade sauce and serve.

Nutrients per serving (2 cups quinoa salad, 2 cups vegetable-tofu mixture, 3 Tbsp sauce): *Calories: 368, Total Fat: 13 g, Sat. Fat: 3 g, Monounsaturated Fat: 3 g, Polyunsaturated Fat: 4 g, Carbs: 43 g, Fiber: 8 g, Sugars: 6 g, Protein: 22 g, Sodium: 278 mg, Cholesterol: 0 mg*

Stuffed Eggplant

WITH TAHINI YOGURT SAUCE

Serves 4. Hands-on time: *35 minutes.* **Total time:** *1 hour, 10 minutes.*

A crispy bread crumb topping and citrusy sesame sauce invite you to dig into this satisfying meatless main, packed with meaty mushrooms, creamy chickpeas and tangy feta. Use any leftover filling as a hearty pasta topper, or enjoy it stuffed in a pita for lunch the next day.

INGREDIENTS:

- Olive oil cooking spray
- 2 Italian eggplants (1 to 1¼ lb each), halved lengthwise
- 1½ tsp olive oil
- 1 red onion, chopped
- 8 oz white button mushrooms, stemmed and sliced
- ¼ tsp sea salt, divided
- 3 cloves garlic, finely chopped
- 3 vine tomatoes, stemmed and chopped
- ¼ tsp dried oregano
- ¼ tsp red pepper flakes, or to taste
- 1 15-oz BPA-free can chickpeas, drained and rinsed
- ¼ tsp fresh ground black pepper
- 2 oz feta cheese, crumbled
- ⅓ cup chopped fresh parsley, plus additional for garnish
- 3 Tbsp whole-wheat panko bread crumbs
- ⅓ cup low-fat plain yogurt
- 2 Tbsp fresh lemon juice
- 1½ Tbsp tahini

INSTRUCTIONS:

ONE: Preheat oven to 425°F. Mist a large baking sheet with cooking spray. Place eggplants cut side down on sheet and roast until flesh is fork-tender and skin is wrinkled but not collapsed, 25 to 35 minutes. Set aside until cool enough to handle.

MAKE AHEAD: Roast eggplant up to 1 day ahead; cover and refrigerate.

TWO: Meanwhile, in a large skillet, heat oil on medium-high. Add onion, mushrooms and ⅛ tsp salt and sauté, stirring occasionally, until tender and golden brown, 10 to 12 minutes. Add garlic, tomatoes, oregano and pepper flakes and sauté until tomatoes are soft and just beginning to break down, about 4 minutes. Stir in chickpeas.

THREE: With a large spoon, scoop out all but a thin layer of eggplant flesh. Add flesh to skillet and season with black pepper and remaining salt. Mix well and remove from heat. Stir in feta and parsley. Spoon mixture into eggplant skins, packing well. Return eggplants to baking sheet and sprinkle with panko. Roast until panko is golden brown, 10 to 12 minutes.

FOUR: Meanwhile, in a small bowl, combine yogurt, lemon juice and tahini. Gradually stir in 2 to 4 Tbsp water, until mixture is thin enough to slowly run off a spoon when dipped. To serve, drizzle yogurt mixture over eggplant and garnish with additional parsley.

Nutrients per serving (½ eggplant and 2 Tbsp yogurt mixture): *Calories: 332, Total Fat: 10 g, Sat. Fat: 3 g, Monounsaturated Fat: 3 g, Polyunsaturated Fat: 2 g, Carbs: 50 g, Fiber: 15.5 g, Sugars: 14 g, Protein: 15 g, Sodium: 350 mg, Cholesterol: 14 mg*

Stuffed Eggplant

Wondering what to marinate your steak in or what to sprinkle over your seafood? *Clean Eating*'s got you covered! Choose any of our sauces or rubs to liven up your meals. Whether you're craving an Asian-style Ginger Teriyaki flavor for your chicken or Indian-inspired veggies with our Curried Buttermilk Marinade, your tastes will be met with our very best! Save any leftover sauces and rubs for your meals throughout the week – a great time-saver!

Curried Buttermilk Marinade

Makes 2 cups.

This adventurous marinade pairs perfectly with our Curried Buttermilk Chicken and Grilled Pineapple found on p. 155.

In a medium bowl, whisk together 2 cups low-fat buttermilk, 2 Tbsp curry powder, 2 tsp fine sea salt and 1 tsp ground black pepper. Store in an airtight container in refrigerator for up to several days.

TRY IT: Use it to marinate pork, chicken, seafood or vegetables.

Balsamic Rosemary Marinade

Makes 2 cups.

This sweet and tart marinade is a match made in heaven with a good steak. Use it to spice up Balsamic Rosemary Steak on p. 132.

In a medium bowl, whisk together 1 cup balsamic vinegar, ¾ cup olive oil, ¼ cup raw honey, 2 Tbsp chopped fresh rosemary, 1 Tbsp garlic powder, 2 tsp fine sea salt and 1 tsp ground black pepper. Store in an airtight container in refrigerator for up to several days.

TRY IT: Use it to marinate beef, pork, chicken or vegetables.

Smoky-Sweet Spice Rub

Makes ¾ cup.

Use this smoky-flavored blend to infuse your steak or chicken with amazing flavor, or shake it up by pairing it with tofu instead! Find Spice-Rubbed Tofu Steaks on p. 215.

In a small bowl, combine ¼ cup ground maple sugar flakes, 3 Tbsp smoked paprika, 3 Tbsp chile powder, 4 tsp granulated garlic powder (or regular garlic powder), 4 tsp granulated onion powder (or regular onion powder), 2 tsp fine sea salt and ½ tsp ground cayenne pepper (optional). Store in an airtight container at room temperature for up to several months.

TRY IT: Rub it on beef, pork, chicken, seafood or vegetables.

Coriander & Fennel Seed Rub

Makes about ½ cup.

This simple seed rub is a snap to prepare, and complements fish perfectly. Try it with Coriander & Fennel Seed Trout on p. 204.

In a small nonstick skillet on medium heat, combine ¼ cup coriander seeds and ¼ cup fennel seeds. Cook, stirring occasionally, for 3 to 4 minutes or until seeds are fragrant and slightly browned. Transfer to a plate and set aside to cool slightly, 1 to 2 minutes. Transfer seeds to a spice grinder or mortar and pestle and pulse or crush to coarsely grind. Stir in 2 tsp sea salt and 1 tsp ground black pepper. Store in an airtight container at room temperature for up to several months.

TRY IT: Rub it on beef, pork, chicken, seafood or vegetables.

Ginger Teriyaki Marinade

Makes 1¾ cups.

A perfect fit for fresh shrimp or chicken, this marinade was made to pair with Ginger Teriyaki Shrimp and Scallion Skewers on p. 187.

In a medium bowl, whisk together ¾ cup aji-mirin sweet cooking rice seasoning, ⅓ cup raw honey, ⅓ cup low-sodium soy sauce, 1 Tbsp grated fresh ginger and 2 Tbsp toasted sesame oil. Store in an airtight container in refrigerator for up to several days.

TRY IT: Use it to marinate beef, pork, chicken, seafood or vegetables.

There's the Rub

A rub is a mixture of herbs, spices and other seasonings – at times also including sugary ingredients – used to add flavor and texture to proteins and vegetables. As its name implies, the coating is often rubbed into food, but rubbing isn't always necessary. Here are a few things to keep in mind:

- **SUGAR BURNS EASILY.** If your rub includes high amounts of clean sweeteners, don't cook over direct, high heat for more than three or four minutes. For foods that require longer cooking times, either use indirect or low heat, or add the rub during the last few minutes of cooking.

- **RUBS ARE TYPICALLY INTENSELY FLAVORED,** so you'll be able to add a lot of vibrancy to your food without adding a great deal of salt.

- **RUBS ARE GENERALLY QUICK AND EASY.**

Marinate on This

Typically, a marinade consists of some type of acid – which could include vinegar, citrus juices, wine, yogurt or buttermilk – oil, herbs and spices. Before marinating your meat for the BBQ, read this:

- **DON'T** cook foods that have soaked in sugary marinades over direct, high heat for more than three or four minutes.

- **MARINADES DON'T REALLY TENDERIZE FOODS** – they don't penetrate deeply enough. They can, however, affect the taste and texture of a food's surface and just below it.

- **MARINATING TIME DEPENDS ON THE MARINADE'S ACIDITY AND THE FOOD'S DENSITY** – more acid and lower density mean a shorter marinating time. Generally speaking, tender fish and smaller pieces of meat can marinate for 15 minutes to one hour; chops and chicken breasts for one to six hours; and tougher and larger cuts for six to 12 hours.

Curried Buttermilk Marinade

Balsamic Rosemary Marinade

Smoky-Sweet Spice Rub

Coriander & Fennel Seed Rub

Ginger Teriyaki Marinade

A World Of Whole Grains

BLACK FORBIDDEN RICE

ORIGIN: Asia.

HEALTH BENEFIT: Anthocyanins, powerful antioxidant plant pigments that lend the grain a dark color (careful, it stains easily). Gluten-free.

USE: Flour in baking or cooked grains in side dishes and salads.

FREEKEH

ORIGIN: Middle East.

HEALTH BENEFIT: Kernels are harvested while young, so freekeh has a higher concentration of vitamins and minerals than brown rice – and up to four times the fiber.

USE: As rice or pasta substitute or in soups and burger patties.

BULGUR

ORIGIN: Mediterranean regions, China and the Middle East.

HEALTH BENEFIT: Manganese, a trace mineral necessary for bone health.

USE: As meat substitute or added to pilafs, soups and baked goods.

There's more to whole grains than brown bread! While you're likely already familiar with the more common varieties – whole oats, brown rice and popcorn (yes popcorn!) – let us introduce you to some of the world's finest lesser-known grains.

FARRO

ORIGIN: Egypt.

HEALTH BENEFIT: Cyanogenic glucosides, a carb that may stabilize blood sugar, lower cholesterol and stimulate the immune system.

USE: Semi-pearled grains in soups, pastas, risottos and casseroles.

MILLET

ORIGIN: Africa.

HEALTH BENEFIT: Gluten-free and contains gut-friendly prebiotics.

USE: In baked goods, porridge, formed into patties and cooked as hot cereal.

STORING TIP: Whole grains contain natural oils, so they can go rancid quickly. Store in an airtight container in a cool, dark place, ideally a pantry or refrigerator, where they will last for three to six months.

KAMUT

ORIGIN: Egypt.

HEALTH BENEFIT: Selenium, an immune system-supporting trace mineral.

USE: Flour in baking or grains in pilaf-style dishes, salads, soups, stews and stir-frys.

WHEAT BERRIES

ORIGIN: No specific origin.

HEALTH BENEFIT: Lignans, plant nutrients that may help reduce risk of breast cancer.

USE: In salads, hot cereal and baked goods, or sauté with mushrooms for a hearty side.

AMARANTH

ORIGIN: South America.

HEALTH BENEFIT: Gluten-free and contains lysine, an amino acid that promotes growth and tissue repair.

USE: In hot cereal, casseroles, baked goods, pancakes, crackers or as a rice substitute.

TEFF

ORIGIN: Ethiopia.

HEALTH BENEFIT: Bone-building calcium.

USE: In baked goods, soups and stews, hot cereal, porridge and polenta. Traditionally used to make injera, Ethiopia's signature flatbread.

Your Summer Produce Shopping Guide

We all know fresh is best, but how exactly do you choose perfect produce and keep it that way at home? Follow our tips to make the most of your market basket.

PLUMS

SELECT: Plump, firm (but not rock hard) fruit with shiny, taut skin. Watch out for bruises and cuts.

STORE: At room temperature in a paper bag until ripe, then refrigerate for up to 3 days.

EAT: Sliced and roasted alongside pork tenderloin or chops.

ARUGULA

SELECT: Vivid green leaves that smell fresh and feel crisp, not soft. Watch out for bruises and mold.

STORE: In a plastic bag in refrigerator crisper for up to 3 days. Wash just before using.

EAT: In a salad with roasted beets, goat cheese, toasted hazelnuts and balsamic vinaigrette.

NEW POTATOES

SELECT: Firm potatoes with smooth skin, free of bruises, sprouts and green discolorations. Small and uniform in size are best for cooking.

STORE: In a cool, dark place (think pantry or basement) with moderate humidity. Do not refrigerate.

EAT: Tangy German-style potato salad dressed with mustard, extra-virgin olive oil, raw honey and white wine vinegar. Add scallions and fresh vegetables of your choice.

MANGOS

SELECT: Firm fruit with no sticky sap on skin. Color may vary from green to red.

STORE: At room temperature until ripe, then eat within 1 to 2 days.

EAT: Pair fresh mango salsa (chopped mango, red onion, tomato, jalapeño, cilantro and lime juice) with grilled turkey burgers.

PEAS

SELECT: Firm, smooth medium pods without any white, yellow or gray blemishes. Avoid mildew spots and water damage.

STORE: In refrigerator for up to 5 days.

EAT: In a barley risotto with shrimp, lemon and fresh herbs.

APRICOTS

SELECT: Plump, firm (but not hard) fruit with velvety skin and uniform color.

STORE: At room temperature until ripe, then refrigerate in a plastic bag for up to 3 days.

EAT: Baked into a crisp with oat and almond topping. Or, chopped and added to a wild rice and pistachio pilaf.

Cheesecake Tartlets, p. 254

Desserts

No need to worry! You can enjoy *Clean Eating*'s nutritious desserts without overindulging in sugars. Full of succulent fruits, wholesome nuts, creamy textures and more, all our sweets are worth saving room for after dinner. Finish off a hefty meal with our light Espresso Crème Brûlée, a lovely finishing touch to any dinner party. Hankering for some chocolaty delight? You and your kids will love our rich Chocolate Walnut Brownies. We offer a treat for everyone's taste.

Nutmeg-Infused Pumpkin Bread

Serves 16. **Hands-on time:** *20 minutes.* **Total time:** *3 hours, 5 minutes.*

This yummy comfort food is made easy with the addition of a slow-cooker. Just 20 minutes of prep work translates into one tasty loaf.

INGREDIENTS:

- Olive oil cooking spray
- ¾ cup 100% apple juice
- ½ cup dried apple juice-sweetened cranberries
- 1¾ cups white whole-wheat flour
- ½ cup maple sugar flakes
- 2 tsp baking powder
- ¼ tsp baking soda
- 1 tsp ground nutmeg
- ¼ tsp ground allspice
- ¼ tsp sea salt
- 1 cup canned organic solid pumpkin or cooked and puréed pumpkin
- ½ cup nonfat plain Greek yogurt
- 4 egg whites
- ¼ cup safflower oil
- 1 Tbsp pure vanilla extract
- 2 oz unsalted pecan pieces, toasted

OPTION: If you don't have pumpkin on hand, swap it for 1 cup cooked and puréed sweet potato.

INSTRUCTIONS:

ONE: Lightly mist an 8½ x 4½-inch nonstick loaf pan with cooking spray; set aside.

TWO: In a small saucepan, combine apple juice and cranberries. Place on high heat and bring to a boil; remove from heat and let sit for 10 minutes to cool slightly.

THREE: In a large bowl, whisk flour, maple sugar flakes, baking powder, baking soda, nutmeg, allspice and salt until combined; set aside.

FOUR: In a medium bowl, stir cranberry mixture, pumpkin, yogurt, egg whites, oil and vanilla until well combined. Add cranberry-pumpkin mixture and pecans to flour mixture and stir until just moistened but no flour is visible; don't over-mix. Spoon into pan, gently smoothing top with back of spoon or a rubber spatula.

FIVE: Place a rack in the bottom of a 6-qt slow cooker to elevate pan from bottom; place pan on top. (Alternatively, form 3 or 4 12-inch pieces of foil into balls and place in bottom of slow cooker to elevate pan.) Cover and cook on high for 2 hours and 45 minutes or until a wooden toothpick inserted in center comes out clean. Transfer pan to a rack and let cool for 10 minutes. Loosen bread from pan by running a spatula around inside edges. Invert onto rack and let cool completely. Slice into 16 pieces.

Nutrients per serving (about ½ inch): *Calories: 159, Total Fat: 6.5 g, Sat. Fat: 1 g, Monounsaturated Fat: 2.5 g, Polyunsaturated Fat: 1 g, Carbs: 21 g, Fiber: 3 g, Sugars: 8 g, wwProtein: 4 g, Sodium: 70 mg, Cholesterol: 0 mg*

Nutritional Bonus:
The potassium found in pump-kins aids in balancing fluid levels in the body and is neces-sary for energy production. The gourd-like squash also contains a good dose of magnesium, which promotes a healthy immune system, contributes to bone strength and helps maintain normal heart function.

Peach Almond
Semifreddo

Peach Almond Semifreddo

*Serves 8. **Hands-on time:** 15 minutes. **Total time:** 2 hours, 15 minutes (includes freezing time).*

Taking its name from the Italian word for semi-frozen, this *CE*-approved dessert is layered with fresh peaches and crunchy almonds, making it a refreshing finale to any meal.

INGREDIENTS:

- 1 cup nonfat plain Greek yogurt
- 1 egg, separated
- ⅓ cup organic evaporated cane juice
- ½ tsp pure almond extract
- 1 tsp pure vanilla extract
- 3 egg whites
- 2 medium peaches, pitted and diced
- ⅓ cup chopped unsalted almonds, toasted

INSTRUCTIONS:

ONE: Line an 8 x 4 x 5-inch loaf pan with plastic wrap.

TWO: In a large bowl, combine yogurt, egg yolk, cane juice and almond and vanilla extracts.

THREE: In a separate large bowl, beat 4 egg whites into stiff peaks with an electric mixer on high speed. Using a rubber spatula, fold egg whites into yogurt mixture, one-third at a time, until combined. Gently stir in peaches and almonds.

FOUR: Pour mixture into prepared pan, smoothing top with spatula. Freeze for 2 to 3 hours, until just frozen. Invert onto a serving tray and gently remove pan. Peel plastic wrap from semifreddo and slice into 8 portions.

TIP: To ease slicing, run your knife under warm water for 1 minute. The heat will allow you to cut through the frozen dessert smoothly.

Nutrients per serving (⅛ of dessert): Calories: 105, Total Fat: 3 g, Sat. Fat: 0.25 g, Carbs: 14 g, Fiber: 1 g, Sugars: 12 g, Protein: 6 g, Sodium: 43 mg, Cholesterol: 0 mg

Nutritional Bonus:
What role does this dessert play in keeping you slim? It's all about the almonds! If your body is nutrient depleted, it sends out hunger signals to the brain telling you to eat. Nutrient-rich foods like almonds properly nourish the body, which stops these signals from being sent, preventing you from overeating.

Caramel Cheesecakes

*Serves 6. **Hands-on time:** 15 minutes. **Total time:** 45 minutes (plus cooling time).*

No wonder this recipe made it into the *CE Comfort Foods* special – it's loaded with creamy Greek yogurt and cream cheese for tartness, along with caramel for perfect sweetness. Dessert is served!

INGREDIENTS:

- ⅓ cup Sucanat
- 6 oz light cream cheese
- 2 large eggs
- ¼ cup nonfat plain Greek yogurt
- ⅓ cup organic evaporated cane juice

INSTRUCTIONS:

ONE: Preheat oven to 350°F.

TWO: In a small saucepan, combine Sucanat and 2 Tbsp water. Place on medium-high heat and bring to a boil. Continue boiling gently until slightly thickened, 30 to 45 seconds. Divide mixture evenly among 6 4-oz ramekins.

THREE: In a food processor fitted with a steel blade, pulse cream cheese, eggs, yogurt and cane juice until well combined. Spoon into ramekins over top of Sucanat mixture, dividing evenly. Set ramekins inside a 9 x 13-inch baking pan and fill pan halfway with warm water. Transfer pan to oven and bake for 22 to 30 minutes or until the tip of a knife inserted into center of cheesecakes comes out clean. Turn oven off and let cheesecakes cool to room temperature inside oven (this will help prevent cracking).

FOUR: To serve, run a knife around the inside edge of each ramekin to loosen cheesecake. Transfer ramekins to a pan of very hot water for 5 minutes to loosen caramel, then remove from water and carefully invert onto serving plates. (NOTE: Don't skip this step! To serve, the caramel must be re-warmed in order to loosen and allow cheesecake to be released from ramekin.)

Nutrients per cheesecake: Calories: 167, Total Fat: 6 g, Sat. Fat: 3 g, Carbs: 23 g, Fiber: 0 g, Sugars: 22 g, Protein: 6 g, Sodium: 173 mg, Cholesterol: 84 mg

Blueberry "Ice Cream"
WITH COCONUT COBBLER CRUMBLE

Serves 6. **Makes** 3 cups ice cream and 2 cups crumble. **Hands-on time:** 30 minutes. **Total time:** 4 hours, 20 minutes (includes freezing time).

Chef Jo couldn't resist taking a classic comfort food, Blueberry Cobbler, and turning it into a refreshing, tangy, warm-weather treat.

INGREDIENTS:

ICE CREAM

- 2 cups fresh blueberries
- 1½ cups nonfat plain Greek yogurt
- ¼ cup raw honey
- ¼ cup 100% orange juice
- Seeds of 1 vanilla bean, pod discarded

CRUMBLE

- ⅓ cup white whole-wheat flour
- ⅓ cup rolled oats
- ½ cup unsweetened medium shredded coconut
- 3 Tbsp Sucanat
- ½ tsp baking powder
- ¼ tsp baking soda
- ¼ tsp sea salt
- 2 Tbsp coconut butter or buttery olive oil spread, chilled
- 3 Tbsp low-fat buttermilk (1%)
- ½ tsp pure almond or vanilla extract
- 1½ cups fresh blueberries, optional

INSTRUCTIONS:

ONE: In a food processor, add all ice cream ingredients. Purée until just combined, about 2 minutes, stopping processor every 30 seconds to scrape down sides of bowl with a rubber spatula.

TWO: With spatula, spoon ice cream mixture into a shallow 9 x 9-inch non-reactive freezer-safe container. Place container in freezer for 30 minutes or until mixture begins to freeze slightly around edges. Remove from freezer, scrape edges with spatula and mix thoroughly with a whisk, blending in ice crystals until creamy again, about 2 to 3 minutes. Return to freezer for an additional 30 minutes. Repeat 2 more times. After third mixing, return to freezer until hardened and ready to eat, 2 to 3 hours.

THREE: Prepare crumble: Preheat oven to 375°F. In a large bowl, whisk together flour, oats, coconut, Sucanat, baking powder, baking soda and salt. Add butter and use your fingertips to rub butter into flour until it resembles coarse crumbs. Stir in buttermilk and almond extract until just combined and mixture forms a loose dough.

FOUR: Scatter dough into an 8 x 8-inch baking dish, pressing lightly into bottom of dish. Bake for 20 to 25 minutes, until golden brown. Let cool completely, then crumble into small pieces.

FIVE: To serve, allow ice cream to soften at room temperature for 5 minutes. Scoop ½ cup ice cream into each bowl and top with 3 Tbsp crumble and, if desired, ¼ cup blueberries. For a clean sugary topping, drizzle with 1½ Tbsp Blueberry Syrup (see recipe below).

MAKER MODIFICATION: If you're using a commercial ice cream maker, skip Step Two. Freeze mixture after completing Step One.

STORE IT: This ice cream can be frozen in a sealable, freezer-safe container for 2 to 3 days. Freeze any unused crumble in a sealable, freezer-safe container for up to 1 month. To serve, simply defrost in fridge overnight.

Nutrients per serving (½ cup ice cream and 3 Tbsp crumble): Calories: 251, Total Fat: 9 g, Sat. Fat: 5 g, Carbs: 37 g, Fiber: 3 g, Sugars: 25 g, Protein: 6 g, Sodium: 189 mg, Cholesterol: 1 mg

Blueberry Syrup

Makes about ½ cup. **Hands-on time:** 10 minutes. **Total time:** 10 minutes

Completely devoid of fat, Chef Jo's Blueberry Syrup is an ice cream revelation! You can also drizzle the sweet sauce atop fresh fruit or clean pastries. Try it on Blueberry "Ice Cream" (see recipe at left).

INGREDIENTS:

- ¾ cup fresh blueberries
- 2 Tbsp raw honey
- 1 Tbsp fresh lemon juice
- 2 tsp arrowroot powder

INSTRUCTIONS:

ONE: In a small saucepan, bring blueberries, honey, lemon juice and 1 Tbsp water to a boil on high heat. Reduce heat to medium-low and simmer for 2 to 3 minutes.

TWO: Meanwhile, in a small dish combine arrowroot powder with 1 Tbsp water to form a slurry (a thickening agent). Whisk or stir arrowroot mixture into blueberry mixture until incorporated. Simmer for 1 minute or until just thickened, carefully mashing blueberries with a fork to extract juice. Remove from heat and let cool completely before pouring over your favorite clean ice cream.

Nutrients per 1-Tbsp serving: Calories: 27, Total Fat: 0 g, Sat. Fat: 0 g, Carbs: 7 g, Fiber: 0.5 g, Sugars: 5 g, Protein: 0.25 g, Sodium: 0.5 mg, Cholesterol: 0 mg

Espresso
Crème Brûlée

Espresso Crème Brûlée

Serves 5. **Hands-on time:** *10 minutes.* **Total time:** *1 hour.*

If you have a food torch, put it to good use tonight to make this favorite dessert even more fancy. You'll wow your guests and get points for presentation at the same time!

INGREDIENTS:

- 13½ oz 1% milk
- 2 tsp instant espresso powder
- 5 large egg yolks
- 1 tsp pure vanilla extract
- 3 Tbsp plus 5 tsp organic evaporated cane juice, divided

INSTRUCTIONS:

ONE: Preheat oven to 300°F. Place 5 4-oz ramekins in a large baking pan. Fill pan with enough hot tap water to cover ramekins halfway.

TWO: In a medium saucepan, combine milk and espresso powder. Place on medium-low heat until mixture just begins to steam, 3 to 4 minutes. Set aside.

THREE: Meanwhile, in a large bowl, combine egg yolks, vanilla and 3 Tbsp cane juice. Whisk or use an electric hand mixer to beat until mixture thickens and turns pale yellow in color, about 2 minutes. Add 1 Tbsp milk-espresso mixture and stir to combine. Slowly add remaining milk-espresso mixture, stirring constantly. Pour mixture into ramekins, dividing evenly. Transfer to oven and bake until set, about 50 minutes. Carefully remove from oven. (NOTE: They may jiggle slightly when removed from oven.) Let cool to room temperature in water bath, about 30 minutes.

FOUR: Arrange oven rack in highest position and preheat broiler. Transfer ramekins to a baking sheet and sprinkle each with 1 tsp cane juice. Transfer to oven and broil until cane juice melts and caramelizes, 3 to 5 minutes (or brown tops with a small torch). Serve immediately.

Nutrients per ramekin: Calories: 136, Total Fat: 5 g, Sat. Fat: 2 g, Carbs: 16 g, Fiber: 0 g, Sugars: 15 g, Protein: 6 g, Sodium: 59 mg, Cholesterol: 210 mg

Nutritional Bonus:
You'll be able to enjoy these creamy desserts guilt-free knowing they provide 13% of your daily calcium need per serving. The bone-building mineral is necessary for nerve impulses and proper muscle function, and supports the structure of your pearly whites.

Mini Cupcakes
WITH LEMONY FROSTING

Serves 8. **Hands-on time:** *30 minutes.* **Total time:** *1 hour (includes cooling time).*

Chock full of the complementary flavors of strawberry, honey and lemon, these tasty minis will go fast once they hit the table!

INGREDIENTS:

- Olive oil cooking spray, optional
- ½ cup quartered fresh strawberries, diced, plus additional slices for garnish
- ½ cup Sucanat
- 2 Tbsp skim milk
- ¼ cup safflower oil
- 1½ tsp pure vanilla extract, divided
- 2 egg whites, at room temperature
- ¾ cup white whole-wheat flour
- ½ tsp baking powder
- ⅛ tsp fine sea salt
- 2 oz light cream cheese, at room temperature
- 1 Tbsp raw honey
- 1 packet stevia
- ¼ cup nonfat plain Greek yogurt
- ½ tsp lemon zest

INSTRUCTIONS:

ONE: Place a rack in center of oven and preheat to 350°F. Fill a mini muffin tin with 16 mini liners or mist with cooking spray.

TWO: Finely chop ½ cup strawberries and place in a medium bowl with any accumulated juices. Stir in Sucanat, mashing strawberries a bit against bowl with a spoon. Stir in milk, oil and ½ tsp vanilla; set aside.

THREE: In a separate clean and dry medium glass or metal bowl, beat egg whites with a hand mixer on high speed just until stiff peaks form, about 5 to 10 minutes; set aside.

FOUR: In a large mixing bowl, whisk together flour, baking powder and salt. Stir in strawberry mixture until well combined. Using a rubber spatula, gently fold in beaten egg whites until completely incorporated.

FIVE: Using a spoon, add rounded tablespoons of batter into each mini muffin cup. Bake for 15 minutes or until cupcakes spring back when lightly touched. Remove from oven and let cool for 5 minutes in tin. Remove to a wire rack and let cool completely before frosting.

SIX: Meanwhile, prepare frosting: In a medium bowl, blend cream cheese, honey, stevia and remaining 1 tsp vanilla until creamy. Add yogurt and lemon zest and blend until combined, scraping down sides with a spatula as necessary. Cover with plastic wrap and chill until ready to use.

SEVEN: Once cooled, top each cupcake with frosting and strawberry slices.

Nutrients per serving (2 mini cupcakes, 2 heaping tsp frosting, 2 strawberry slices): Calories: 190, Total Fat: 8 g, Sat. Fat: 1 g, Monounsaturated Fat: 5 g, Polyunsaturated Fat: 1.5 g, Carbs: 25 g, Fiber: 2 g, Sugars: 14 g, Protein: 4 g, Sodium: 90 mg, Cholesterol: 3 mg

Chocolate Chunk Banana Bread

Serves 12.

Determined to mimic classic banana bread, we cleaned this favorite up by ditching the calorie-laden Crisco for raw honey, applesauce and healthy oils.

INGREDIENTS:

- 1½ cups whole-wheat flour
- 1¼ tsp baking powder
- ½ tsp baking soda
- 1 Tbsp cinnamon
- 1 Tbsp ground flaxseed
- Pinch of sea salt
- 3 ripe bananas, mashed with a fork
- 2 egg whites
- ¼ cup unsweetened applesauce
- ½ cup raw honey
- ¼ cup flaxseed oil
- ⅓ cup chopped dark chocolate
- Olive oil cooking spray, optional

INSTRUCTIONS:

ONE: Preheat oven to 350°F. In a medium bowl, combine flour, baking powder, baking soda, cinnamon, flaxseed and salt.

TWO: In a large bowl, with a hand mixer, beat bananas until smooth. Add egg whites and beat until combined. Gradually mix in applesauce, honey and flaxseed oil.

THREE: Mix dry ingredients into banana mixture; stir in chocolate.

FOUR: Mist a 9 x 5-inch loaf pan with cooking spray. Pour batter into pan and bake for 25 minutes, or until browned on top.

Nutrients per slice: Calories: 182, Total Fat: 6 g, Sat. Fat: 1 g, Monounsaturated Fat: 1 g, Polyunsaturated Fat: 3 g, Carbs: 32 g, Fiber: 3 g, Sugars: 16 g, Protein: 3 g, Sodium: 74 mg, Cholesterol: 0 mg

Chocolate Frosted Cupcakes

*Makes 18 cupcakes. **Hands-on time:** 25 minutes. **Total time:** 40 minutes.*

This *CE* take on the classic favorite is sure to hit the spot, whether you're eight or 98!

INGREDIENTS:

- ½ cup unsweetened cocoa powder
- 2 large eggs
- ½ cup organic evaporated cane juice
- 2 Tbsp safflower oil
- 1 cup nonfat plain Greek yogurt
- 1 tsp pure vanilla extract
- 1½ cups light spelt flour
- ¼ tsp fine sea salt
- ½ tsp baking powder
- 1½ tsp baking soda

FROSTING

- 3 Tbsp organic unsalted butter, room temperature
- 4 oz light cream cheese, room temperature
- 3 Tbsp organic evaporated cane juice
- ¼ cup unsweetened cocoa powder
- 1½ Tbsp 1% milk

INSTRUCTIONS:

ONE: Preheat oven to 375°F. Bring a small saucepan or kettle of water to a boil. Line a muffin tin with medium paper muffin liners.

TWO: In a 1-cup measure or small heat-proof bowl, combine ½ cup boiling water and ½ cup cocoa powder; stir to dissolve. Set aside.

THREE: In a large bowl, beat eggs, ½ cup cane juice and oil with an electric hand mixer until fluffy, 2 to 3 minutes. Add yogurt and vanilla and beat until combined. Add cocoa mixture and beat for 30 more seconds. In a separate large bowl, whisk flour, salt, baking powder and baking soda. Add flour mixture to cocoa mixture and beat until just combined, 30 to 45 seconds. Spoon mixture into muffin liners, dividing evenly. Transfer tin to oven and bake for 12 to 15 minutes or until a toothpick inserted in center comes out clean. Let cool completely in tin.

FOUR: Meanwhile, prepare frosting: In a medium bowl, beat butter, cream cheese and 3 Tbsp cane juice with electric hand mixer until light and fluffy, 2 to 3 minutes. Gradually add ¼ cup cocoa powder in 3 batches, beating until combined between each, and scraping down sides of bowl with a rubber spatula if necessary. Add milk and beat until smooth, about 45 seconds. Top each cooled cupcake with ½ Tbsp frosting.

Nutrients per cupcake: Calories: 128, Total Fat: 5.5 g, Sat. Fat: 2.5 g, Carbs: 17 g, Fiber: 2 g, Sugars: 8 g, Protein: 5 g, Sodium: 179 mg, Cholesterol: 32 mg

Chocolate
Frosted
Cupcakes

Clafoutis

Clafoutis

*Serves 8. **Hands-on time:** 10 minutes. **Total time:** 30 minutes.*

A *clafoutis* is commonly made with un-pitted cherries, as the pits add an almond flavor. Try our version with pitted cherries and almond extract, and you can save on the dental work!

INGREDIENTS:

- 2 eggs
- 2 egg whites
- ¾ cup skim milk
- ½ cup spelt flour
- ¼ tsp fine sea salt
- ½ tsp pure almond extract
- ¼ cup organic evaporated cane juice, divided
- Olive oil cooking spray
- 30 cherries, pitted

INSTRUCTIONS:

ONE: Preheat oven to 425°F.

TWO: In a blender, combine eggs, egg whites, milk, flour, salt, almond extract and all but 1 Tbsp cane juice.

THREE: Mist a 9-inch ovenproof skillet with cooking spray and place on medium-high heat. Add cherries to skillet and sprinkle with remaining 1 Tbsp cane juice. When cane juice has just begun to melt, about 45 seconds, pour prepared batter over cherries. (Since skillet is on stovetop, batter will immediately begin to set.) Transfer skillet to oven and cook for 20 minutes, until set in center. Serve warm.

OPTIONS: Try your clafoutis served with a spoonful of nonfat plain Greek yogurt and a drizzle of pure maple syrup.

Nutrients per serving (⅛ of recipe): *Calories: 74, Total Fat: 1.5 g, Sat. Fat: 0.5 g, Carbs: 11 g, Fiber: 1 g, Sugars: 5 g, Protein: 5 g, Sodium: 103 mg, Cholesterol: 53 mg*

Nutritional Bonus:
Cherries are loaded with antioxidants, making them a veritable power fruit. Not only do they contain nearly 19 times more beta-carotene than blueberries or strawberries, but they can also ease the symptoms of arthritis and help you get a better sleep because of the anthocyanins and melatonin they contain.

Caramel Pudding Cake

*Serves 8. **Hands-on time:** 15 minutes. **Total time:** 45 minutes.*

The name says it all with this ingenious cross between velvety pudding and soft cake. But be warned: Serve this gem to your dinner guests and they'll never want to leave!

INGREDIENTS:

- Olive oil cooking spray
- 1 cup light spelt flour
- ⅓ cup organic evaporated cane juice
- 2 tsp baking powder
- ¼ tsp sea salt
- 1 large egg
- ⅓ cup 1% milk
- 1 tsp pure vanilla extract
- 3 Tbsp organic unsalted butter, melted
- ¼ cup Sucanat

INSTRUCTIONS:

ONE: Preheat oven to 350°F. Coat an 8-inch square baking pan with cooking spray. Bring a small saucepan or kettle of water to a boil.

TWO: In a medium bowl, combine flour, cane juice, baking powder and salt. In a measuring cup or small bowl, whisk egg, milk, vanilla and butter. Add milk mixture to flour mixture and stir until combined. Spoon batter into pan, spreading evenly to cover bottom. Sprinkle with Sucanat, then pour 1 cup boiling water over top. Transfer to oven and bake for 25 minutes, until water is gone yet cake still appears soft. Serve warm.

Nutrients per serving (2 x 4-inch piece): *Calories: 160, Total Fat: 5 g, Sat. Fat: 3 g, Carbs: 25 g, Fiber: 1 g, Sugars: 14 g, Protein: 3 g, Sodium: 84 mg, Cholesterol: 38 mg*

Cheesecake Tartlets

Makes 36 tartlets.

Chef Phillip Dell of Sin City Chefs had it right with these little tarts – the perfect balance of tart cheesecake and sweet fruit makes this dessert a hit among even his celebrity customers!

INGREDIENTS:

- 6 Tbsp all-natural, no-sugar-added fruit preserves of your choice
- 36 fresh berries (raspberries, large blueberries or quartered strawberries)

CHEESECAKE FILLING

- 4 oz low-fat cream cheese, softened
- 4 oz fresh goat cheese, softened
- 2 Tbsp raw honey
- ¼ tsp pure vanilla extract

LEMON SHORTBREAD

- 2 cups whole-wheat pastry flour
- ⅔ cup organic unsalted butter, softened
- ½ cup raw honey
- 2 tsp finely grated lemon zest

INSTRUCTIONS:

ONE: Prepare Cheesecake Filling: In a food processor, blend both cheeses, honey and vanilla, stopping to scrape sides of bowl, until smooth. Spoon mixture into a piping bag. (Alternatively, use a small resealable bag with a corner snipped off). Refrigerate for at least 30 minutes.

TWO: Preheat oven to 350°F. Prepare Lemon Shortbread: In a large bowl, add flour, butter, honey and lemon zest; mix with a fork until well blended and a dough is formed.

THREE: Form into 36 tablespoon-size balls. Place balls in cups of a nonstick mini muffin or mini tartlet pan. Use the back of a spoon or your thumb to press each ball onto bottom and partway up side of each cup (dough should be quite thin) to make an indentation to hold preserves. Spoon ½ tsp fruit preserves into each cup.

FOUR: Bake for about 15 minutes or until golden and firm. Transfer pan to a rack and let cool for 5 minutes. Remove tartlets from pan and let cool completely on rack, about 20 minutes.

FIVE: Pipe about 1 tsp Cheesecake Filling onto each tartlet, then top with berries. Leftover 4 oz Cheesecake Filling can be kept, covered, in refrigerator for up to 2 days.

FREEZE IT: This dough is excellent for freezing! Roll the dough into a log with wax or parchment paper. Wrap the log tightly with plastic wrap and freeze until needed. For a quick treat, remove the dough from the freezer, cut the log into slices, place the slices onto a parchment-lined cookie sheet and proceed to baking.

Nutrients per tartlet: Calories: 90, Total Fat: 4.5 g, Sat. Fat: 3 g, Carbs: 12 g, Fiber: 1 g, Sugar: 5 g, Protein: 2 g, Sodium: 20 mg, Cholesterol: 10 mg

For a photo of this recipe, see page 240.

Apple-Pecan Blondies
WITH MAPLE GLAZE

Makes 16 squares. **Hands-on time:** *20 minutes.* **Total time:** *50 minutes.*

A lighter, sweeter alternative to brownies, these moist dessert bars are packed with scrumptious chunks of apple and pecans. To keep them low fat, we've halved the butter and doubled up on applesauce to deliver a smooth, flavorful batter.

INGREDIENTS:

- 1¼ cups whole-wheat pastry flour
- ⅔ cup plus ¼ cup organic evaporated cane juice, divided
- 1 tsp baking powder
- 1 tsp ground cinnamon
- ¼ tsp sea salt
- 1 large egg, lightly beaten
- ¼ cup unsweetened applesauce
- 4 Tbsp organic unsalted butter, melted and slightly cooled
- 1 tsp pure vanilla extract
- 1 apple (such as Fuji, Gala, McIntosh or Golden Delicious), peeled and cut into ¼-inch dice (about ¾ cup)
- ⅔ cup toasted unsalted pecans, chopped, divided
- ¼ cup pure maple syrup

INSTRUCTIONS:

ONE: Preheat oven to 350°F. Line a 9-inch square baking dish with nonstick foil or parchment, leaving 6 inches hanging over two opposite sides.

TWO: In a large bowl, whisk flour, ⅔ cup cane juice, baking powder, cinnamon and salt. In a medium bowl, whisk egg, applesauce, butter and vanilla. Add to flour mixture and stir until just moistened. Fold in apple and all but 2 Tbsp pecans.

THREE: Spoon mixture into baking dish, shaking pan several times to distribute evenly. Bake for 20 to 25 minutes, until edges begin to pull away from pan and a toothpick inserted in center comes out with just a few moist crumbs. Remove from oven and let cool in pan for 10 minutes. Lift both sides of overhanging foil and carefully transfer blondies to a cooling rack. Let cool slightly.

FOUR: In a small saucepan, combine maple syrup and remaining ¼ cup cane juice. Heat on medium-low and cook, stirring, until cane juice dissolves, 3 to 5 minutes; do not let simmer. Pour over top of blondies, spreading evenly. Immediately sprinkle with remaining 2 Tbsp pecans, pressing lightly to adhere. Let cool completely. Cut into 16 squares.

Nutrients per serving (1 square): Calories: 163, Total Fat: 7 g, Sat. Fat: 2 g, Monounsaturated Fat: 2 g, Polyunsaturated Fat: 1 g, Carbs: 25 g, Fiber: 2 g, Sugars: 16 g, Protein: 2 g, Sodium: 35 mg, Cholesterol: 21 mg

Apple-Pecan
Blondies

Chocolate
Walnut
Brownies

Chocolate Walnut Brownies

*Makes 16 brownies. **Hands-on time:** 15 minutes. **Total time:** 30 minutes.*

Perfect for a bake sale or just to enjoy at home, these brownies are a surefire way for your kids to make friends. Save one for yourself before they all vanish!

INGREDIENTS:

- Olive oil cooking spray
- 3 oz dark chocolate (70% cocoa or greater)
- 3 Tbsp organic unsalted butter
- ¼ cup strongly brewed coffee (warm or room temperature; not hot)
- ½ cup organic evaporated cane juice
- 1 tsp pure vanilla extract
- 2 large eggs
- ⅓ cup light spelt flour
- ¼ cup chopped unsalted walnuts

INSTRUCTIONS:

ONE: Preheat oven to 350°F. Coat an 8-inch square baking pan with cooking spray.

TWO: In the top of a double boiler, melt chocolate and butter on medium-low heat, 1 to 2 minutes. Once melted, stir gently to combine. (Alternatively, set a metal bowl over top of a pot of gently simmering water, ensuring bowl does not touch water.)

THREE: Remove from heat and add coffee, cane juice and vanilla, stirring. Stir in eggs, flour and walnuts until just combined and no egg is visible. Pour mixture into pan, transfer to oven and bake for 15 to 18 minutes, until just beginning to set; do not over-bake. Let cool completely before cutting into 16 squares.

Nutrients per brownie: Calories: 102, Total Fat: 6 g, Sat. Fat: 3 g, Carbs: 10 g, Fiber: 1 g, Sugars: 7 g, Protein: 2 g, Sodium: 12 mg, Cholesterol: 32 mg

Nutritional Bonus:
Not only does the dark chocolate in these moist brownies satisfy your sweet tooth, but it also might help lower your blood pressure. Numerous studies link consuming small amounts of dark chocolate on a regular basis with a reduction in blood pressure and a reduced risk of developing heart disease, thanks to the antioxidant-rich flavonoids found in cocoa beans.

Mini Spiced Ginger Cupcakes
WITH LEMON CREAM CHEESE FROSTING

*Makes 48 cupcakes. **Hands-on time:** 25 minutes. **Total time:** 1 hour, 40 minutes (includes cooling time).*

Chef Jo's clean mini cupcakes pack enough zing to end any meal with a punch of excitement.

INGREDIENTS:

- ¾ cup maple sugar flakes
- ½ cup olive oil buttery spread
- 2 large eggs
- 1 tsp pure vanilla extract
- 1 tsp white vinegar
- ½ cup nonfat plain Greek yogurt
- ½ cup skim milk
- 2 cups gluten-free flour blend, sifted
- 1 Tbsp ground ginger
- 2 tsp pumpkin pie spice
- 1 tsp baking soda
- ½ tsp sea salt
- ¼ tsp baking powder

FROSTING

- 4 oz low-fat plain cream cheese, softened
- ⅓ cup maple sugar flakes
- ⅓ cup nonfat plain Greek yogurt
- 2 Tbsp fresh lemon juice
- Zest 1 lemon

INSTRUCTIONS:

ONE: Preheat oven to 350°F. Line 48 mini muffin cups with paper liners.

TWO: In a large mixing bowl, add ¾ cup maple sugar flakes, buttery spread, eggs, vanilla and vinegar, and beat with a hand mixer on medium-high speed until smooth, fluffy and opaque and maple flakes are dissolved. (Alternative: Use a stand mixer with paddle attachment on medium-high speed, then scrape into a large mixing bowl.)

THREE: In a small bowl, whisk ½ cup yogurt and milk. In a medium bowl, whisk flour, ginger, pumpkin pie spice, baking soda, salt and baking powder. Beginning with flour mixture, alternately fold flour mixture and yogurt mixture into egg mixture, making 3 additions of flour and 2 additions of yogurt. Fold only until flour is smooth and mixture is just combined; do not over-mix.

FOUR: Spoon about 1½ Tbsp batter into each cupcake liner. Bake in center of oven for 12 to 14 minutes, or until a toothpick comes out clean when inserted in center. Remove from oven and let cupcakes cool in muffin tin on a wire rack for 15 minutes. Remove cupcakes from tin and let cool completely on rack for at least 1 hour.

FIVE: Meanwhile, prepare frosting: In a stand mixer or food processor, blend cream cheese, ⅓ cup maple sugar flakes, ⅓ cup yogurt and lemon juice until smooth and maple flakes are dissolved. Spoon 1 tsp icing onto each cooled cupcake. Top each with lemon zest, dividing evenly. Serve immediately.

TIP: Cupcakes are best when iced just before serving. Keep icing refrigerated and store cupcakes in a sealed container in a cool, dark place until needed. Cupcakes and icing will keep for up to 2 days.

Nutrients per 2 cupcakes: Calories: 103, Total Fat: 5 g, Sat. Fat: 2 g, Carbs: 11 g, Fiber: 1 g, Sugars: 3 g, Protein: 3 g, Sodium: 148 mg, Cholesterol: 20 mg

Upside-Down Ginger Apple Coffee Cake

Serves 10. **Hands-on time:** 15 minutes. **Total time:** 1 hour.

We guarantee you'll fall for this rich, comforting, ginger-infused upside-down cake with its mix of tangy and sweet flavors.

INGREDIENTS:

- Olive oil cooking spray
- 2 Tbsp pure maple syrup, plus additional for garnish
- 1 medium apple (such as Northern Spy, Granny Smith or Cortland), cored and thinly sliced
- 2 cups spelt flour
- 1 tsp baking powder
- 1 tsp baking soda
- 1 tsp ground cinnamon
- ½ tsp fine sea salt
- ¼ cup safflower oil
- ½ cup Sucanat
- 1 egg
- ½ cup unsweetened applesauce
- 1 cup low-fat plain yogurt
- 2 Tbsp fresh grated ginger

INSTRUCTIONS:

ONE: Preheat oven to 350°F. Mist an 8-inch round cake pan with cooking spray. Drizzle bottom of pan with maple syrup, swirling pan to coat bottom. Arrange apple slices in a single-layer circle over top, allowing each slice to overlap slightly, until bottom is covered. Set aside.

TWO: In a medium bowl, combine flour, baking powder, baking soda, cinnamon and salt. Set aside.

THREE: In a large bowl, beat oil, Sucanat, egg, applesauce, yogurt and ginger with an electric hand mixer until smooth, 1 to 2 minutes. Add flour mixture and beat until just combined. Pour batter over top of apples and bake for 35 to 45 minutes or until a toothpick comes out clean when inserted in the center. Let cool in pan on a wire rack for 10 minutes, then invert onto a serving platter.

Nutrients per 2½-inch slice (¹⁄₁₀ of cake): *Calories: 230, Total Fat: 7 g, Sat. Fat: 1 g, Monounsaturated Fat: 4 g, Polyunsaturated Fat: 1 g, Carbs: 36 g, Fiber: 4 g, Sugars: 16 g, Protein: 5 g, Sodium: 250 mg, Cholesterol: 25 mg*

Coconut Cream Pie

Serves 8. **Hands-on time:** 20 minutes.
Total time: 2 hours, 30 minutes (includes chilling time).

Who doesn't love this classic indulgence? Skip the guilt and enjoy this *CE*-approved version of the creamy, coconutty treat.

INGREDIENTS:

CRUST

- 1 cup old-fashioned rolled oats
- ¼ cup spelt flour
- ¼ cup whole unsalted almonds
- 2 tsp raw honey
- 3 Tbsp safflower oil

FILLING

- ⅓ cup light coconut milk
- ½ cup coconut water
- 1 cup low-fat milk
- ⅓ cup organic evaporated cane juice
- ¼ cup brown rice flour
- 1 tsp pure coconut extract
- ½ tsp pure vanilla extract
- 1 Tbsp unsweetened flaked coconut, toasted, optional

INSTRUCTIONS:

ONE: Preheat oven to 375°F. Prepare crust: In the bowl of a food processor fitted with a steel blade, blend oats, spelt flour and almonds until a fine grind has been reached, about 3 minutes. Add honey and oil and pulse until mixture becomes crumbly and sticks together when squeezed in your palm. Turn mixture out into a 9-inch pie pan and press into bottom and sides of pan. Bake for 10 minutes or until lightly browned. Remove from oven and let cool.

TWO: Prepare filling: Combine all filling ingredients in a medium saucepan and bring to a boil on medium, stirring constantly with a whisk. Continue stirring and let boil for 1 minute. Remove from heat and allow mixture to stand for 1 minute without mixing. Pour into baked pie shell. Chill in fridge until set, at least 2 hours.

Nutrients per serving (⅛ of pie): *Calories: 196, Total Fat: 9 g, Sat. Fat: 1 g, Monounsaturated Fat: 6 g, Polyunsaturated Fat: 1 g, Carbs: 23 g, Fiber: 2 g, Sugars: 10 g, Protein: 4 g, Sodium: 22 mg, Cholesterol: 0 mg*

Nutritional Bonus:
In a recipe or alone as a post-workout drink, coconut water is a great way to replenish your electrolytes and load up on potassium. And at only 19 calories per 100 g serving you'll be feeling refreshed, nourished and guilt-free!

Sticky Buns

Sticky Buns

Makes 12 buns. **Hands-on time:** *15 minutes.* **Total time:** *2 hours, 30 minutes (includes rising time).*

One of the most famous (and least healthy) treats around is the comforting sticky bun. With this *CE* update, you can have your gooey sticky bun and eat it too!

INGREDIENTS:

- Olive oil cooking spray
- 2 cups light spelt flour, plus additional for rolling
- ¼ tsp fine sea salt
- 2 tsp plus 2 Tbsp organic evaporated cane juice, divided
- 2 tsp quick-rise active dry yeast
- 3 Tbsp organic unsalted butter, divided
- ¼ cup pure maple syrup
- 1 tsp raw honey
- ½ tsp Sucanat
- ¼ cup chopped unsalted pecans
- 1 Tbsp ground cinnamon

INSTRUCTIONS:

ONE: Mist a large bowl with cooking spray; set aside.

TWO: In the bowl of a food processor fitted with a steel blade, combine flour and salt (do not process yet).

THREE: In a 1-cup measure, combine ½ cup lukewarm water and 2 tsp cane juice; stir to dissolve. Sprinkle with yeast and stir until combined. Let sit for 5 minutes, until foamy. With food processor running, add yeast mixture to flour mixture and pulse for 1 to 2 minutes. Once a dough ball forms, process for 1 more minute. Transfer dough to bowl, turning to coat. Cover with plastic wrap and let dough rise until doubled in volume, about 1 hour.

TIP: Letting dough rise in a warmer spot will yield quicker results.

THREE: Meanwhile, coat an 8-inch square baking pan with cooking spray. In a small saucepan or pot, melt 1½ Tbsp butter on medium-low heat. Pour butter into bottom of baking pan. Add maple syrup and swirl with a spoon to evenly distribute and combine. Drizzle with honey and sprinkle with Sucanat and pecans; set aside.

FOUR: On a lightly floured surface, roll dough into an 8 x 12-inch rectangle. Spread remaining 1½ Tbsp butter over top and sprinkle with remaining 2 Tbsp cane juice and cinnamon. Roll dough up lengthwise, pinching along the length of the folded edge to help roll hold its shape. Cut into 12 equal portions. Place each portion into pan, flat side down, evenly spaced and, preferably, not touching. Cover with plastic wrap and let rise at room temperature until doubled in volume, about 45 minutes.

FIVE: Preheat oven to 375°F. Remove plastic wrap from pan, transfer to oven and bake until golden, 20 to 25 minutes. Remove from oven, invert onto a large plate and gently remove pan. Serve warm.

Nutrients per bun: Calories: 145, Total Fat: 5 g, Sat. Fat: 2 g, Carbs: 24 g, Fiber: 2 g, Sugars: 9 g, Protein: 3 g, Sodium: 41 mg, Cholesterol: 8 mg

Cape Gooseberry Crumble

Serves 8. **Hands-on time:** *15 minutes.* **Total time:** *1 hour, 5 minutes.*

Cape gooseberries are also known as physalis, Incan berries, ground cherries, goldenberries, Peruvian ground cherries and Chinese lanterns.

INGREDIENTS:

- 2 6-oz pkg fresh gooseberries, papery skins discarded and stems removed
- 4 medium peaches, pitted, peeled and thinly sliced
- ¼ cup chopped unsalted pecans
- ½ cup spelt flour
- ½ cup old-fashioned rolled oats
- ⅓ cup organic evaporated cane juice
- ½ tsp ground cinnamon
- ¼ tsp sea salt
- 1 tsp pure vanilla extract
- 3 Tbsp safflower oil or grapeseed oil
- 1 cup nonfat plain Greek yogurt, optional
- 1 Tbsp raw honey, optional

INSTRUCTIONS:

ONE: Preheat oven to 350°F. Line bottom of an 8 x 8-inch glass dish with gooseberries and peaches.

TWO: In a medium bowl, combine pecans, flour, oats, cane juice, cinnamon and salt; mix well. Add vanilla and oil and mix until a crumble is formed.

THREE: Sprinkle pecan mixture evenly over fruit in dish and bake on middle rack in oven for 40 to 45 minutes, until topping turns golden brown and edges start bubbling. Let cool slightly.

FOUR: If desired, prepare topping: In a small bowl, combine yogurt and honey; mix well and add a dollop on top of crumble to serve.

Nutrients per serving (⅛ of crumble): Calories: 193, Total Fat: 9 g, Sat. Fat: 1 g, Monounsaturated Fat: 4 g, Polyunsaturated Fat: 1 g, Carbs: 28 g, Fiber: 4 g, Sugars: 14 g, Protein: 3 g, Sodium: 60.5 mg, Cholesterol: 0 mg

Nutritional Bonus:

Use this tasty recipe to load up on cape gooseberries. These tangerine-colored morsels contain cryptoxanthin, a carotenoid and anticarcinogenic that protects cells and DNA from free radical damage.

All About Berries

This handy berry guide will show you how to use your favorite berries in new and unexpected ways!

Fresh berries add vibrant color and flavor and are chock full of nutrients like vitamin C, fiber and heart-healthy antioxidants. Berries are best when in season because they pack the most flavor punch.

One of the best things about berries is their versatility – you can use them in both sweet and savory dishes. To show you just how easy it is to incorporate berries into your cooking, we've put together a go-to berry guide to keep handy when you're buying or cooking with berries.

RASPBERRIES

FLAVOR PROFILE: Fruity and sweet with a hint of tartness.

BEST USES: Pair with balsamic vinegar, brie or mint. Great for preserves, coulis, sorbets and frozen yogurt, or adding whole to your morning yogurt or cereal.

CAPE GOOSEBERRIES
(also called ground cherries)

FLAVOR PROFILE: Mildly sweet, tangy, light grape tomato flavor.

BEST USES: Enjoy fresh or baked into pies, in compotes or sauces for savory dishes. Also beautiful as a garnish on tarts, cakes and dessert plates.

BLACKBERRIES

FLAVOR PROFILE: Sweet and burst-in-your-mouth juicy.

BEST USES: Excellent flavor-booster for iced teas and lemonades or as a topper for frozen yogurts, salads or cereal. Delicious addition to scones, muffins, preserves, pies and tarts.

TABLE GRAPES & WINE GRAPES

FLAVOR PROFILE: Sweet, firm, juicy, with bitter seeds.

BEST USES: Excellent with cheese, fruit platters and as a snack. Table grapes are ideal in jams and pies.

KIWI FRUIT & GOLD KIWI FRUIT

FLAVOR PROFILE: Tart, slightly sweet with crunchy seeds. The gold variety is less tart with hints of mango, citrus and melon.

BEST USES: Excellent for smoothies, juices, fruit platters, fresh fruit tarts and ice pops. Pair perfectly with strawberries; can also be used to tenderize meats.

STRAWBERRIES

FLAVOR PROFILE: Sweet, firm and juicy.

BEST USES: A lovely complement to feta or goat cheese, toasted nuts, mint, black pepper, chicken and spinach. Excellent for baking into pies (especially with rhubarb), shortcake and angel food cake, as well as preserves.

BLUEBERRIES

FLAVOR PROFILE: Sweet, slightly tart, firm and juicy.

BEST USES: Delicious on salads, with granola and as a topper for hot and cold cereals. Perfect for baking into scones, muffins and pies and an excellent accompaniment to salmon, lean game meats and beef. Great for making preserves, juice and chutney.

Credits

Contributors:

Peter Agostinelli, Robin Asbell, Elizabeth Brown, MS, RD, CPT, CDE, Emily Christopher, Gabriele Corcos, Phillip Dell, Tara Mataraza Desmond, Allison Fishman, Aliza Green, Julie O'Hara, Nadia G., Nicole Hamaker, Ryan Hardy, Jessica Goldbogen Harlan, Jill Silverman Hough, Lisa Howard, Nancy S. Hughes, Alison Kent, Soo Kim, Signe Langford, Joanne Lusted, Linda Malone, CSCS, Debi Mazar, Robin Miller, MS, Kate Parham, Victoria Abbott Riccardi, Aarón Sánchez, Dominic Tedesco, Lisa Turner, Laura Walsh, Diane Welland, MS, RD, Marianne Wren, Allison Young

All new recipes created by Julie O'Hara.

Photographers:

Buceta, Paul: 95

Duivenvoorden, Yvonne: 10-11, 17, 23, 61, 69, 70, 72-75, 96-97, 121, 138, 141, 147, 150-151, 162, 166, 169, 182-183, 186, 201, 205-206, 208-209, 210-211, 213-214, 235-239, 246-247, 252, 259, 272

Griffith, Donna: 14, 24, 65, 86, 93, 107-108, 111-112, 126, 134, 137, 173-174, 193, 217, 226, 229, 233, 255

iStockphoto.com: 237 (grains in jar, upper right)

James, Gregory: 56, 148, 167

Masterfile: 265,

Pond, Edward: 13, 30-31, 33, 38-39, 41, 49, 52-53, 57-58, 62, 66, 78, 80-81, 90, 100, 103, 116-117, 125, 129, 130, 145-146, 149 (sandwich), 153, 178, 185, 190, 221, 225, 230, 243, 245, 247-248, 251, 260

Pudge, Jodi: 18, 21, 42, 51 (prep shots), 77, 104, 118-119, 122, 157, 161, 170, 177, 180-181, 218, 244, 250

Reynolds, Bradley: 196

Shutterstock: 26-27 (woman: Leonid and Anna Dedukh, chocolate: Patrick Krabeepetcharat, salt: Olga Miltsova, wheat: Elena Schweitzer, vitamin D: Kellis), 29 (Yuri Arcurs), 50 (Igor Sokolov), 51 (bottom right, Lik Studio), 94 (Anna Sedneva), 146 (Elena Gaak), 149 (baking sheet: Nordling, spoon: plo3, frying pan: Anastasia_Fisechko, thermometer: Milos Luzanin)

Szulc, Ryan: 142, 158, 222

Tonner, Ashley: 34-35, 37, 45-46, 82, 99, 115, 133, 165, 189, 194, 198, 253, 256

Tsakos, Joanne: 71, 85, 154, 197, 202

Visnyei, Maya: 262-263

Cover Photography: Broccoli Rabe Linguine with Feta (p. 227, photo: Donna Griffith, styling: Claire Stubbs)

Back Cover Photography (clockwise from top-left): Cauliflower & Clams in Parsley Broth (p. 76, photo: Jodi Pudge, styling: Nicole Young), Sticky Buns (p. 261, photo: Edward Pond, styling: Claire Stubbs), Chicken BLT Salad (p. 67, photo: Edward Pond, styling: Marianne Wren), Lamburgers with Tzatziki & Fresh Mint (p. 120, photo: Yvonne Duivenvoorden, styling: Nicole Young), Kale Barley Soup (p. 81, photo: Edward Pond, styling: Marianne Wren), Lobsta Roll (p. 48, photo: Edward Pond, styling: Ashley Denton), Lamb Osso Bucco with Herbed Couscous (p. 124, photo: Edward Pond, styling: Marianne Wren), Thai Pork & Papaya Couscous (p. 145, photo: Edward Pond, styling: Claire Stubbs)

Food Stylists:

Colley, Jessica: 148

Denton, Ashley: 18, 30-31, 33, 49, 74-75, 138, 141, 166, 169, 213, 238-239, 244, 250

Grenier, David: 51, 72-73

Hagan, Adele: 122, 146-147, 149, 182-183, 246-247

Stubbs, Claire: 13-14, 17, 24, 38-39, 41, 52-53, 61, 65, 78, 80, 86, 90, 93, 96-97, 100, 103, 107-108, 111-112, 126, 130, 134, 137, 142, 145, 153, 158, 162, 173-174, 178, 180-181, 185, 190, 193, 201, 206, 208-211, 217, 222, 225-226, 229-230, 233, 236-237, 243, 248, 251, 255-256, 260, 262-263

Sugar Tart: 69, 71, 197, 202

Wren, Marianne: 10-11, 21, 23, 34, 37, 42, 56-58, 62, 66, 81, 104, 125, 129, 157, 161, 167, 177, 189, 221, 245, 252-253, 259, 272

Young, Nicole: 35, 45-46, 77, 82, 85, 99, 115, 116-119, 121, 133, 150-151, 154, 165, 170, 186, 194, 198, 205, 214, 218, 235

Prop Stylists:

Laura Branson, Catherine Doherty, Madeleine Johari, Laura McGraw, Carolyn Souch, Cheryl Thompson, Genevieve Wiseman

Models:

Pamela Graver (hand model), Jennifer Mackenzie (hand model), Saori Niwa (Sutherland Models), Tosca Reno, Charity Woodrome (Sutherland Models)

Hair & Make-up:

Valeria Nova

Model Styling:

Rachel Matthews Burton

Index

THE BEST OF CLEAN EATING 3

BREAKFAST, BRUNCH & BEVERAGES

Light and Easy Prawn Pasta, p. 195